Springer Texts in Business and Economics

Springer Texts in Business and Economics (STBE) delivers high-quality instructional content for undergraduates and graduates in all areas of Business/Management Science and Economics. The series is comprised of self-contained books with a broad and comprehensive coverage that are suitable for class as well as for individual self-study. All texts are authored by established experts in their fields and offer a solid methodological background, often accompanied by problems and exercises.

Léo-Paul Dana • Christian Keen •
Veland Ramadani
Editors

Entrepreneurship in South America

Context, Diversity, Constraints, Opportunities and Prospects

Springer

Editors
Léo-Paul Dana
Rowe School of Business
Dalhousie University
Halifax, NS, Canada

Christian Keen
Département de management, Faculté des sciences de l'administration
Université Laval
Québec, Canada

Veland Ramadani
Faculty of Business and Economics
South East European University
Tetovo, North Macedonia

ISSN 2192-4333 ISSN 2192-4341 (electronic)
Springer Texts in Business and Economics
ISBN 978-3-030-97059-8 ISBN 978-3-030-97060-4 (eBook)
https://doi.org/10.1007/978-3-030-97060-4

This Springer imprint is published by the registered company Springer Nature Switzerland AG
The registered company address is: Gewerbestrasse 11, 6330 Cham, Switzerland

This book is dedicated to Michelle Brandstrup

Foreword

Understanding the cultural, economic, and institutional differences between developed and emerging economies is key for conducting international business and entrepreneurial activities. Understanding the extreme diversity of contexts and strong institutional differences in each of the South American countries is another extra challenge that investors and entrepreneurs unexpectedly face when visiting this region for their first time, as they imagine a homogeneous place in terms of culture, institutions, politics, and business environments.

This book offers much-needed insights into each of the South American markets and how they differ from each other. During this challenging times that we are all facing in this post-pandemic economy, both business students and entrepreneurs need to develop a deep understanding of the experiences that small entrepreneurial firms in each of these countries face, particularly in the South American context, where the business practices and entrepreneurial skills under crisis are relatively under-explored. Additionally, these practices may significantly differ from the traditional US and European developed economies practical way of thinking. This book presents new insights that I will use when advising my students, executives, investors, and entrepreneurs going to South America.

EDEM Business School
Valencia, Spain

International University of Monaco
Rue Hubert Clerissi, Monaco

Founder CEO, Stein Global Consulting
Valencia, Monaco

Christian Felzensztein

Editorial Board

Contents

Introduction to Entrepreneurship in South America

Léo-Paul Dana, Christian Keen, and Veland Ramadani

Abstract

Understanding context is essential to succeed in entrepreneurship. South America is a land of contrasts, and context is perhaps even more important here than elsewhere. It is a continent of superlatives, home to rain forest and desert. Influenced by the environment, entrepreneurship varies greatly across this vast continent. Entrepreneurship can be considered a vehicle to foster inclusive economic development.

Understanding context is essential to succeed in entrepreneurship. Among early studies to focus on context and entrepreneurship, Dana (1995) showed that the culture of an individual influences that person's response to opportunity for entrepreneurship and is, therefore, a highly relevant explanatory variable. In a similar vein, Dana (1996) showed that individuals from different cultures view the same opportunity for entrepreneurship differently; that which is an opportunity for one person is not for another of a differing culture.

For some, South America might be a place on the globe (Fig. 1), but it is no ordinary place. Revolutions have been many and military rule has not been unknown

L.-P. Dana (✉)
Rowe School of Business, Dalhousie University, Halifax, NS, Canada
e-mail: lp762359@dal.ca

C. Keen
Département de management, Faculté des sciences de l'administration, Université Laval, Québec, Canada
e-mail: christian.keen@fsa.ulaval.ca

V. Ramadani
Faculty of Business and Economics, South East European University, Tetovo, North Macedonia
e-mail: v.ramadani@seeu.edu.mk

L.-P. Dana et al. (eds.), *Entrepreneurship in South America*, Springer Texts in Business and Economics, https://doi.org/10.1007/978-3-030-97060-4_1

Fig. 1 South America on globe in Montpellier; photo © 2021 by Léo-Paul Dana

here. Figure 2 features a military parade in Chile. In Fig. 3, men directing traffic in Peru hold machine guns.

South America is a land of contrasts, and context is perhaps even more important here than elsewhere. It is a continent of superlatives, home to rain forest and desert (Fig. 4). The Andes (Fig. 5) form the world's longest continuous mountain chain. Lake Titicaca is the world's highest navigable lake. Iguacu Falls (Fig. 6) constitute the largest waterfall in the world. Venezuela's Angel Falls are the world's tallest uninterrupted water falls. The Amazon is the second-longest river in the world; among the rivers of the Amazon Basin is the Urubamba River (Fig. 7), sacred to the Incas. La Paz is the highest national capital in the world.

The continent is home to very rich and very poor people (Fig. 8). For some entrepreneurs, business means the stock exchange (Fig. 9), while for others good business is selling a few kilos of cheese (Fig. 10). Banks are many (Fig. 11), but some areas have few if any motor vehicles (Fig. 12). Many people use animals for transport (Fig. 13). Entrepreneurs include self-employed farmers (Fig. 14), retailers (Fig. 15), and informal traders (Fig. 16).

Fig. 2 Outside La Moneda Government Palace; photo © 2021 by Léo-Paul Dana

Figure 17 shows an informal vendor just outside a formal shop. Some entrepreneurs in South America are ambulant merchants meandering in search of clients (Fig. 18) or pushing a cart along a street (Fig. 19). Others have sidewalk stalls (Fig. 20) or impromptu stands (Fig. 21). While Fig. 22 shows a Western-style pharmacy in Santiago, the indigenous entrepreneur in Fig. 23 sells traditional indigenous medication in La Paz. Rubber (Fig. 24) is grown in South America; aeroplanes (Fig. 25) are also manufactured here.

Indigenous people have been entrepreneurs here, well before contact with Europeans (Dana, 1988). The Inca Empire had a sophisticated trade network and introduced Quechua to regions where this language is used to this day (Fig. 26). Indigenous traders often sell in open markets (Fig. 27), much as in former times.

The following chapters introduce entrepreneurship across South America. The next chapter focuses on Argentina, the flag of which features the Sun of May, representing the sun that shone on May 25, 1810, when demonstrations began against Spanish rule. Following that, Chapter 3 features entrepreneurship in Bolivia—until 1825, known as Upper Peru. Chapter 4 is about entrepreneurship in Brazil, the fifth largest country in the world and the world's largest coffee producer. Chapter 5 discusses entrepreneurship in Chile, a country 2160 miles long, and therefore with much diversity. Chile has the world's largest reserves of copper. Next is a chapter about entrepreneurship in Colombia, named after Christopher

Fig. 3 Lima; photo © 2021 by Léo-Paul Dana

Fig. 4 Atacama Desert; photo © 2021 by Léo-Paul Dana

Columbus. Chapter 7 is about entrepreneurship in Ecuador, the country that includes the Galapagos Islands. Chapter 8 explains entrepreneurship in French Guiana–officially a region of France. Chapter 9 is about entrepreneurship in Guyana, a former British colony where 90% of the people live along the coast. Chapter 10 discusses entrepreneurship in Paraguay, a country 60% of which is shrub land. Chapter 11 is about entrepreneurship in Peru, once home to the Inca civilisation.

Fig. 5 Snow on the Andes; photo © 2021 by Léo-Paul Dana

Fig. 6 Iguacu Falls; photo © 2021 by Léo-Paul Dana

Fig. 7 Urubamba River; photo © 2021 by Léo-Paul Dana

Fig. 8 Wealthy client having shoes polished; photo © 2021 by Léo-Paul Dana

Fig. 9 Stock exchange, Santiago; photo © 2021 by Léo-Paul Dana

Chapter 12 discusses entrepreneurship in Suriname, a former Dutch colony, the economy of which includes alumininum, rice and sugar; Suriname was acquired by the Netherlands in 1667, in exchange for New Amsterdam, today's New York. It became independent republic in 1975. Chapter 13 focuses on entrepreneurship in Uruguay, where praire grassland is ideal for raising cattle and sheep; exports include beef, leather and wool. In contrast, Venezuela exports oil; Chapter 14 discusses entrepreneurship in this country. Finally Chapter 15 features banking services for entrepreneurs.

Fig. 10 Selling cheese; photo © 2021 by Léo-Paul Dana

Fig. 11 Citibank facing Banco del Estado de Chile; photo © 2021 by Léo-Paul Dana

Fig. 12 No vehicle traffic photo; © 2021 by Léo-Paul Dana

Fig. 13 Horses in Temuco; photo © 2021 by Léo-Paul Dana

Fig. 14 At work on the farm; photo © 2021 by Léo-Paul Dana

Fig. 15 Montevideo, Uruguay; photo © 2021 by Léo-Paul Dana

Fig. 16 Informal traders; photo © 2021 by Léo-Paul Dana

Fig. 17 Selling outside a shop; photo © 2021 by Léo-Paul Dana

Fig. 18 No need to pay rent; photo © 2021 by Léo-Paul Dana

Fig. 19 With cart; photo © 2021 by Léo-Paul Dana

Fig. 20 Stall; photo © 2021 by Léo-Paul Dana

Fig. 21 Impromptu stands; photo © 2021 by Léo-Paul Dana

Fig. 22 Pharmacy in Santiago; photo © 2021 by Léo-Paul Dana

Fig. 23 La Paz; photo © 2021 by Léo-Paul Dana

Fig. 24 Rubber tree; photo © 2021 by Léo-Paul Dana

Fig. 25 Embraer190 made in Brazil for export to Canada; photo © 2021 by Léo-Paul Dana

Fig. 26 Speaking Quechua; photo © 2021 by Léo-Paul Dana

Fig. 27 Open air market in Peru; photo © 2021 by Léo-Paul Dana

References

Dana, L.-P. (1988). More small business is not the answer for Peru. *Journal of Small Business Management, 26*(3), 68–70.

Dana, L.-P. (1995). Entrepreneurship in a remote sub-Arctic community: Nome, Alaska. *Entrepreneurship: Theory & Practice, 20*(1), 55–72. Reprinted in Norris Krueger, Ed., *Entrepreneurship: Critical Perspectives on Business and Management*, Volume IV, London: Routledge, 2002, pp. 255–275.

Dana, L.-P. (1996). Self-employment in the Canadian sub-Arctic: An exploratory study. *Canadian Journal of Administrative Sciences, 13*(1), 65–77.

Léo-Paul Dana is Professor at the Rowe School of Business of Dalhousie University, Canada. As well, he holds titles of Professor at Montpellier Business School, and Visiting Professor at Kingston University. He is also associated with the Chaire ETI at Sorbonne Business School. A graduate of McGill University and HEC-Montreal, he has served as Marie Curie Fellow at Princeton University and Visiting Professor at INSEAD. He has published extensively in a variety of journals including: *Entrepreneurship: Theory & Practice; International Business Review; International Small Business Journal; Journal of Business Research; Journal of Small Business Management; Journal of World Business; Small Business Economics;* and *Technological Forecasting & Social Change.*

Christian Keen is an Assistant Professor at the Département de Management, Université Laval, Canada. Christian has an extensive research and working experience in Europe, Latin America, and North America. His professional experience includes being member of several the Board of Directors of private companies and NGOs. His research interests are in the areas of international entrepreneurship, entrepreneurship, emerging economies, and rapidly growing firms. Christian is a member of the editorial board of the International Journal of Entrepreneurship Small Business, European Journal of Family Business, Journal of Enterprising Communities, and associated editor at TIM Review.

Veland Ramadani is Professor of Entrepreneurship and Family Business at Faculty of Business and Economics, South East European University, North Macedonia. His research interests include entrepreneurship, small business management and family businesses. He authored or co-authored around 140 research articles, 11 textbooks and 20 edited books. He has published in *Journal of Business Research, International Entrepreneurship and Management Journal, International Journal of Entrepreneurial Behavior & Research, Technological Forecasting and Social Change,* among others. Dr. Ramadani has recently published the book *Entrepreneurial Family Businesses* (Springer). Dr. Ramadani is Editor-in-Chief of *Journal of Enterprising Communities* (JEC). During the period of 2017–2021, he served as a member of Supervisory Board of Development Bank of North Macedonia, where for 10 months served as an acting Chief Operating Officer (COO) as well.

Entrepreneurship in Argentina

Gustavo Birollo

Abstract

Argentina possesses many natural resources, a large and educated middle-class, and an innovative and entrepreneurial culture; however, over the last century, the country has struggled to achieve steady economic growth. This chapter describes how in a particular location of Argentina, the city of Rafaela, the entrepreneurial dynamics brought by the first Italian and Swiss immigrants at the end of the nineteenth century set the pace for the development of this thriving city. This entrepreneurial dynamic is catalyzed by the conjoint work of actors from the public and private sectors supported by the contribution of academic institutions. This entrepreneurial ecosystem allows the city to formulate policies and innovate technology and processes for the development of a sustainable economy.

1 Introduction

Argentina is a South American country rich in natural resources, possesses a large and educated middle-class, and an innovative and entrepreneurial culture (Anchorena & Ronconi, 2012; Pradilla, 2012). However, after a promising economic start at the beginning of the twentieth century (Fleming, 1979), Argentina had an elusive economic development consequent of a series of political crisis that already has lasted almost a century. Consequently, even if the conditions were set for the development of the entrepreneurial activity and for the country to progress, many other factors have threatened this development, such as the high level of corruption,

G. Birollo (✉)
Department of Management, Faculty of Business Administration, Université Laval, Québec, Canada
e-mail: gustavo.birollo@fsa.ulaval.ca

L.-P. Dana et al. (eds.), *Entrepreneurship in South America*, Springer Texts in Business and Economics, https://doi.org/10.1007/978-3-030-97060-4_2

the more than often burdensome regulatory environment, and the difficulty of accessing financial markets (Pradilla, 2012).

Argentina has a population of 44,938,712 inhabitants[1] and an area of 2.78 million square kilometers, being the eighth largest country in the world and second after Brazil in South America. Argentina is a federal republic consisting of 23 provinces and the autonomous city of Buenos Aires. By 1850, post-colonial Argentina had only an estimated population of one million people with 80% of these living in rural areas. After the boom of meat export around the 1880s and its strong and flourishing commercial ties with Europe, Argentina received a massive affluence of European immigrants finding itself in 1914 with 7,800,000 inhabitants (Fleming, 1979). These immigrants populated the country in different ways and faced different realities, such as building a society anew (this chapter) or faced an already settled Spanish post-colonial society (see Fleming, 1979). This chapter aims, first, to describe how the entrepreneurial spirit of these immigrants, acting as intermediary among natural resources, capital and labor (Anchorena & Ronconi, 2012), helped to build the economy of a particular society, the city of Rafaela. And second, to show how the entrepreneurial dynamics brought by these pioneers is still nourishing the development of this thriving city.

2 Historical Overview

The city of Rafaela is located in the Department of Castellanos, in the center west of the Province of Santa Fe (Argentina), about 540 km north of Buenos Aires, the capital of Argentina and about 300 km of the two others most important cities in the country, Córdoba and Rosario. The settlement was established on a plain that until 1880 was almost inhabited. The process of colonization began with the arrival of Italian immigrants, predominantly from the Piemonte region, and Swiss immigrants, from the German's cantons, who came to exploit these lands, which were excellent for cereal cultivation (Costamagna & Garrappa, 2010).

Most of the Santa Fe territory was populated through a system known as private colonization (Gob Rafaela, 2021). The lands where Rafaela settled were properties of Carlos Saguier, Manuel Quintana and Félix Egusquiza. They sold their lands to eleven Italian families through Guillermo Lehmann's Colonizing Company, a Swiss-German businessman. The first bill of sale dates from 1881, so this date is considered to be the year the city was founded (Casabella & Zaragozi, 2010). The sale system Mr. Lehmann used in his company consisted of offering agricultural producers land concessions to be paid for with the yields of the harvests. Many farmers quickly became interested in the opportunity offered by Mr. Lehmann of paying for the land on a long-term basis. Thus, in only 8 months after the first land was put up for sale, 53% of the available concessions had already been sold (Region Litoral, 2021). According to historical data, in 1882, in Rafaela there were only

[1] Data for 2019 from The Word Bank (https://data.worldbank.org/country/AR)

Fig. 1 Downtown Rafaela (1905) © Municipality of Rafaela (https://www.rafaela.gob.ar/Archivos/Arc_18493.jpg)

63 people living in 15 precarious dwellings. Two years later, the population totalled 512 inhabitants, and there were 150 dwellings, as well as 13 shops and a flour mill (Casabella & Zaragozi, 2010).

The city had a very fast demographic and economic growth between 1885 and 1890, mainly thanks to the railway system laid out in the city (Fig. 1). It had three stations and four train lines, which connected the city both intra- and extra-regionally. By the end of this period, various economic activities and social institutions had set in, such as banks, newspapers, printing presses, government offices, health services, notaries, consular representation, cooperatives, social clubs, etc. (Vincenti, 2019). The initial economic activity of the city was agricultural; however, over the years, it diversified by also focusing on livestock breeding. By 1913, reaching a population of 8242 people, the provincial government declared Rafaela a city and formed the Municipal Council, which was democratically elected (Castellanos, 2019).

During the years of the First World War (1914–1918), dairy farms became very popular and along came the creation of the first creameries and dairies, entrepreneurial initiatives that would be consolidated toward 1925 shaping the industrial profile of the city. In the same period, with the development of the livestock farms, there was the launch of the first meat-processing industry. These operational, agricultural, and commercial entrepreneurial initiatives were key factors to the city's progress and the attraction of new immigrants that would increase the population of the city (Casabella & Zaragozi, 2010).

By the crisis of 1930s, the industrial profile of the city, which until then was connected to the transformation of local primary products (meat and milk), starts their diversification toward the production of agricultural machinery to support the primary production. However, entrepreneurs' incursion into the metal-mechanic industry is consolidated by the 1970s, and it added the manufacture of auto-parts and the production of industrial machinery to refrigerate food (Costamagna & Garrappa, 2010). By the end of the 1980s, many of Rafaela's enterprises managed to start exporting their products and gaining participation in foreign markets.

The strength of the local enterprises became evident in the 1990s when companies pushed back the strong competition from abroad that arose from a drastic opening-up process designed by the national government. The productive structure of the city in the second half of the 1990s represented 40% of the gross domestic product (GDP), mainly through the food and the metal-mechanic industry (Costamagna & Garrappa, 2010). About ten years later, following the collapse of the convertibility system (2001), Rafaela took advantage of the favorable exchange policy and the prosperous global scenario and increased its exports in 2004 by 75% (Costamagna & Garrappa, 2010; Casabella & Zaragozi, 2010) with the dairy and the meat industry leading the growth (Casabella & Zaragozi, 2010).

By 2010, the population of Rafaela was 90,200 inhabitants (see Figs. 2 and 3). At that time, the city had 1880 commercial establishments. In addition, the city had 378 industries and manufactured 296 different processed products (Casabella & Zaragozi, 2010). In the last decades, several migratory currents arrived in the city from other provinces and countries causing a demographic explosion and a geographical extension of the city. Currently, Rafaela is facing a new phenomenon in the metropolitan area as it seeks to integrate surrounding towns such as Bella Italia, Lehmann, Roca, and Susana, from where people commute every day to work, to study or to run different errands (Grande, 2019).

Fig. 2 Panoramic Rafaela (2020) © Municipality of Rafaela (https://www.rafaela.gob.ar/Archivos/Arc_18545.jpg)

Fig. 3 Downtown Rafaela © 2021 Abelardo Vercesi

Based on data from the 2019 socioeconomic survey, Rafaela has approximately 107,000 inhabitants. Of these, 51.9% are women and 48.1% are men, and 44.1% of the total is people under 30 years of age; 48.3% of the population is in the labor market and 51.7% represents the economically inactive population (Gob Rafaela, 2021). Nowadays in Rafaela, there are 93 educational establishments: 34 preschools, 31 primary, 15 secondary, five university campuses and six special needs schools. In total, there are about 30,000 students (in all educational levels). More than 500 industries currently make up the city's productive base; this number has increased by 32% in the last decade. Forty-six companies export to some 90 destinations worldwide (Gob Rafaela, 2021).

3 The Environment for Entrepreneurship

From its settlement, Rafaela was a fertile land for entrepreneurs. The entrepreneurial spirit of the first immigrants coming from Piemonte and Switzerland set the stage for the growth of one of the most thriving cities in Argentina. Just as an example, the city's dairy industry is mainly related to European immigrants: the German-Swiss José Maria Williner and the Italians brothers Juan, Constancio and Mario Molfino. These entrepreneurs and their families are intimately connected to the development of Rafaela and, consequently, to the growth of the dairy industry in Argentina as the companies they founded are nowadays in the top five national dairy firms. Rafaela's success has always been related to entrepreneurs aiming not only to add value to

Table 1 Presence of active industrial firms 2000–2018

Year	Number of firms
2000	375
2006	432
2012	496
2018	540

Source: Informe preliminar Instituto de Capacitación y estudios para el desarrollo local (ICEDeL), 2018

Table 2 Distribution of industrial firms by sector in 2018

Industrial sector	Percentage
Food and beverages	29,1%
Metal-mechanic	32,8%
Printing and reproduction	7,5%
Furniture and mattresses	6,3%
Textile and garment	5,9%
Others	18,4%

Source: Informe preliminar Instituto de Capacitación y estudios para el desarrollo local (ICEDeL), 2018

primary products, mainly in the dairy industry and in the meat industry, but also to generate goods to support these industries. For example, Giuliani S.A. that produces equipment for primary production or IMAI S.A. that started manufacturing tanks for the dairy industry and now supplies entire lines of food processing. Moreover, this metal-mechanical experience prompted entrepreneurs' incursions into another important industry for Rafaela: auto-parts, which gave way to the formation of companies such as Válvulas Edival or Válvulas 3B.

The first Industrial Census of Rafaela, carried out in the year 2000, showed the presence of 375 firms producing industrial goods, among which we can highlight a clear specialization in the food and refrigeration industries, and also in the metal-mechanical sector, where we can distinguish the building of agricultural equipment and machinery, the manufacture of machinery for the food industry and the production of auto-parts. Table 1 shows the evolution of the industrial firms present in Rafaela from 2000 until 2018, and Table 2 the distribution of these firms by business sector in 2018 (ICEDeL, 2018).

Rafaela and its industries stand out by their social and environmental responsibility. Several actions to incorporate the use of clean energy have been implemented as a conjoint work between the municipality and local entrepreneurs. For example, the use of LED technology in public luminaires to save energy, the promotion of the use of solar thermal energy, the recycling of Used Vegetable Oils (UVO) by hotels and gastronomic businesses in the city to produce biodiesel. All these initiatives represent not only economic savings and an improvement to environmental quality, but also the activation of a new economy, which includes companies that manufacture the devices, companies that commercialize them, and the technicians that install and carry out maintenance services. In a nutshell, this implies the creation of an environment for the development of "green" (ecological and sustainable) entrepreneurs (Corach, 2019). Moreover, in 2015, a group of diverse organizations, public and private, created the Institute for Sustainable Development of Rafaela (IDSR). This institute carries out various functions of assistance and advice in sectors related to sustainable development in the city. The main lines of action of the IDSR are water resource management, waste management, environmental education and communication, sustainable mobility, energy efficiency and urban biodiversity (IDSR, 2021).

4 Moving toward the Future

The immigrants that arrived at the beginning of the twentieth century generated an entrepreneurial dynamism that is still the cornerstone of the social and economic growth of Rafaela. This dynamism is the mortar of the entrepreneurial ecosystem underpinned by the conjoint work of actors from the public and private sectors supported by the contribution of academic institutions. Their conjoint work allows the city to formulate policies and innovate technology and processes for the development of a sustainable economy (Basara et al., 2013).

Moreover, in the last decades, the city started the implementation of programs to encourage entrepreneurial spirit and to help the germination of new small enterprises. Particularly, the city has a dedicated office that offers supports regarding procedures for the opening and operation of economic activities, information on sources of financing for the project, as well as advice on access to markets and business opportunities. From 2003 until 2005, the city ran the program "*Emprendiendo Sueños*" (Undertaking Dreams) focused on training people over 18 years of age with secondary education to launch productive enterprises in any activity or sector of their choice. This program resulted in 8 productive enterprises, most of them led by university students. This program was managed by the Municipality of Rafaela, the Rural Society of Rafaela and several academic institutions (Gob Rafaela, 2021).

Since 2009, the Municipality of Rafaela together with academic institutions and non-profit organizations coordinate the program "*Rafaela emprendre*" (Entrepreneurship Rafaela) which seeks to stimulate economic activity and employment (Castellanos, 2021a). On the selected projects, the entrepreneurs are followed by young professional mentors that help them to implement what they have learnt in the formal training program. They can also have the assistance of professionals from the universities to help them solve technical problems and professionals from the chamber of commerce to discuss their experiences and general business perspectives (Rafaela.com, 2010). Since its creation, this program has helped more than 450 entrepreneurs. Only in 2020, the program had 250 candidates from where 57 ventures were accepted (Gerbaudo, 2021). Following the success of this program, the city has implemented in 2020, "*Rafaela verde*" (green Rafaela) aiming to enhance the sustainability commitment of Rafaela's entrepreneurs (Gerbaudo, 2020a). Moreover, in 2021 the program "*Rafaela Digital*" was created and its goal was to support young people who wanted to become entrepreneurs in the digital sector (Castellanos, 2021b).

It is important to point out the contribution of the academic and research and development (R&D) institutions in the success of the entrepreneurial ecosystem of Rafaela. These institutions are always important stakeholders in the development of the cited entrepreneurial programs and in the support of established industries. Among the academic institutions we can name: UTN (Universidad Tecnológica Nacional), Rafaela campus; UNRaf (Universidad Nacional de Rafaela); U.C.E.S. (Universidad de Ciencias Empresariales y Sociales), Rafaela campus, U.C.S.F. (Universidad Católica de Santa Fe), Rafaela campus, U.C.S.E. (Universidad Católica de Santiago del Estero). It is noteworthy that the latter offers a one-year-program for entrepreneurship based on the start-up and management of an enterprise that follows the principles of social responsibility. Further, the INTI-*Lácteos* (National Institute of Industrial Technology—Dairy division) and the INTA Rafaela (National Institute of Agricultural Technology) are two R&D centers based in Rafaela that support the entrepreneurial ecosystem by running research programs, technology transfer, and technical assistance (Erbes et al., 2019).

5 Case Study

Jose Maria Williner, originally from Switzerland, immigrated to Rafaela (in Argentina) at the end of the nineteenth century. He pioneered the dairy farm business with the aim of producing the best dairy products in the country. After his death, his son Alfredo Williner, who shared his fathers' goals, started to process milk from his dairy farms in a small factory in Bella Italia, 10 km east from Rafaela, in 1928 (Ilolay, 2021) (Fig. 4). Ten years later, by 1939, Alfredo Williner was running four creameries in the area, producing the raw material for the production of butter

Fig. 4 First Williner's creamery—Bella Italia 1928 © A.P. Suc. de A. Williner S.A

Fig. 5 Williner's Bella Italia central plant—2019 © A.P. Suc. de A. Williner S.A

and incorporating the production of *dulce de leche* (milk caramel), that over the years would become a very popular product for the firm (Ilolay, 2021). His sons continued the family business, and created the firm *Sucesores de Alfredo Williner S. R. L.* Armando Williner took the direction of the company when he was only 21 years old (Litoral, 2000).

The 1950s were very important for the company as they centralized their production in a new factory, which at that time was in the outskirts of Rafaela. With this new plant, the company began an era of technology integration to improve their processes and to incorporate new consumer markets, hence they also added new production lines to offer to the market various products under the brand Ilolay, such as pasteurized milk, different types of cheese, yoghurt, etc. In 1967, they inaugurated the first milk powder plant to be able to capture and process more milk to reach more distant markets. As this product was a great success, they started up a second milk dehydration plant in 1970 and a third one in 1975 (Ilolay, 2021).

In 1978, the company starts expanding to the cheese production and acquired the company *Victorio and Esteban de Lorenzi Ltda,* which allowed them to start offering a wider range of cheeses to the market (Algaba, 2015).

In 1976, a green field was acquired in Bella Italia with the intention of consolidating all the production in just one modern, state-of-the-art plant and this became a reality in 1993 (Fig. 5). This new plant is equipped with brand new areas of milk reception, milk powder processing, long-life milk processing, butter production, cheese processing, fractioning areas, and multi-purpose storage chambers (Ilolay, 2021). This plant also holds a quality control central laboratory. From 1986 until 1990, Williner introduced major changes in its cheese production techniques, incorporating the ultra-filtration system for milk which allowed for an increase in its production capacity. In 2000, they added areas for the production of fresh products such as yoghurt, ricotta, cream, pasteurized milk and dairy desserts (Ilolay, 2021). This new plant has a drying capacity of 600,000 liters of milk per day

(Bidegaray, 2003; Bidegaray, 2004). In 2005, they added an area for the production of grated and processed cheese (Ilolay, 2021). According to the company's president at that time, Alfredo Curiotti, the investment for the milk powder drying, the cheese production lines and the installation of the new milk reception system alone was around 15 million dollars (Bidegaray, 2006).

By 2003, the company and all its plants processed more than 380 million liters of milk per year and had more than 1200 direct employees. About 60 to 70% of its products were commercialized in the national market (Litoral, 2003), the company obtained 30% of its sales in Buenos Aires and 70% in the rest of the country (Bidegaray, 2006). The remaining was exported to several countries such as the USA, Canada, Australia, Algeria, Mexico, Brazil, Bolivia, Chile, and Paraguay (El Litoral, 2003, Bidegaray, 2004). Their biggest market for hard cheese was the USA, while Algeria was their main destination for milk powder (Bidegaray, 2006).

The strategic focus of the firm was to center their production in Bella Italia plant. So, in 2007 a new plant was built for the production of soft cheese and mozzarella cheese, equipped with French technology. It was able to process 250,000 liters of milk per day (Ilolay, 2021). In 2012, the production of dulce de leche done in the Rafaela plant was moved to this industrial complex. This allowed for an increase in production capacity and greater control of the different production parameters (Ilolay, 2021).

Williner is recognized in the industry for its management and administration skills with healthy and balanced economic conditions (Infocampo, 2007). The family's third generation had always been in charge of the company's strategic direction and operative management. However, in 2008, the company restructured the top management and decided that the fourth generation, which consisted of 30 members, would only be in charge of the company's strategic direction. The operative management would be in the hands of 14 trusted employees who had been working in the company for a long time in management positions. These measures aimed to clarify internally and externally the responsible parties for the different managerial tasks (TodoAgro, 2008).

In 2018 the company had 1300 direct employees in its industrial plants, branches, and distribution centers. As a strategy to increase its competitiveness they invested 20 million dollars in its Bella Italia plant and closed its factory in the city of Suardi, where 68 people worked. Some workers were relocated to the company's other plants and those who did not accept relocation were given financial compensation through voluntary retirement (Ulman, 2018). In 2020, the company processed 540 million liters of milk per year, which were transformed into 234 million kilos of product (Devincenzi, 2021) positioning Williner as the third dairy producer in the country (OCLA, 2020).

Thus, at present, Williner has dairy processing plants in El Trébol, Rafaela, Arrufó and Bella Italia, all in the province of Santa Fe. It has eleven warehouses for the maturation and conservation of dairy products, located in the provinces of Santa Fe, Neuquén, Corrientes, Salta, Mendoza, Córdoba and Buenos Aires. It also has an important dairy farm: Las Taperitas S.A. (Infocampo, 2007). The company employs 1300 employees and supplies a network of more than 40 distributors and representatives from its nine logistics centers. It participates in the international market (with a presence) among more than 30 countries (Devincenzi, 2021).

Throughout the growth of the firm, since its beginnings, the company has been an important player not only in its community but also for the technological environment. Many of their technological initiatives were the fruit of close relations with universities and research centers.

Relation with the technological environment: In 2004, the company succeeded in developing and patenting a unique product in the world: a probiotic cheese. The product was developed through the joint work of the company with researchers from the National Universities of Litoral (UNL), Tucumán (UNT) and the Reference Center for Lactobacilli (Ce.Re.La) in Tucumán (UNL News, 2004). In 2006, they signed an agreement with the Favaloro Foundation, coronary medical research and teaching institution, to launch its healthy Ilolay Vita line on the market, which was to carry the foundation's logo (TodoAgro, 2006).

In 2014, Williner signed with the INTI (National Institute of Industrial Technology) an associative agreement to form a public-private consortium for the energetic use of organic waste and its transformation into biofertilizers (TodoAgro, 2014). Likewise, in 2015, together with other companies in the region, they signed an environmental commitment agreement with institutions of the city and the municipality of Rafaela for the sustainable management of solid urban waste (CCIRR, 2015).

Commitment to society: The Williner family actively participated in their social environment and contributed to various fields. Armando Williner (Alfredo Williner's son) was involved in various activities related to the progress of the area. He was president of the Santa Fe Dairy Industry Association and the Chamber of Dairy Farmers, vice-president of the Dairy Industry Center and member of the Santa Fe Provincial Dairy Council, director of the Municipal Power Plant (El Litoral, 2000). Over the years, the Alfredo Williner Foundation has been consistently committed to society. In 1985, the company donated the "Swiss republic Plaza" (La Opinión, 2011). In 2011, the foundation supported the construction and equipping of the Miguel Alfredo Williner library at the National Technological University. It also participated in the construction of the community health center "Laura Williner de Bañón," which was inaugurated in 2017. This center covers gynecology, kinesiology, dentistry, cardiology, psychology, pediatrics, and a laboratory, with the possibility of extending their services to other specialties (La Opinión, 2017). More recently, in 2020, together with several companies from Rafaela, Williner donated 16 artificial respirators to face the Covid crisis (Gerbaudo, 2020b).

6 Conclusion

Through this chapter we have seen how, since the settlement of the first Italian and German-Swiss immigrants, Rafaela has grown and created a fabric of entrepreneurial initiatives. The first immigrants that arrived at the last decades of the nineteenth century devoted their life to the primary production work, however, rapidly the dairy and livestock farms gave birth to the first industrial entrepreneurial initiatives, dairy and meat processing. The emergence of these industries catalyzed other entrepreneurs' initiatives principally in the metal-mechanic industry to support their growth. Moreover, the knowledge accumulated in this area created the possibility for the entrepreneurial incursion into the auto-part sector. Rafaela has been able to exploit this web of opportunities in order to develop an entrepreneurial ecosystem that has supported its growth since its foundation. The case of *Sucesores de Alfredo Williner S.R.L.* is just an example of the entrepreneurial activities that germinated in Rafaela and became flagships for the country's economy. It is noteworthy that this entrepreneurial ecosystem remains active thanks to the conjoint work of actors from the public, private, and academic sectors. These actors promote the creation of entrepreneurial programs and set the pace for the development of a sustainable economy.

References

Algaba, F. (2015, February 19). Historia del queso Trebolgiano. *La opinión*. https://diariolaopinion.com.ar/contenido/246265/historia-del-queso-trebolgiano.

Anchorena, J. & Ronconi, L. (2012). Entrepreneurship, entrepreneurial values and public policy in Argentina. IDB Working Paper Series, No IDB-WP-316. *Inter-American Development Bank (IDB)*, Washington DC.

Basara, P. A, Maresca, G. & Baldacchino, P. (2013). Cluster–El caso de Rafaela. *Edutecne*. http://www.edutecne.utn.edu.ar/coini_2013/trabajos/COD15_TC.pdf

Bidegaray, F. (2003, December 19). La láctea Williner amplía su planta de Rafaela. *El cronista*. https://www.cronista.com/impresa-general/La-lactea-Williner-amplia-su-planta-de-Rafaela-20031219-0029.html.

Bidegaray, F. (2004, May 7). Williner sube la producción de leche en polvo y queso. *El cronista*. https://www.cronista.com/impresageneral/Williner-sube-la-produccion-de-leche-en-polvo-y-queso-20040507-0035.html.

Bidegaray, F. (2006, September 25). Williner amplía la producción de quesos con una nueva planta. *El cronista*. https://www.cronista.com/impresa-general/Williner-amplia-la-produccion-de-quesos-con-una-nueva-planta-20060925-0015.html.

Casabella, C. & Zaragozi, M. E. (2010). Rafaela, un milagro de la pampa gringa. *Universidad Nacional del Litoral*. https://www.fhuc.unl.edu.ar/portalgringo/crear/gringa/archivo/pdf/Rafaela,%20un%20milagro%20de%20la%20pampa%20gringa.pdf

Castellanos. (2019, October 24). La declaracion de ciudad, un hito singular. *Castellanos*. https://diariocastellanos.com.ar/2019/10/la-declaracion-de-ciudad-un-hito-singular/.

Castellanos. (2021a, January 30). Rafaela emprende 2021 continua con las inscripsiones. *Castellanos*. https://diariocastellanos.com.ar/2021/01/rafaela-emprende-2021-continua-con-las-inscripciones/

Castellanos. (2021b, Aril 22). El municipio avanza con el programa Rafaela emprende digital. *Castellanos*. https://diariocastellanos.com.ar/2021/04/el-municipio-avanza-con-el-programa-rafaela-emprende-digital/

CCIRR. (2015, June 8). Centro comercial e industrial Rafaela y región. Empresas comprometidas con el ambiente. *Centro comercial e industrial de Rafaela y región*. https://www.ccirr.com.ar/w9/VerNoticia.aspx?i=1671

Corach, M. (2019, October 24). Repensar y actuar para promover una nueva matriz energética. *Castellanos*. https://diariocastellanos.com.ar/2019/10/repensar-y-actuar-para-promover-una-nueva-matriz-energetica/

Costamagna, P. & Garrappa, M. (2010). *La experiencia de desarrollo local de Rafaela, Argentina.* Programa regional de formación para el desarrollo económico local con inclusión en América Latina y el Caribe (conectadel.org)

Devincenzi, A. (2021, March 12). Ilolay reestructuró su deuda y lanza un plan para darle batalla a la crisis. *El cronista.* https://www.cronista.com/apertura-negocio/empresas/nueva-etapa/

El Litoral (2000, November 9). Armando José Williner. *El litoral.* https://www.ellitoral.com/index.php/diarios/2000/11/09/informaciongeneral/INFO-02.html

El Litoral (2003, November 22). El regalo de cumpleaños de Williner fue una nueva sala para el hospital. *El litoral.* https://www.ellitoral.com/index.php/diarios/2003/11/22/regionales/REGI-01.html

Erbes, et al. (2019). *Industria 4.0: oportunidades y desafíos para el desarrollo productivo de la provincia de Santa Fe. Documentos de Proyectos.* CEPAL (Economic Commission for Latin America and the Caribbean).

Fleming, W. J. (1979). The cultural determinants of entrepreneurship and economic development: A case study of Mendoza Province, Argentina, 1861-1914. *Journal of Economic History, 39*(1), 211–224.

Grande, E. (2019, October 24). Los hitos en la formación de la colonia Rafaela en 1881. *Castellanos.* https://diariocastellanos.com.ar/2019/10/los-hitos-en-la-formacion-de-la-colonia-rafaela-en-1881/

Gerbaudo, A. (2020a, September 17). Mas de 90 emprendedores se sumaron al "Rafaela emprende Verde." *Viapais.* https://viapais.com.ar/rafaela/2001697-mas-de-90-emprendedores-se-sumaron-al-rafaela-emprende-verde/

Gerbaudo, A. (2020b, March 24). Empresas rafaelinas donaron respiradores. Viapais-Rafaela. *Viapais.* https://viapais.com.ar/rafaela/1658130-empresas-rafaelinas-donaron-respiradores/

Gerbaudo, A. (2021, April 16). Casi 60 emprendimientos participaran de la edición de "Rafaela emprende". *Viapais.* https://viapais.com.ar/rafaela/casi-60-emprendimientos-participaran-de-la-edicion-de-rafaela-emprende/

Gob Rafaela. (2021). *Ciudad de Rafaela, Gobierno Municipal.* Accessed May 24, 2021, from https://www.rafaela.gob.ar/Sitio/#/Inicio

ICEDeL. (2018). La industria de Rafaela y el desafío de la creación de empleo local. *Instituto de capacitación y estudios para el desarrollo local.* http://icedel.rafaela.gob.ar/archivos/ORDICEdel/Informe%203.1.%20con%20formato%20final.pdf

IDSR. (2021). *Instituto de desarrollo Sustentable de Rafaela.* Accessed May 24, 2021, from http://rafaela-sustentable.com.ar/sitio/#instituto

Ilolay. (2021). *Historia.* Accessed May 24, 2021, from http://institucional.ilolay.com.ar/institucional/Historia/

Infocampo. (2007, December 14). Williner: una láctea familiar que factura $ 500 M por año. *Infocampo.* https://www.infocampo.com.ar/williner-una-lactea-familiar-que-factura-500-m-por-ano/

La Opinion. (2011, August 30). *Plazoleta Republica Suiza.* La Opinion. https://diariolaopinion.com.ar/contenido/102388/plazoleta-republica-suiza.

La Opinion. (2017, April 8). Centro de salud que es orgullo de la comunidad. *La Opinion.* https://diariolaopinion.com.ar/contenido/177377/centro-de-salud-que-es-orgullo-de-la-comunidad

OCLA. (2020, August 3). Argentina: Ranking de Industrias lácteas 2019–2020. *Observatorio de la cadena láctea Argentina.* https://www.ocla.org.ar/contents/news/details/16607593-argentina-ranking-de-industrias-lacteas-2019-2020

Pradilla, M. (2012). Entrepreneurship in Argentina. In E. R. Brenes et al. (Eds.), *The future of entrepreneurship in Latin America* (pp. 57–76). Palgrave Macmillan.

Rafaela.com. (2010, September 21). Rafaela emprende: programa de asistencia integral a emprendedores. *Rafaela.com.* https://www.rafaela.com/cms/news/ver/2079/1/Rafaela-Emprende:-programa-de-asistencia-integral-a-emprendedores.html

Region Litoral. (2021). *Historia fundación de Rafaela, Santa Fe.* Accessed May 24, 2021, from https://www.regionlitoral.net/2014/11/historia-fundacion-de-rafaela-santa-fe.html

TodoAgro. (2006, October 12). Williner presenta su línea ilolay Vita con sello de Alimentos Fundación Favaloro. *TodoAgro*. https://www.todoagro.com.ar/williner-presenta-su-linea-ilolay-vita-con-sello-de-alimentos-fundacion-favaloro/

TodoAgro. (2008, November, 27). *Williner: ocho décadas de tradición láctea*. TodoAgro. https://www.todoagro.com.ar/williner-ocho-decadas-de-tradicion-lactea/

TodoAgro. (2014, January 30). Forman consorcio para reducir el impacto ambiental y agregar valor a los residuos orgánicos. *TodoAgro*. https://www.todoagro.com.ar/forman-consorcio-para-reducir-el-impacto-ambiental-y-agregar-valor-a-los-residuos-organicos/

Ulman, P. (2018, February 4). "La reestructuración estratégica de Williner tiene como objetivo crecer". *La opinion*. https://diariolaopinion.com.ar/contenido/210144/la-reestructuracion-estrategica-de-williner-tiene-como-objetivo-crecer

UNLNews. (2004, August 18). Logran producir un bioqueso único en el mundo. *UNLNews*. https://www.unl.edu.ar/noticias/news/view/logran_producir_un_bioqueso_único_en_el_mundo#.YLD5ay_pNWO

Vincenti, M. I. (2019, October 24). Rafaela, la región más gringa. *Castellanos*. https://diariocastellanos.com.ar/2019/10/rafaela-la-region-mas-gringa/

Gustavo Birollo, PhD, is a professor and Director of International Relations at the Faculty of Business Administration, Laval University, Canada. His research focuses on strategy implementation, strategy-as-practice, and middle managers. His research has been published in the International Journal of Project Management and presented at international conferences such as those of the Academy of Management, EGOS (European Group of Organization Studies) and the Strategic Management Society. Prior to joining academia, he worked as a project manager in the agro-industry in South America, North America, and Europe. In particular, he has managed integration projects in cross-border acquisitions.

Entrepreneurship in Bolivia

Sergio Garcia-Agreda B., Mariana Pérez Escobar, and Alejandro Zegarra Saldaña

Abstract

The Plurinational State of Bolivia is known to be a developing country with a rebellious population and rich in natural resources. It is known in an international context regarding its entrepreneurial ecosystem, which has been rapidly developing during the last 15 years, even during the COVID-19 pandemic which accelerated the technological transformation and created articulations between institutions in order to give a merged and integral support to entrepreneurs.

Because of its strategic geographical position, Bolivia is an important connector in Latin America, allowing not only entrepreneurship to flourish into neighboring countries, but also, by being the shortest route for international ventures to grow in the country as well.

In the last 6 months, during the COVID-19 pandemic, Bolivia has been able to adapt and confront the crisis, rapidly being part of the world's vision of virtual businesses, however, there is still the need to improve various factors of doing business, such as taxation, bureaucracy, and construction permits.

Even though the current entrepreneurial situation of the country doesn't offer a positive perspective, changes are being made to adapt and support entrepreneurs in the country. Today, more than 35 "hubs" exist, demonstrating the capacity of involved institutions to articulate and strategically plan their support.

S. Garcia-Agreda B. (✉) · M. Pérez Escobar · A. Zegarra Saldaña
Olave School of Business, Universidad Privada Boliviana, Cochabamba, Bolivia
e-mail: sgarciaagreda@upb.edu; marianaperez@upb.edu; alejandrozegarra@upb.edu

L.-P. Dana et al. (eds.), *Entrepreneurship in South America*, Springer Texts in Business and Economics, https://doi.org/10.1007/978-3-030-97060-4_3

1 Introduction

The Plurinational State of Bolivia is known to be a developing country with a rebellious population and rich in natural resources. It is known in an international context regarding its entrepreneurial ecosystem, which has been rapidly developing during the last 15 years, even during the COVID-19 pandemic, which accelerated the technological transformation and created articulations between institutions in order to give a merged and integral support to entrepreneurs.

2 Historical Context

Bolivia's entrepreneurial ecosystem is strongly influenced by the socio-political, cultural, and economic evolution of the country. Since its foundation, Bolivia has constantly been involved in both international and national conflicts that has shaped Bolivian's insubordinate attitude towards conflicts (Asebey Claure & Mamani Siñani, 2015).

The Spanish came to conquer Bolivia in 1535 with Spanish Diego Almagro arriving to the Charcas Audience in nowadays Sucre, and a few years later, in 1545, Diego Huallpa discovered the Cerro Rico de Potosí (Fig. 1), where colonials

Fig. 1 Arco de Cobija and Cerro Rico de Potosí, Bolivia. Source: ©André Manjón—Photofox, used with permission

exploited an immense quantity of silver that brought important wealth to the Spanish crown. In 1825, Simon Bolivar liberated the country from Spanish rule, with a vast newly independent area of 2,363, 769 km^2.

Today, Bolivia's territory is 1,098,581 km^2 and it has frontiers with five countries: Argentina, Brazil, Chile, Paraguay, and Peru (Naboer Fjerne, n.d.).

Bolivia faced internal socio-political and cultural conflicts. Even before the independence, there were revolts from indigenous people against the creoles and mestizos that came with the Spanish crown. New political parties with national, socialist, and revolutionary points of view start gaining support from the Bolivian population resulting in the National Revolution of 1952. (Mercado et al., 2005).

The following years are characterized by constant military coup d'état, peasant uprising with guerrilla leaders such as Ernesto "Che" Guevara, dictatorships, and populations' general discontent. (Mercado et al., 2005). During this period, the economy was fluctuating, based on "cheap" external debt, and good exporting prices on tin, petroleum, and of the newly found natural gas reserves. Due to the international tin market collapse in 1985, the worst hyperinflation of the country, and of Latin American history, escalated to 24,000% (Dana, 2011).

After this, Bolivia started a period of uprising and political instability because of constant changes of Presidents, violent protests against energy management and taxes. In 2005, new elections were called where socialist leader Evo Morales Ayma won the presidential elections, becoming the first indigenous Bolivian to take office. An era of nationalization starts, where the government gets involved with gas operation, land reform bills are passed to expropriate up to one-fifth of Bolivian land for redistribution, a new constitution is drafted to give more wealth and greater voice to the indigenous majority, an increase of the national minimum wage, the launch of Bolivia's first telecommunication satellite, and a reduction of the miners and coca producers revolts. After a year of an interim conservative government due to Morales resignation after controversial results in the 2019 presidential elections, in October 2020, former colleague of Morales, Luis Arce, won the presidential elections with the same political party. (BBC News, 2018).

3 Environment for Entrepreneurship

3.1 Understanding Bolivia's Social Context

Because of the constant social revolts, wars, and fight for equal rights of people, Bolivians are known to be hard workers and rebellious towards social and political statements that they do not like. In that sense, this insubordinate spirit demonstrates that the Bolivian population has developed the capacity to transform the country through actions like social revolts; for example, the regime into a socialist government, led by a former cocalero leader.

However, this spirit has also compelled Bolivians to live with a lack of a unified vision, which has an impact on the country in a social and economic way. Likewise, there is an important ethnical discrimination in education and labor market, where indigenous usually access schools of lower educational quality, and it hass been demonstrated that in the labor market, they usually occupy low-skilled labor and are in less paid sectors, facing different labor market structures from non-indigenous ones (Mercado et al., 2003). It is important to recognize three important economic activities that co-exist in Bolivia: the firm-type sector (focused on impersonal transactions, competitions between sellers, prices are settled by vendors and no negotiation takes place in this sense), the Bazaar sector, and the State-controlled sector (focus on bureaucracy, competition unnecessary since the states declare monopoly, prices are dictated by the state and no negotiation is necessary). The Bazaar sector is "deemed as a social and cultural system, a way of life and a general mode of commerce activity" (Dana, 2011) where the focus is on personal relationships rather than activities or prices, and negotiation takes place between seller and buyer to fix a price. Firms in the Bazaar do not see each other as competition, even though there is little brand differentiation among merchants, and they create cluster-like sectors depending on the products. Because of the lack of developed market institutions, Bolivia developed a strong informal economy due to its underground activities, such as street vending. (Dana, 2011).

3.2 Role of the Informal Economy

The social and economic problem has led the country to have a strong informal economy (Fig. 2), representing 60% of GDP in 2015 (Velasco Valdez, 2015), increasing to 73.2% in 2018, with a greater representation of the women population (75.2%) than men population (71.5%), placing Bolivia as the first in the world in the ranking of informal economy (Figueroa Cárdenas, 2020). This popular economy is

Fig. 2 Avenida Tumusla, Bazaar-type sector in La Paz. Source: ©André Manjón—Photofox, used with permission

part of a network of social relations both horizontal, with the potential to become a "broad-based economy" (similar to the definition of clusters), and vertical, towards larger companies and multinational companies (Müller, 2017). This informal commerce goes beyond the illicit goods and cross-borders flow and is mainly based on commerce (Figueroa Cárdenas, 2020), creating a complex relationship between the government and the merchants (Müller, 2017). It has an impact on the entrepreneurial ecosystem of the country, since it facilitates the creation of new ventures without the weight of the law and the need to pay taxes, thus creating opportunities.

The importance on the informal economy presented relies on its impact on the entrepreneurship environment, where it has been proven that entrepreneurs that come from informal markets do not have a clear concept of entrepreneurship and entrepreneurs (Bailey et al., 2020).

3.3 Difficulty of Doing Business in Bolivia

The World Bank Group (2020) develops the Doing Business magazine each year in which it compares quantitative indicators on business regulations and the protection of property rights between 190 economies. In 2020, it scored Bolivia with 51,7 Doing Business score (an economy's ease of doing business score is reflected on a scale of several indicators, from 0 to 100, where 0 represents the lowest and 100 represents the best performance), and ranked 150 from 190 economies. Bolivia's ranking is lowered mainly by the score of 21.6 DB in Paying Taxes indicator, and 69.4 DB in Starting a Business indicator, which measured the procedure to legally start and formally operate a company, time required to complete each procedure, cost required per procedure, and paid-in minimal capital. (World Bank Group, 2020).

Bolivia has a total of seven incubators and four accelerators installed in the country, which demonstrates a growth regarding the previous year (2019) through the number of actors involved, including one accelerator that focuses in technological advances. There are 160 actives start-ups in the country, where 95,62% operate in Santa Cruz, La Paz, and Cochabamba, the three main cities of the countries. The main difficulties these start-ups face are lack of finance (24,23%), strategic allies (19,38%), and networking (14,54%). (Bolivia Emprende, 2020).

3.4 Entrepreneurship in Bolivia: Its Development

Bolivia's entrepreneurial ecosystem evolved per region, and it slowly headed to a national unity, since these alliances "multiplies the effect of the support for entrepreneurs, compared to the individual support that each institution may give" (Salomón, 2020).

In 2002, in Santa Cruz (Fig. 3), an alliance conformed by the *Gobernación* (municipal prefecture at the time), the Autonomous University Gabriel René Moreno, Industrial and Commerce Chamber, Exporters' Chamber, and the

Fig. 3 City of Santa Cruz de la Sierra, Bolivia. Source: ©Evelyn Cabrera—Photofox, used with permission

Polytechnic University of Valencia (Spain) created the *Trabajo Empresa* Foundation, with the purpose of promoting economic development and the labor market, through the articulation of all the involved parts, resources, trainings, the integral development of the businesses they supported, among others (Fundación Trabajo Empresa, 2011). At the time, they supported mainly small commerce entrepreneurships like jewelry stores or bakeries since they were essential to the economy. However, people started moving towards technology, web pages, and system developments since it was the new need of the environment (Salomón, 2020). In 2006, the *Red Bolivia Emprendedora*, later renamed *Bolivia Emprende*, was created, which is an entity that "brings together governments, companies and society for the entrepreneurial development of Bolivia, encouraging an entrepreneurial culture" (Fundación Emprender Futuro, 2013). They focused mainly on working with universities and schools to inform and educate students regarding entrepreneurship, as well as creating different entrepreneurial opportunities like fairs to promote their services or products.

Having different public, private and mingled networks created on a national scale, Global Entrepreneurship Network (GEN) initiated different activities to enhance entrepreneurship in each city through Start-up Weekends, starting in 2008, even though the strongest city on the subject continued to be Santa Cruz.

In 2016, Hub Santa Cruz was created, an ecosystem that rewards the inspiration of various initiatives and provides the necessary support to the community, specifically in the subjects of innovation, technology, science and entrepreneurship (Hub

Fig. 4 City of Nuestra Señora de La Paz, Bolivia. Source: ©André Manjón—Photofox, used with permission

Santa Cruz, 2020a, b). First of the kind in the country, this hub consolidates the support of various institutions, private and public, the government, municipalities, universities, in order to support entrepreneurships in a direct way. Thus, the biggest Bolivian network was created, with the support of institutions like *Generaknow*, Entrepreneurial Women Institute, Red *Bolivia Emprendedora*, among others; by being part of the ecosystem, it has departmental allies and events focused on Santa Cruz' ventures (Hub Santa Cruz, 2020a, b), and aims to be part of the international network as well. This model will later be reproduced in other cities, like Tarija, Sucre, Cochabamba, La Paz (Fig. 4), with different names depending on its locations, since it proved to be an excellent source for entrepreneurs to promote, articulate, and learn about entrepreneurships (Salomón, 2020). These hubs not only focuses in making an entrepreneurial networking, but also, in creating conscience, share resources, and provide trainings to potential entrepreneurs around the world, since today, they articulate with speakers or hubs from others countries, such as Argentina, Paraguay, or Peru (Hub Santa Cruz, 2020a, b).

Since, there has been an important focus on the fact of belonging to a cluster, but with actions and not only as a passive participant, where a data flux has to be developed in order to link everyone to the ecosystem (Infantas, 2020). The geographical distribution has been solved with internet connection, which allows inclusions of all sectors, rural or urbans, allowing a major scope of the entrepreneurial ecosystem. The fact of belonging to a cluster has numerous advantages as alliances, capital to pay for services, education, or high-level providers that individually would be difficult to pay for, among others (Infantas, 2020).

Méndez (2020) highlights that media coverage of entrepreneurial activities is insufficient, which is why the development of the ecosystem was significantly slowed down. It is not but recently that media start gaining interest in the sector, in how they are working and what innovations can be found, according to the impact in the economy that Start-Ups or ventures can have. It is because of this lack of interest that the magazine *Emprendedores* was created, being a pioneer in giving limelight to the Bolivian entrepreneur. It is a "white page" in which ventures are explained and promoted (Méndez, 2020). An alternative channel of communication are social networks, where entrepreneurs started to use this system as an alternative to traditional media (Arzabe, 2020).

Likewise, an "entrepreneurial mindset is missing, which is developed with a set of skills that enable entrepreneurs to identify and make the most of opportunities, overcome and learn from setbacks, and succeed in a variety of settings" (NFTE, 2020). Universities are working to mold the entrepreneur vision and mentality, for example, the Forum: Bolivian Entrepreneurial Ecosystem and challenges (Facultad De Postgrado UPB, 2020) which united the entrepreneur ecosystem's actors nationwide, from entrepreneurs themselves, to institutional organizers.

On the other hand, new entreprises are working cross-country, like *Emprendexito*, which is a Training Center that develops the skills of young professionals, entrepreneurs, and independent professionals to face the challenges of the market and sales (Emprendexito, 2020). However, it is important to have an international education on the subject, "since the traction entrepreneur has the potential to open international markets and will compete at a regional level for funds" (Angulo, 2018). The culture of selfless mentoring to entrepreneurs is beginning to appear thanks to events with experts in the field, but there is a need to increase them in order to have more access to international mentors, experts in this area (Angulo, 2018). Education should reach all the structure of the ecosystem (Angulo, 2018).

Salinas (2020) points out that all the advance on the ecosystem was crucial to highlight its importance but it is fundamental to have a greater government's support in order to have a greater impact. This effort can be measured through investment in innovation, research, and technological development. Bolivia presented its Patriotic Agenda 2025—Bolivia's General Economic and Social Development Plan for Living Well (PDGES), compiling 13 pillars are presented to implement a Sovereign and Dignified Bolivia (CEPAL—Naciones Unidas, 2013), where pillar 4 refers to the Scientific and Technological Sovereignty. In order to follow this goals, various approaches have been made, like the *Intervenciones Urbanas* program in 2019, which supports and promotes the talent and creativity of Bolivians through competitive funds that the State has available, covering areas like Cultural industries, cinema and audiovisuals, sports, social and technological innovation (Rivera Caballero & Caballero, 2019). Likewise, the Municipal Autonomous Government of La Paz has an ongoing program since 2015 to support cultural entrepreneurships generating encounters between producers and others actors of the area, where "the idea is to generate an internal market that in La Paz and Bolivia is still small, but also to generate international connections with other markets, especially in the Southern Cone" (Rivera Caballero & Caballero, 2019). However, even though there are specific actions from the government, the biggest support for the entrepreneurial ecosystem in the country at the moment came from the networks presented beforehand, and that a strategy of technology, digital transformation and orange economy is fundamental to develop this ecosystem as well (Salinas, 2020). The future of technology is based on capacities, and thus, in "a change of form and background" meaning, not only the use of technological tools, but also, the change of attitude towards technology and its implementation (Santander, 2020). Even though the COVID-19 pandemic was a major drawback in the economy, Bolivia has been able to adapt and slowly develop its technology and entrepreneurial ecosystem.

Finally, it is important to highlight the necessity of legal security, which has not been yet developed in the country. Even though there are drafts of possible laws that will pass in labor, administrative and commercial aspects of entrepreneurships, at the moment, no law has passed to protect entrepreneurs and their creation.

Today, there are six incubators and four accelerators that allow Start-Ups to develop, where most of the finance is directed to hire professionals for software development, marketing, or expansion of the business. The majority of the support needed is of finance, strategic allies, and networking, however, the described ecosystem has helped entrepreneurs to develop faster and with more tools at hand (Fundación para la Producción (FUNDA-PRÓ); Fundación Solidaridad y Desarrollo Sostenible (Solydes); Fundación Emprender Futuro; BIM Asset Management, 2020).

4 Towards the Future

Multinational organizations are starting to invest in developing countries in Latin America; for example, CAF and BID will be investing 400 million dollars in 2021, mainly for entrepreneurships focused on subsistence and innovation, referring to entrepreneurships that industrialize and help local communities (Ventures Pulse, 2020).

In order to attract more seed capital to the country, important advances are being made through education with the support of the academic body of different institutions, that helps the population to understand what entrepreneurship is and the mentality regarding ventures focused on triple impact (sustainability, social, and technological entrepreneurships). Universities are the main drivers of this education, even though there is a need for government's involvement to impact on a larger scale in order to attract more seed capital and support to the entrepreneurial ecosystem (Salomón, 2020) (Salinas, 2020). In the one hand, education is needed to develop an entrepreneurial mindset, to motivate and inspire possible entrepreneurs to take the risk, in the other hand, which is slowly but steadily being developed as well, is the project management skills to carry out the business day to day, with the support of the technological platforms to have a major scope of the project (Santander, 2020).

5 Case Study: YAIGO

Where some fail, others succeed. This is particularly true for the development of a company that was established by four founders who worked hard in their Start-Up, in the middle of the COVID-19 pandemic.

Ariel Valverde, a 34-year-old system engineer, had experience working first as an informatic security, then as a contact center manager of one of the most important telecommunication companies in the country, TIGO. He and his brother, Erick, started thinking about ideas they could develop as a Start-Up, as they believe that they had the knowledge and the ideas might have the potential to become important international companies someday. They started off with a software company, but did not have a valid business model, which is why they closed this first company.

Ariel and Carlos Barrera, two friends at the time, were in a meeting discussing what Bolivia needed, and they established that the country needed a delivery system solution. The company was founded by Ariel, Carlos, Erick and another long-time friend, Saul Paniagua. Keeping in mind the international aspect they wanted the company to have in the near future, they chose a name that would directly connect their business model, an e-commerce and delivery model, to the name: YAIGO (You Ask, I Go). The mission: To be the most used delivery application in the country, integrating all regions. The vision: To deliver anything the client needs in the least amount of time.

Back in 2016, there was only local delivery competition, no transnational companies that were established in Bolivia. The first thing they did, first individually, then as a group in order to complement the idea, was to research what those international companies did, what they did not do, and what were the client's complaints in order to understand the key points of the company they were developing. During 2 years and 8 months, these four founders dedicated their time and money to develop the platform themselves, so as to be sure that everything works as they have planned, which is a major difference since usually these platforms are usually outsourced. Likewise, they studied the market of non-main cities, since time was passing and other international competitors, like Uber Eats and *Pedidos Ya*, were entering the country but only in the main cities. They completed the team adding one operational manager and four developers, and in May 2019, they were finally ready to launch their company with an application that linked the client, the commerce and the delivery man online.

YAIGO had to adapt its business model to the varying socio-cultural reality present in the country, since it started changing to a digital era where payments were made through bank transfers, QR payments, among others; consumers massively started using applications platforms, and the transportation was severely limited for all. They had to familiarize with the difficulties of obtaining the government's permits to work during the pandemic and where deliveries of various products had to be made promptly and efficiently. Said business model also had to go beyond what the competition (national and international) offered. Goods such as medicine, school supplies, groceries, and even drinks had to be adapted to the need of Bolivians through delivery system, in a certain way confronting the social paradigm where access to differentiated goods was only given to medium or high-class Bolivians.

Once the company launched their operations, they started expanding to other non-main cities, so when they arrived to the main cities where major transnational companies had established, they already had a path and were recognized by Bolivians. YAIGO was following the spread of the COVID-19 pandemic, which is why they decided to act before it hit, as to assure that the company would continue operations even when the country would enter the rigid quarantine[1] period. They decided to approach the Commerce Chamber and directly offer them discounts during the quarantine period, in one hand to support the commerce that would close because of the rigid quarantine, and in the other hand, to create loyalty from the clients. At the time, they decided to approach the biggest pharmacy chains from the country in order to be able to deliver medicine during the pandemic.

When the pandemic was upon the country, the founders of YAIGO decided to rapidly organize the main tasks that cannot be delegated since they are crucial to the well-function of the company. For example, one of the founders was in charge of negotiating the government's permission to operate during the rigid quarantine, another was in charge of the logistics of the deliveries, the need of materials to operate like backpacks or uniforms when everything is closed, among others. They met at 5 am and at 12 am every day during the crisis in order to discuss what they awaited, and the conclusion of the operations of the day. This allowed a rapid decision making based on crucial information each of the founders had. At the beginning of the rigid quarantine, there were more commands than the platform supported, or even YAIGO could take care of, so YAIGO sent individual apology messages to the 25% of the commands they could not comply, and gave them a purchase vouchers. Informal markets were closed at first, but were later secretly opened for consumers, giving lower prices, selling through Marketplace (Facebook), and offering their own delivery system that did not charge the consumer, thus becoming a new competitor for YAIGO.

YAIGO focused on the following in order to survive the growing commands and the critical situation of the pandemic, and consequently, the rigid quarantine, through the agility on processes, technology, and continuous improvements, innovation, and corporate social responsibility. Processes were reviewed in order to make it more efficient; the technology of the platform was developed and updated every week in order to give the best platform experience to their clients (consumers, commerce and delivery men); innovation came from the fact that they had to think in ways to deliver all of what the consumers required; and corporate social responsibility by participating in community pots or contributing to causes such as pediatric oncological support. (Valverde, 2020) Not only was the company able to survive the pandemic crisis, where other companies had to close, but they were able to

[1] The rigid quarantine in Bolivia was from March 22nd to May 31st, where there was almost a total paralysis of activities. The country entered a more flexible quarantine in the following months, until August 31st, where there was the first "post-confinement" status.

become leaders in delivery throughout the country, main and non-main cities included, establishing the regional inclusion they established in their mission. YAIGO was also able to support other ventures through their delivery system, allowing them to grow in a challenging time.

As for the expansion, with the now validated model of e-commerce and delivery that YAIGO has, they were able to open operations in other countries, ending 2020 with seven countries in operation, or to be operated: Guatemala, Paraguay, El Salvador, Chile, México, Nicaragua, and proximately, Spain. Not only are they starting to buy other delivery companies in said countries, but they are gaining international recognition that spots this Start-Up in the Latin American entrepreneurial context. This acknowledgment has situated YAIGO in the view of Start-Up accelerators, attracting financial investment of a million dollars as well as an interesting team to implement their model in other countries. INCAE has named YAIGO as part of the 20 best Start-Ups of 2020, which is important to denote since it is the year where the pandemic crisis hit the country. (CAINCO, 2020) This Start-Up also won the InnovaTIC 2020, a nationwide award for TIC solutions (FUNDETIC-BOLIVIA, 2020). Today, this 100% Bolivian company is worth more than 20 million dollars. (CAINCO, 2020).

6 Conclusion

Even though the current entrepreneurial situation of the country does not offer a positive perspective, changes are being made in order to adapt and support entrepreneurs in the country. Today, more than 35 "hubs" similar to the one in Santa Cruz exist, demonstrating the capacity of involved institutions to articulate and strategically plan their support.

Salomón (2020) stated that entrepreneurs started pointing out the necessity of constructing a national politic regarding entrepreneurship in order to be supported, to promote the cultural entrepreneurship ecosystem that has already advanced in the last 15 years, and the need to have a safe context for entrepreneurs to develop. Even though in the last 6 months, during the COVID-19 pandemic, Bolivia has been able to adapt and confront the crisis, rapidly being part of the world's vision of virtual businesses, there is still the need to improve various factors of doing business, such as taxation, bureaucracy, and construction permits.

The current entrepreneurial education should start before higher education studies in order to introduce some seeds to start a business. Education should emphasize in innovation and the need to develop a creative mindset, there are some initiatives such as Quantum (electric cars), Mamut (recycling of tires to park floors), the lithium boom, and the high-technological services that could be developed and exported that proved that there are many blue oceans to be exploited.

Finally, because of its strategic geographical position, Bolivia is an important connector in Latin America, allowing not only entrepreneurship to flourish into neighboring countries, but also, by being the shortest route for international ventures to grow in the country as well.

References

Angulo, V. (2018, December 12). *El despegue del emprendedor boliviano*. Retrieved from Revista Emprendedores: https://emprendedores.bo/el-despegue-del-emprendedor-boliviano/

Arzabe, G. (2020, December 19). *Foro: Ecosistema Emprendedor Boliviano, retos y desafíos*. Retrieved from Online Forum post: https://www.facebook.com/facultadde.postgradoupb/videos/1358593901150262

Asebey Claure, R. C., & Mamani Siñani, R. L. (2015). Violence and conflict in the history of Bolivia. *T'inkazos*, 129–150.

Bailey, A. B., Nogales, C. S., Murillo, S. L., & Arroyo, G. C. (2020). Entre el emprendedurismo y la subsistencia. *Revista Investigación y Negocios*, 112–121.

BBC News. (2018, January 10). *Bolivia profile–Timeline*. Retrieved from BBC News: https://www.bbc.com/news/world-latin-america-18727510

Bolivia Emprende. (2020, Septiembre 18). *Crecen las startups en Bolivia: La mayoría está en Santa Cruz de la Sierra, Cochabamba y La Paz*. Retrieved from Bolivia Emprende: https://boliviaemprende.com/noticias/crecen-las-startups-en-bolivia-la-mayoria-esta-en-santa-cruz-de-la-sierra-cochabamba-y-la-paz

CAINCO. (2020, December 10). *Yaigo: la startup boliviana valorada en más de 20 millones de dólares continúa expandiéndose*. Retrieved from Empresa y Desarrollo–CAINCO: https://www.cainco.org.bo/empresaydesarrollo/2020/12/10/yaigo-la-startup-boliviana-valorada-en-mas-de-20-millones-de-dolares-continua-expandiendose/

CEPAL–Naciones Unidas. (2013). *Agenda Patriótica 2025- Plan de Desarrollo General Económico y Social para el Vivir Bien (PDGES) de Bolivia*. Retrieved from Observatorio Regional de Planificación para el Desarrollo: https://observatorioplanificacion.cepal.org/es/planes/agenda-patriotica-2025-plan-de-desarrollo-general-economico-y-social-para-el-vivir-bien

Dana, L.-P. (2011). Entrepreneurship in Bolivia: An ethnographic enquiry. *International Journal Business and Emerging Markets*, 75–88.

Emprendexito. (2020, December 10). *Emprendexito*. Retrieved from Emprendexito: https://www.facebook.com/emprenderexito

Facultad De Postgrado UPB. (2020, December 19). *Foro: Ecosistema Emprendedor Boliviano, retos y desafíos*. Retrieved from Facultad de Postgrado UPB: https://www.facebook.com/facultadde.postgradoupb/videos/1358593901150262

Figueroa Cárdenas, M. (2020, May 1). *Renaciendo de la crisis: Visibilizando las oportunidades de la economía informal*. Retrieved from PNUD Bolivia: https://www.bo.undp.org/content/bolivia/es/home/blog/renaciendo-de-la-crisis%2D%2Dvisibilizando-las-oportunidades-de-la-e1.html#:~:text=Con%20respecto%20a%20este%20%C3%BAltimo,pa%C3%ADses%2C%20exceptuando%20Brasil%20y%20Uruguay.

Fundación Emprender Futuro. (2013). *Bolivia Emprende*. Retrieved from Bolivia Emprende: https://boliviaemprende.com/

Fundación para la Producción (FUNDA-PRÓ); Fundación Solidaridad y Desarrollo Sostenible (Solydes); Fundación Emprender Futuro; BIM Asset Management. (2020, September). *Mapeo del Ecosistema de Tecnología Digital en Bolivia 2020*. Retrieved from Bolivia Emprende: https://boliviaemprende.com/noticias/crecen-las-startups-en-bolivia-la-mayoria-esta-en-santa-cruz-de-la-sierra-cochabamba-y-la-paz

Fundación Trabajo Empresa. (2011). *Misión y Visión*. Retrieved from Fundación Trabajo Empresa: http://www.fte.org.bo/Principal/VisionesYMision

FUNDETIC-BOLIVIA. (2020). *InnovaTIC Bolivia*. Retrieved from Fundacion para el Desarrollo de las Tecnologias de Informacion y Comunicacion en Bolivia: https://premioinnovaticbolivia.org.bo/

Hub Santa Cruz. (2020a). *Hub Santa Cruz*. Retrieved from Hub Santa Cruz: https://hubsantacruz.com/

Hub Santa Cruz. (2020b, noviembre 16–23). *Semana Mundial del Emprendimiento*. Retrieved from Hub Santa Cruz: https://l.facebook.com/l.php?u=https%3A%2F%2Femprendedoreslatam.com%2Fgew2020%2F%3Ffbclid%3DIwAR1Gf_9hbPCLd5jXpPHxFDujf76DNqFu1lIzBQJQMmNZcJlm3bhdhmai2qc&h=AT2L8H7ymCy4rh_T0X_SeZMl7W6o0pvhh8WncHGLGSCOPoNewnweKUmDU9PkWGLc0-yWslANQ0QrOlKnvMUycW0H9iOpeP6b3Io

Infantas, K. (2020, December 19). *Foro: Ecosistema Emprendedor Boliviano, retos y desafíos*. Retrieved from Online Forum post: https://www.facebook.com/facultadde.postgradoupb/videos/1358593901150262

Méndez, W. J. (2020, December 19). *Foro: Ecosistema Emprendedor Boliviano, retos y desafíos*. Retrieved from Online Forum post: https://www.facebook.com/facultadde.postgradoupb/videos/1358593901150262

Mercado, A. F., Andersen, L. E., Muriel, H., & B. (2003). Discriminación étnica en el sistema educativo y el mercado de trabajo de Bolivia. *Revista Latinoamericana de. Desarrollo Económico*, 69–98.

Mercado, A. F., Leitón, J. G., & Chacón, M. F. (2005). El crecimiento económico en Bolivia (1953-2003). *Revista Latinoamericana de Desarrollo Económico*, 9–42.

Müller, J. (2017). *La regulación del comercio en Bolivia: de la economía informarl al mercado extralegal*. IAJED.

Naboer Fjerne. (n.d.). *Bolivia Bajo Cambio*. Retrieved from Vecinos Remotos–Naboer Fjerne: http://www.fjernenaboer.dk/index.php?PID=276

NFTE. (2020). *Entrepreneurial Mindset*. Retrieved from NFTE: https://www.nfte.com/entrepreneurial-mindset/

Rivera Caballero, M. J., & Caballero, A. (2019, October 7). *Cinco sectores son clave para el desarrollo de la economía naranja*. Retrieved from Guardiana: https://guardiana.com.bo/especiales/cinco-sectores-clave-para-el-desarrollo-de-la-economia-naranja/

Salinas, M. (2020, December 19). Foro*: Ecosistema Emprendedor Boliviano, retos y desafíos*. Retrieved from Online Forum Post: https://www.facebook.com/facultadde.postgradoupb/videos/1358593901150262

Salomón, R. (2020, December 19). *Foro: Ecosistema Emprendedor Boliviano, retos y desafíos*. Retrieved from Online Forum Post: https://www.facebook.com/facultadde.postgradoupb/videos/1358593901150262

Santander, J. (2020, December 19). *Foro: Ecosistema Emprendedor Boliviano, retos y desafíos*. Retrieved from Online Forum post: https://www.facebook.com/facultadde.postgradoupb/videos/1358593901150262

The World Bank Group. (2020). *Ease of Doing Business Scores*. Retrieved from The World Bank: https://www.doingbusiness.org/en/data/doing-business-score

Valverde, A. (2020, November 17). Desarrollo de YAIGO. (S. García-Agreda, Interviewer).

Velasco Valdez, D. (2015). *Economía informal en bolivia: Análisis, evaluación y cuantificación en base al enfoque monetario de la demanda de efectivo (Periodo 1994–2014)*. Investigación & Desarrollo.

Ventures Pulse. (2020, September 6). *Salvo en America Latina, se mantiene el nivel de inversión en capital de riesgo*. Retrieved from El Cronista: https://www.cronista.com/finanzasmercados/Salvo-en-America-latina-se-mantiene-el-nivel-de-inversion-en-capital-de-riesgo-20200906-0031.html

World Bank Group. (2020). Economy profile bolivia. *Doing business 2020–Comparing business regulation of 190 economies*, 4–9.

Sergio García-Agreda B. is a Doctor in Business from the Polytechnic University of Valencia (UPV). Professor on Business Strategy and Digital Business at Universidad Privada Boliviana (UPB). International Speaker, Coach, Mentor and Senior Advisor in global and digital business. Director of International Department UPB, Director MBA double degree in Digital Business UPB—UPV. Managing Director of Garcia Agreda Corporation, a company focused on the development of companies and entrepreneurs with a global vision. Director of Global Business Academy—GBA World (under development) and Past Chair and founder of the Academy of International Business in Bolivia (now AIB LAC in Bolivia).

Mariana Pérez Escobar earned a MSc degree in Process Engineering in France and a MBA with an International Management specialization at Universidad Privada Boliviana (UPB) in Bolivia. Professor of Process Management and Business Management, currently works as International Network Manager, Academic Coordinator of the International Young Entrepreneurship Program and case writing with the Harvard methodology for MBA subjects in collaboration with Oscar Molina Tejerina Ph.D. at UPB. She is interested in research regarding processes, environmental subjects, and entrepreneurship.

Alejandro Zegarra Saldaña has a Ph.D. in ITC implementation in organizations from the Polytechnic University of Valencia in Spain, a Master in Economics from Tilburg University in the Netherlands, another Master in Excellency and quality of Education from Santiago de Compostela University in Spain. Professor of Innovation and Entrepreneurship of Universidad Privada Boliviana (UPB), he has practical experience in Strategic Management and Financial Services. He is currently part of the board in various financial institutions in Bolivia and the USA. He is the CEO of the Club Tenis La Paz.

Entrepreneurship in Brazil

Pedro Tonhozi de Oliveira, Rubens Mussolin Massa, Daniel do Prado Pagotto, Candido Vieira Borges Junior, and Marcus Alexandre Yshikawa Salusse

Abstract

This chapter depicts a glance picture of Brazil's state of entrepreneurship. It begins with a historical overview and establishment of the state. It describes the challenges that Brazil has faced as well as its current issues. The current state of entrepreneurship, the business environment, and entrepreneurs and small business owners' problems are discussed. The chapter concludes with suggestions for further development of entrepreneurship in Brazil.

1 Introduction

Brazil—a republic with over 8.5 million square kilometers and 211 million people—is one of the most multicultural and ethnically diverse nations in the world. This diversity has a significant impact on the entrepreneurial environment. People from all over the world came to Brazil to seek a new life and job opportunities. Its cities are huge, for example, São Paulo with a population of 12.18 million (Fig. 1). And, while it is true that the language—Portuguese—is a barrier for new entrants, in the last five years, the number of startups in Brazil grew by over 200% (Carrilo, 2020).

P. T. de Oliveira (✉)
Industrial Production and Operations Administration Department, FGV EAESP, São Paulo, SP, Brazil
e-mail: pedro.tonhozi@fgv.br

R. M. Massa · M. A. Y. Salusse
Center for Entrepreneurship and Business Venturing Research, FGV EAESP, São Paulo, SP, Brazil
e-mail: rubens.massa@fgv.br

D. d. P. Pagotto · C. V. Borges Junior
Entrepreneurship and Innovation Research Laboratory, Universidade Federal de Goiás, Goiás, GO, Brazil

L.-P. Dana et al. (eds.), *Entrepreneurship in South America*, Springer Texts in Business and Economics, https://doi.org/10.1007/978-3-030-97060-4_4

Fig. 1 São Paulo; Photo ©2021 Pedro Tonhozi de Oliveira

And, in 2018, for the first time, a Brazilian startup reached the mark of a Unicorn—a privately held startup company valued at over one billion dollars (Tunes, 2019). This achievement was an essential step for entrepreneurship in Brazil. Its consequence was that among Latin American countries, Brazil was the country that raised the most venture capital investments of 2019. In that year alone, 50.5% of venture capital investments in Latin America involved Brazilian startups. This represents 2.5 billion US dollars invested in over 220 deals (LAVCA's Annual Review of Tech Investment in Latin America, 2019).

Though we concede that those numbers make the impression that most Brazilian businesses are successful, characterized by innovation, accelerated growth, and high impact, most of the ventures are founded by necessity entrepreneurs with small businesses and high levels of informality (Greco et al., 2019). This reflects the average entrepreneur profile of low education and income. According to SEBRAE (2020), 82.75% of founders do not have a Bachelor's degree, and 89% have a monthly income under R$ 6,000.00 reais.

2 Historical Context

The first record of Brazil's history dates from 1500 when Portugal colonized the country. In 1822, it conquered its independence from Portugal, and in 1889, it became the Republic of Brazil. This period was marked by emerging characters

Fig. 2 Barão de Mauá; Lithographia de S. A. Sisson 1861 © Public Domain

that contributed to the consolidation of its entrepreneurial scenario. Before becoming a republic, the population was represented by over 2000 unique Indigenous groups, Portuguese settlers, and Africans brought in as slaves (Ribeiro, 2000).

In this pre-republic period, one pioneer entrepreneur was the remarkable *Irineu Evangelista de Sousa*, known as the Viscount of Mauá (Fig. 2). Born in 1813, he was even recognized as a Rothschild of the South American continent (The New York Times, 1871). After 20 years of working for the British company Carruthers, he resigned and built—at the age of 32—his first company—the *Companhia Ponta da Areia*—to accelerate Brazil's industrialization. Next, he expanded his empire to transportation, gaslighting, and railroad construction. He also pioneered many other industries (e.g., shipyards, banking, telecommunications, tannery) (Bertero & Iwai, 2005; Caldeira, 1995; Marchant, 1965).

In 1888, after the *Lei Áurea* or Golden Law that ended slavery in Brazil was passed, the need for labor to replace the slaves freed led to the influx of immigrants. They came not only from many European countries (e.g., Italy, Germany, and Spain) but also all over the world (e.g., Japan, Syria, and Turkey) (IBGE, 2000). This movement completely changed the population landscape (Fig. 3). Those immigrants came to the new land searching for better living conditions, cheaper and vast lands, and labor (Marriott, 2012). Those immigrants and their descendants led to accelerated industrialization, which generated many entrepreneurs (Marcovitch,

Fig. 3 Musiciens allemands à bord du Tyne 1862 © Public Domain

2012; Pereira, 1964). While the list is extensive, we highlight a few names that marked this period of industrial modernization.

Nami Jafet, representing the Syrian and Lebanese community, supported the textile industry's advancement and retailing—including adopting an itinerant sales approach. Later, his family made substantial investments in areas like health care, culture, and education. For instance, the Jafet family was involved in creating the "Hospital Sírio-Libanês" (Syrian-Lebanese Hospital), known as one of Brazil's most important medical centers (Guru, 2020). Another remarkable entrepreneur was Francisco Matarazzo, an Italian immigrant that established the Matarazzo Industries (Fig. 4). At its peak, his corporation held over 350 companies in the most diverse industries (e.g., textile, chemistry, commercial, banking, and food) and employed 6% of São Paulo's population at the time. In 1937, he was the fifth richest person (Marcovitch, 2012).

At first glance, one may say that the population embraced the entrepreneurial culture. But on a closer inspection, it was limited to only a few people and at a nascent stage. Professors were instructing university students to work for big companies or to the public administration. The latter being the most respected and desired path, as a public servant's career was a guarantee of stability and high wages. After all, creating a venture was neither ambition nor an activity valued by society at that time. All of that was about to change at the beginning of the 1970s. The conservative politicians, driven by the international entrepreneurial cases, changed the Brazilian public policies toward new business and created the first makers' movement.

Fig. 4 Indústrias Reunidas Francisco Matarazzo; photo Secretaria da Cultura do Estado de SP © Public Domain

One remarkable change was the creation of the Micro and Small Business Support Service, also known as Sebrae, in 1972. Sebrae is a non-for-profit private entity operating across the whole country with the mission of "promoting the competitiveness and sustainable development of small businesses and stimulating entrepreneurship." Its flagship services are around entrepreneurship education, business consulting, research, and enhancing the entrepreneurial ecosystem. If you plan to start a venture in Brazil, Sebrae might be a good starting point, as it helps millions of entrepreneurs every year. Between January and June of 2020, Sebrae has assisted about 2,3 million entrepreneurs and small business owners ("Cresce busca por serviços do Sebrae: primeiro semestre registra 2,3 milhões de atendimentos," 2020). Another one was the inclusion of entrepreneurship education courses into undergraduate programs, which started in 1998 with the University Network Program for Entrepreneurship Education. The program was a partnership between Sebrae and Instituto Euvaldo Lodi. Fernando Dolabela was the first to introduce a methodology for entrepreneurship education at Brazilian universities (Filion & Dolabela, 2007).

The growth of the entrepreneurial ecosystem drove the third wave. It involved creating business incubators, venture capital funds, co-working spaces, and maker spaces (Fig. 5). The result was the development of innovative and high-impact enterprises. For example, there was a significant increase in the volume of investment from venture capital and the emergence of the first Brazilian unicorn, *99 Tecnologia* (Tunes, 2019).

Fig. 5 Distrito Spark Co-working Space; Curitiba © Pedro Tonhozi de Oliveira

We recently hit three milestones with new public policies, enacted in 2006, 2009, and 2019. Each one had a unique impact on the creation of different tax regimes for startups. The first policy was called Simples Nacional. It created a tax reduction regarding cost and the bureaucracy for micro-companies—revenue of up to R$ 360,000—and small companies—those with up to R$ 3.6 million (Lopes et al., 2017). The second one was called MEI, which is a legal framework created for microentrepreneurs. On the one hand, it simplified the company registration process entirely online, making a cheaper and simpler taxation model. On the other hand, MEIs are limited to a single employee, to revenues of less than R$ 81,000 per year, and only a handful of business activities can be registered in this framework (Brazilian Government, 2021). The last one is the "Marco Regulatório das Startups" or Startup Act of 2019 ("Marco Legal das Startups," 2020). The last framework created the Simple Credit Company and Inova Simples. It introduced the Brazilian definition of a startup as "business organizations, newborn or early stage, whose main activity area is innovation in the business model, product, or service." It also regulated angel investors, public procurement requirements, federal commission sandboxes—which allow some controlled and limited experimentation before applying for health or telecommunication permits—and more stock options for employees (Julio, 2020).

Beyond the contributions listed above, Brazil has many entrepreneurs acting as role models. Jorge Paulo Lemann, from 3G Capital, and Luiza Helena Trajano, from Magazine Luiza, to name a few, have been catalysts of Brazilian entrepreneurial

Table 1 List of the Brazilian Unicorns © Daniel Pagotto

Name	Industry	Year of foundation	Year that reached US$ 1 billion
99	Urban mobility	2012	2018
Nubank	Finance	2013	2018
Arco Educação	Education	2006	2018
Movile/iFood	Multiple sector/food delivery	1998	2018
Stone	Finance	2012	2018
Gympass	Health and wellbeing	2012	2019
Loggi	Logistics	2013	2019
QuintoAndar	Real estate	2012	2019
Ebanx	Finance	2012	2019
Wildlife	*Games*	2011	2019
Loft	Real estate	2018	2020
Vtex	e-commerce	1999	2020
C6 Bank	Finance	2018	2020
Creditas	Finance	2012	2020
MadeiraMadeira	e-commerce	2008	2021

culture and vital to spread entrepreneurship in Brazil. Likewise, the thousands of entrepreneurs and the newborn unicorns in Brazil enhanced this vision's formation. These have made Brazil one of the most dynamic places for innovative entrepreneurs in recent years. We conclude our review of Brazil's entrepreneurial historical overview with the beginning of 2021, fifteen unicorns, as shown in Table 1.

3 The Environment for Entrepreneurship

Some studies allow us to have an important historical perspective on the development of entrepreneurship in Brazil. Run since 2002, the Global Entrepreneurship Monitor presents annual rates for entrepreneurs in the country and allows to analyze its evolution (Fig. 6). In an increasing trajectory since 2002, the total rate of entrepreneurs in Brazil was 39.46% of the adult population in 2019, which corresponds to an estimate of 53,437,971 million individuals out of a total of 208.3 million (Greco et al., 2019).

Among the more than 53 million entrepreneurs, there is a great diversity of businesses and important contrasts. On the one hand, traditional entrepreneurs and necessity entrepreneurs, and on the other, innovative entrepreneurs and startups. Those who start a business in Brazil still do it, mainly due to the lack of opportunities in the formal market. These entrepreneurs tend to act informally (73.6%) in the entrepreneur's own city, focusing on product and services to final customers (B2C), and are less innovative. Most of these businesses work for just providing enough income for the entrepreneur, thus, generating a limited economic impact in terms of

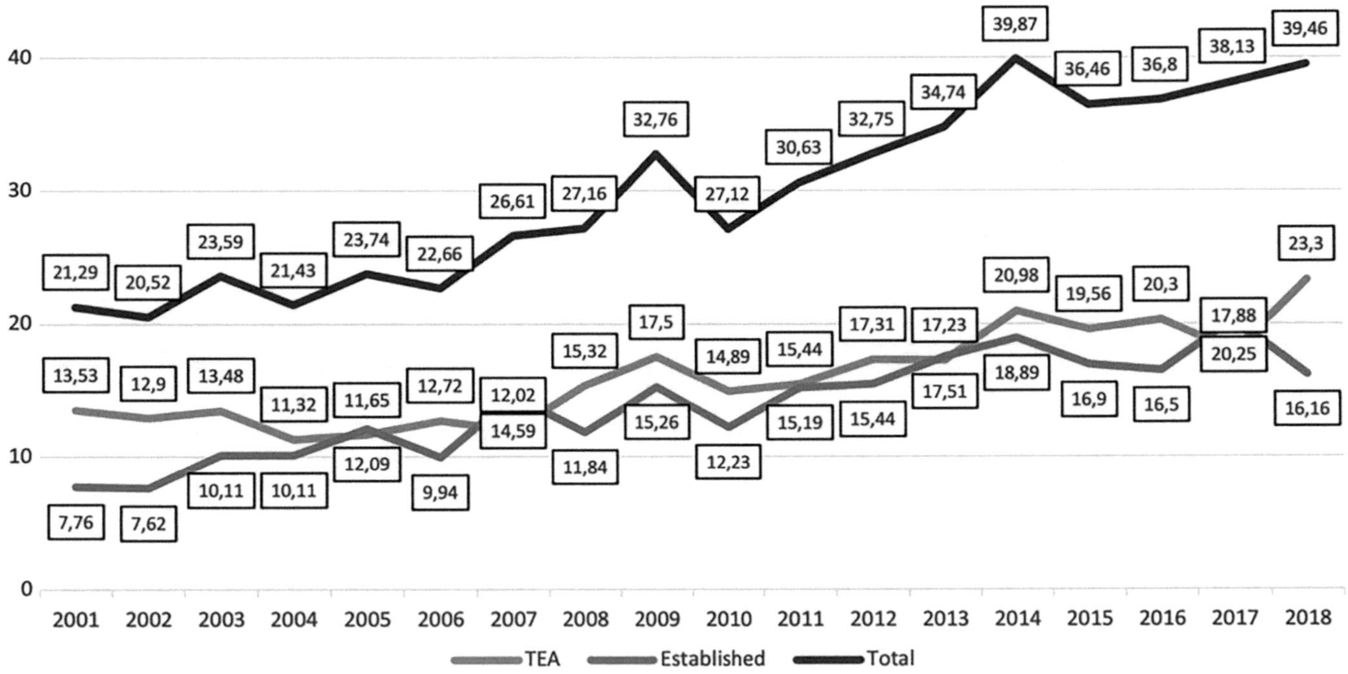

Fig. 6 Nascent Ventures, established business, and total activity rates in Brazil, 2002–2019; GEM 2019; ©Daniel Pagotto

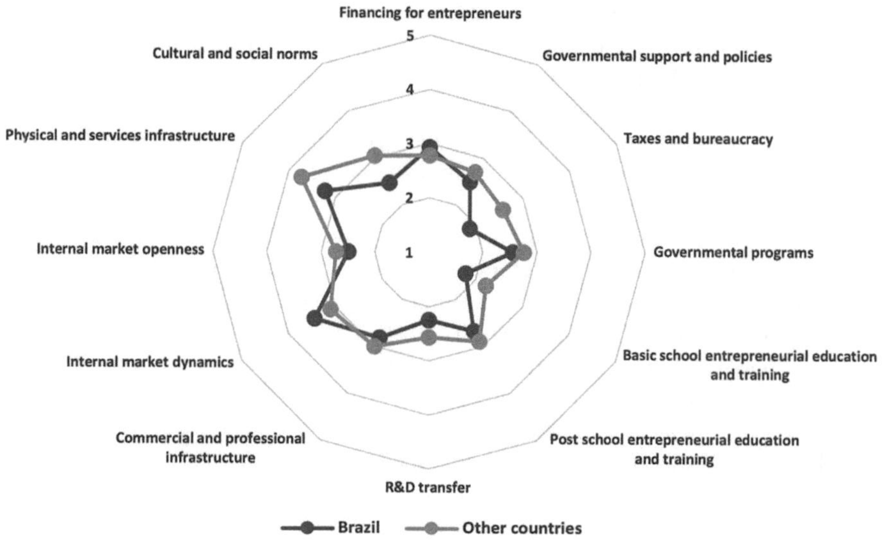

Fig. 7 Ratings of entrepreneurship environment conditions in Brazil; GEM 2019 © Daniel Pagotto

job and income generation. For illustration, these are the small neighborhood stores, bars, restaurants, street vendors, and countless other individuals who work in the gig economy through apps around the country.

On the other side, there are Brazilian startups and unicorns. Startups are innovative businesses that often use venture capital, out of the box business models and technology to grow exponentially and generate high impact. In Brazil, innovative entrepreneurs represent a low percentage of the total, but in the past decade, this pattern started to change especially due to the increasing support of important players, such as business incubators, accelerators, and technology parks.

The facts listed in the last subsection contribute to understanding how the entrepreneurial activity is configured nationally and its historical evolution. However, to broaden this understanding, we bring GEM 2019 data on Entrepreneurial Framework Conditions, which compiles indicators of conditions that enable entrepreneurial activity in Brazil (Fig. 7). In general, Brazil still has important challenges to create a favorable environment for entrepreneurship, with an NECI Score[1] of 3.98 against 4.61 in Chile and 5.89 in China.

Among the main challenges Brazil has to overcome to develop a better business environment, government policies stand out, especially through reducing bureaucracy and reducing taxes; the economic climate and political context, due to institutional insecurity; and financial support, mainly with the cost reduction and expansion of access to credit (Greco et al., 2019). The main enablers to the opening and

[1] GEM NECI is the Global Entrepreneurship Monitor's National Entrepreneurship Context Index.

maintenance of new businesses in Brazil, the entrepreneurial capacity of individuals stands out, which refers to the personality traits of the Brazilian, such as their creativity and the ability to adapt to adverse situations, the so-called "the Brazilian way." Also worthy of mention is the opening of the market and the composition of the population, which are associated with the size and diversity of the population, as well as the existence of opportunities and a friendly environment to entrepreneurship.

Another important reference on the business environment in Brazil is the World Bank Doing Business study, which measures how laws and regulations promote or restrict business activities through quantitative indicators on regulation and protection of property rights (World Bank, 2020). In 2019, Brazil fell fifteen positions, from 109th to 124th in 190 economies, approaching the position it occupied during 2017 and 2018, after an improvement in 2019. By way of comparison, nations like Mexico (60th), India (63rd), and South Africa (84th) reached better positions than Brazil. In one of the main indicators, the opening of companies—which measures the number of procedures, the cost, and the time required for a company to start its operation in the country formally—there was a small improvement compared to 2018, which indicates actions from the state government—specifically São Paulo and Rio de Janeiro—intending to try to improve the conditions for doing business in the country. Among the challenges that still exist, we highlight the complexity of taxation. Brazil remained among the tenth worst country, occupying 184th place, and access to capital, which is still expensive and uncompetitive, in addition to bringing few guarantees to creditors and legal uncertainty.

Despite the advances and governmental initiatives envisioned in recent decades, there is still a long way to reach an ideal business environment in Brazil. In general, both through the Entrepreneurial Framework Conditions and the NECI Score and through the Doing Business 2020 ranking, Brazil still has challenges. However, the country has kept initiatives to reduce bureaucracy and build a simpler and more transparent business environment for entrepreneurs, like the creation of SIMPLES and MEI mentioned above. There are two entrepreneurial realities in Brazil, and for both, it is of vital importance to develop a business environment that enables entrepreneurial activity. On the one hand, traditional entrepreneurs will benefit from the simplicity of the processes needed to create and operate their small businesses, and on the other, the favorable environment helps the flourishing of high-impact entrepreneurs through startups, which have benefited from the entrepreneurial capacity of Brazilian and national markets to create the first Brazilian unicorns.

4 Toward the Future

Anyone familiar with the Brazilian entrepreneurial market should agree that we are in a fertile time. As we discussed, Brazil has had many unicorns ranging from fintech, real estate rental, delivery companies, mobility apps to health, logistics, agribusiness, and artificial intelligence industries. The challenge posed to new ventures is to address the United Nations' Sustainable Development Goals. Those unfamiliar with those goals may be interested to know that it basically boils down to ending poverty, improving health and education, reducing inequality, spur economic growth, tackling climate change, and preservation of our oceans and forests (UN General Assembly, 2015). Plainly put, Brazil has many social and environmental challenges that need to be addressed. In our view, among the most important ones are the income disparity, access to education, and access to the internet.

While it is known that only one-quarter of the population does not have access to the internet, there is a meaningful difference across different income, gender, race, and geographical regions. In this realm, it is worth clarifying that the market for digital products in Brazil is enormous despite the challenges regarding connection. One indicator raised by the last census is that this internet access is heavily focused on mobile devices, with one-third of the population accessing the internet using their phones (Valente, 2020).

In addition to high-impact entrepreneurship, which highlights Brazil as one of the largest generators of unicorns in the world, there is an economy based on agribusiness, multinationals, and micro and small companies, which together account for more than 30% of the country's GDP and more than 50% of the number of formal jobs. These companies are, in essence, natural entrepreneurship out of necessity and face great structural difficulties: restricted access to credit, technical unpreparedness, lack of planning, high tax burdens, significant family involvement without clear functions, and, in essence, face the constant challenge of basic survival, often with the objective of generating jobs for the generating family itself or the entrepreneur. This fact can be seen from the GEM 2019 data, which shows that 90% of Brazilian entrepreneurs agree that one of the biggest motivations for entrepreneurship is the scarcity of jobs. The scarcity, present in contexts like this, generates, despite the problems, a creative and vigorous entrepreneurial environment.

This entrepreneurial vocation, albeit with its limitations, is clear when analyzing at GEM 2019 that having one's own business is the fourth biggest dream of the Brazilian being behind even making a career in organizations. The study also shows that 23.5% of the population is involved in their own business in its initial phase. Looking more closely at the numbers, it is clear that this phenomenon is related to periods of economic crisis, such as those between 2008 and 2009 and 2014 and 2016. Still looking at the GEM, it is observed that three out of ten adults who have not yet are entrepreneurs would like to open their own business in the next 3 years. Still, Brazil is highlighted as the fourth country with the highest rates of initial entrepreneurship and in second place among the businesses already established, occupying the leadership in the BRICS.

The challenge of a continental country, with a population of more than 200 million inhabitants and with a plurality of profiles, including economic ones, generates an environmental complexity that needs to be understood by anyone who wants or needs to undertake in Brazil. It is not possible to discuss entrepreneurship without highlighting the great nuances between the high impact power, especially of scale-ups and Brazilian unicorns, and the prevalence of entrepreneurship out of necessity as one of the important bases of the Brazilian economy.

Although there is no warm and inviting legal and bureaucratic environment, Brazil is one of the largest markets in the world and offers opportunities to develop solutions for micro and small entrepreneurs as well as social and high-impact entrepreneurs and has growing rates of growth in the world. However, to act in the peculiar cultural and legal environment, it is important to recognize at the national and regional level its plurality in different dimensions, nationally speaking, and micro-regionally speaking.

5 Case Study for Students

Miss Zica is the stereotypical black Brazilian woman from Tijuca, Rio de Janeiro, from a poor suburb neighborhood (Assis, 2021). She is one of 12 siblings, Afro-American. She has endured her whole life with the challenge of having tightly curled strands, like frizz, flyaways, split ends, tangles, and too much volume. Against all Brazilian media and social pressure of perfect hair being perfectly straight, she had zero desire to straighten her hair. She just wanted a solution to enhance and shine her natural style and its beauty characteristics.

She browsed and tried all different solutions available on the market and was caught off guard with one piece of information—70% of the Brazilian women had curly hair. Back then, harsh hair habits like daily blow-drying, wielding hot tools like curling irons, and getting chemical straightening treatments were the to-go solution pushed by hair salons around the country. But working full-time as a housekeeper, her first challenge was getting into the hairstyling community. "With only 21 years old, I went to follow my dreams. I said enough is enough; I quit everything, and I cut my hair very short. Next, I enrolled in a hairdresser course to learn why my hair was so thick? Why was it so curly? I couldn't even use a comb; only a fork would work for me," said Zica.

Her hair has always intrigued her. She liked its characteristics and was proud of its origins. But the enormous difficulties in taking care of her, and even with the hairdressing course in hand, a natural rebelliousness of her hair seemed to have no solution. Restless and unhappy with not finding products on the market that would help her solve her problem—they just promised this—she decided to look for a solution herself. Based on the basic knowledge in hair chemistry she acquired in her course, she started experimenting with formulas that could help it. It went on for years without much pretension.

After 10 years of carrying out various homemade experiments, Zica seemed to have found a different formula between successes and mistakes. In 1993, Zica returned from work when she saw her cousin, who instantly noticed the difference in her hair. It seemed lighter but without losing its features. Her cousin, very interested, questioned how she had reached that result. Zica said that she had done it herself with a formula she created. It was an aha moment, Zica discovered something that worked not only for herself but for other people. Those, who like her, faced difficulties in dealing with their unruly hair—often giving in to straightening and other techniques. "I want it too!" said the cousin." That's why I say that day was my day one. I found out that I had done something. I discovered that I had developed something," said Zica.

She was already tired of the housemaid routine. The several requests from friends desiring the same results achieved by Zica led her to arrive at home with an idea: develop and expand her formula. But one question lingered on her mind. How can I do this? Her poor neighborhood and social class made it difficult for her to have access to credit, and her family could not help her. She even reports that she was unaware of any financing. Her husband worked full time, but they had no spare money. Intrigued, she slept that day with the question in her head, determined to solve it.

Analyzing all possible scenarios, the only thing that came to her mind was her husband's VW Beetle 1978, which was worth around R$ 3000 at the time. Furthermore, the only resource was her knowledge as a hairdresser and her experience in preparing the formula, which she managed to file a patent with a chemist's help. Despite her limitations, she decided to go all-in and put her idea into practice. Her first move was to call some friends to her house and test whether her product had the same effect on them. It confirmed its efficacy and left her friends delighted with the results. In less than a month, Zica decided it was time to talk to her husband about selling their car to invest in her business. She opened her beauty salon as a hairdressing salon specialized in offering esthetic treatments to black women of her poor neighborhood. This was when Beleza Natural came into existence; her desired beauty salon.

Those steps were enough to convince her husband to sell their car. He was supportive and enthusiastic about the idea. In a short time, they had received the money from the car sale. After much research, Zica found a small commercial spot near her community in the Tijuca region to set up his salon. "It was a tiny room in the backyard," said Zica, "there was another room in the front, and I had to go through a different corridor to get there." She rented the place and bought the essential items that she could afford, which were not many. With zero money for advertising, she wrote on a ruled paper from her notebook. She made a dozen copies of it and flyposted it to her community to inform them about her formula and business proposal. (NOTE: Flyposting is a guerrilla marketing tactic where advertising posters are put up in the street.) She also posted them on city buses. Her focus was on lines that she knew her peers passed by daily on their way to work or to take their children to school. With friends' help, the idea was carried out entirely informally, without any concern with legal or commercial implications. Those concerns were still far away as Zica did not even have an EIN (Employer Identification Number).

The advertising and the word-of-mouth made her company known all around the Tijuca community in just a few days. As the opening day arrived, Zica was shocked; there was a long queue in front of her salon. Zica found it hard to believe what she saw, but it was real. She confirmed her assumptions that she had created a valuable product. Her dissemination strategy, although amateurish, was proved to be extremely efficient. Soon, she realized that she needed to professionalize her business or not meet the increasing demand. Aware of her limitations, she began to look for answers to how she could take this step. The first person that came to her mind was her brother. He not only was in her immediate circle but also had the most technical and practical knowledge running a business due to the experience of managing a McDonald's franchise. Excited by the opportunities and the challenge of running a company with more autonomy to apply what he had learned, Zica's brother accepted the challenge.

The challenges were (1) increasing the offer of her product and service, (2) how to grow and maintain quality, (3) keeping Rio de Janeiro's typical personality, and (4) maintaining affordable and attractive prices. The production of products was not a problem Zica faced, as she dominated the formula. However, she needed a way of doing it more efficiently, and her brother's previous experience with fast food "fitted like a glove." They built an assembly line where the client passed through the hands of several professionals. Each one specialized in a part of the process, increasing efficiency, speed, and safety while maintaining the process's quality. This also reduced the operating costs. They need to teach employees to carry out only a specific job instead of hiring more experienced and expensive professionals to do everything. At the same time, they kept the know-how of the entire process for themselves, avoiding the risk of copycats.

"We had a very high-quality control; we wanted to be the best, we wanted to have a standard of production. I wanted everyone to be specialized in what they do. Because in addition to developing the product, I developed a technique for applying the product." recounts Zica.

The model as executed, brought work opportunities to Zica's colleagues and acquaintances from the community. Soon, keeping the initial trend, the expansion was inevitable. Many people huddled at the door to the salon to receive the "miraculous" formula, dubbed "Super Relaxant." It was capable of giving lightness to wavy hair without resorting to straightening and other treatments that disfigured the characteristics of black beauty. This growth process brought significant daily challenges and learning opportunities without time for much planning. One assumption was that black women in lower social classes had self-esteem problems, perhaps derived from how they were treated in their jobs and even in Rio, where prejudice was latent despite the existing miscegenation. From this perception coming from the company's day-to-day life, she gave special attention to bringing self-esteem to these women, creating a self-worth experience that increased the degree of relationship and empathy between *Beleza Natural* and its customers.

"The Hall opened at 8 AM, and when it was 5 AM, the line had already started. At 9 AM, there were already over 100 people in line. I developed a technique for applying this product. I managed to train four people with me, and these four people were no longer able to cope because there were just too many people. We left there around midnight, one o'clock in the morning, from Monday to Saturday. It was a success!" said Zica. However, Zica has one problem: she feels that there were many opportunities for expanding her business. Some of her ideas are creating a cosmetics factory to manufacture the products on a larger scale, moving to a franchise model, and opening stores outside Rio de Janeiro. Now she needs your help.

Discussion questions:

1. How did Zica's personality and environment affect her business?
2. What was key in Zica's knowledge, and how did it enable her to grow?
3. Who was instrumental in Zica's business creation and expansion?
4. How do you evaluate the way the company has developed?
5. Is experimentation, or learning by doing, a valid form of business creation? Is it sustainable for expansion and in the long term?
6. How important are contingencies and day-to-day learning in the success of your business?
7. What would be the other alternatives in the creation and development of the business?
8. What are Zica's main limitations, and what challenges will it bring in the future?
9. Considering Brazil's business environment, what do you think would be the next steps for "Beleza Natural" to continue its expansion?

6 Conclusion

Brazil is a country that offers different nuances to the entrepreneur, and this is a historical construction that needs to be understood to be incorporated into the culture of any organization that intends to invest in the plural and peculiar environment existing in its continental area.

Historically, the country has always dealt with two parallels: great inventions and inventors that created markets and brought solutions that are still important for humanity today and relevant organizations in the world economy. A large part of the population making micro and small companies in need of survival is the base of the country's economic pyramid today. This characteristic also gave rise to large companies that operate in the country and have consolidated over time.

The entrepreneur here encounters substantial bureaucratic and legal barriers, with Brazil not being a country well-positioned in the economic freedom indexes, with a lot of bureaucracy in its structure in all stages of creating new businesses, from the opening of the company to access credit, support from agencies responsible for promoting and hiring people. However, the country has a tremendous entrepreneurial vocation. Much of the population plans to open their own business. The market, still in development, offers great opportunities, either because they have not been explored yet or poorly explored. These can be found in different sections: by region, by socio-economic profile, by social classes of interest, or by cultural fit. In conclusion, despite the challenges, Brazil is a great country for entrepreneurs and a great country to live (Fig. 8).

Fig. 8 Pirambuzios Beach, view of the place where part of this article was written, 2021 © Pedro Tonhozi de Oliveira

References

Assis, H. (2021). *Beleza natural: Uma Fábrica de Autoestima*. Retrieved from https://www.belezanatural.com.br/institucional/sobre-nos/

Bertero, C. O., & Iwai, T. (2005). A visit to the baron. *BAR–Brazilian Administration Review, 2*(2), 1–16. https://doi.org/10.1590/s1807-76922005000200002

Brazilian Government. (2021). *Empresas & negócios*. Retrieved from https://www.gov.br/empresas-e-negocios/pt-br

Caldeira, J. (1995). *Mauá: empresário do império* (1st ed.). Companhia das Letras.

Carrilo, A. F. (2020). *Crescimento Das Startups: Veja O Que Mudou Nos Últimos Cinco Anos!* Retrieved from https://abstartups.com.br/crescimento-das-startups/

Cresce busca por serviços do Sebrae: primeiro semestre registra 2,3 milhões de atendimentos. (2020). Retrieved from http://www.agenciasebrae.com.br/sites/asn/uf/NA/cresce-busca-por-servicos-do-sebrae-primeiro-semestre-registra-23-milhoes-de-atendimentos,62cc3ead53b73710VgnVCM1000004c00210aRCRD

Filion, L. J., & Dolabela, F. (2007). The making of a revolution in Brazil: The introduction of entrepreneurial pedagogy in the early stages of education. In A. Fayolle (Ed.), *Handbook of research in entrepreneurship education* (Vol. 2). Edward Elgar Publishing.

Greco, S. M. D. S. S., da Cunha, C. R., Onozato, E., Guimarães, M. L., Bastos Jr, P. A., & de Souza, V. L. (2019). *Global entrepreneurship monitor "Empreendedorismo no Brasil: 2018"*. Retrieved from https://atendimento.sebrae-sc.com.br/wp-content/uploads/2019/05/1551466386GEM_2018.pdf

Guru, S. (2020). *Best hospitals–Brazil*. Retrieved from https://www.newsweek.com/best-hospitals-2020/brazil

IBGE. (2000). *Brasil: 500 anos de povoamento*. Instituto Brasileiro de Geografia e Estatística.

Julio, R. A. (2020). O que realmente muda com o novo Marco Legal das Startups. *Revista PEGN*. Retrieved from https://revistapegn.globo.com/Startups/noticia/2020/12/o-que-realmente-muda-com-o-novo-marco-legal-das-startups.html

LAVCA's Annual Review of Tech Investment in Latin America. (2019). Retrieved from https://lavca.org/industry-data/inside-the-4th-consecutive-peak-year-lavcas-annual-review-of-tech-investment-in-latam/

Lopes, M. A., Pinto, E. D. C., & Tiossi, F. M. (2017). Simples nacional: Vantagens E Desvantagens Para Microempresas E Empresas De Pequeno Porte. *Organizações e Sociedade, 6*(6). https://doi.org/10.29031/ros.v6i6.298

Marchant, A. (1965). *Viscount Mauá and the empire of Brazil. A biography of Irineu Evangelista de Sousa (1813–1889)*. University of California Press.

Marco Legal das Startups, PLP 146/2019 (2020).

Marcovitch, J. (2012). Pioneiros e Empreendedores. In *A Saga do Desenvolvimento no Brasil* (Vol. 3). EDUSP.

Marriott, E. (2012). *The history of the world in bite-sized chunks*. Michael O'Mara Books.

Pereira, L. C. B. (1964). Origens étnicas e sociais do empresário paulista. *Revista de Administração de Empresas, 4*(11), 83–106. https://doi.org/10.1590/s0034-75901964000200002

Ribeiro, D. (2000). *The Brazilian people: The formation and meaning of Brazil (G. Rabassa, trans.)*. University Press of Florida.

SEBRAE. (2020). *DataSebrae Indicadores: Empreendedores*. Retrieved from: https://datasebraeindicadores.sebrae.com.br/resources/sites/data-sebrae/data-sebrae.html#/Empreendedores

The New York Times. (1871). *Railway loans and Amazonian navigation contracts. The New York times* (p. 5) Retrieved from https://www.nytimes.com/1871/08/22/archives/south-america-the-great-coffee-product-of-brazil-newyork-losing-the.html

Tunes, S. (2019). The land of the unicorns. *Pesquisa FAPESP, 1*, 66–69. Retrieved from https://revistapesquisa.fapesp.br/en/the-land-of-the-unicorns-2/

UN General Assembly. (2015). *Transforming our world: The 2030 Agenda for Sustainable Development*. Retrieved from https://www.refworld.org/docid/57b6e3e44.html

Valente, J. (2020). *Brasil tem 134 milhões de usuários de internet, aponta pesquisa.* . Retrieved from https://agenciabrasil.ebc.com.br/geral/noticia/2020-05/brasil-tem-134-milhoes-de-usuarios-de-internet-aponta-pesquisa

World Bank. (2020). *Doing business 2020*. World Bank.

Pedro Tonhozi de Oliveira is an assistant professor at the FGV EAESP in São Paulo, Brazil. He earned a Ph.D. in Entrepreneurship and Innovation from the University of Missouri-Kansas City. Afterwards, he was a postdoctoral fellow in the Department of Global Entrepreneurship and Innovation at the Henry W. Bloch School of Management and a Visiting Assistant Professor at Western Kentucky University. Pedro's expertise spans the entrepreneurship field, focusing on entrepreneurial crowdfunding and finance, new product development, innovation, blockchain, and big data.

Rubens Massa is a professor at the FGV EAESP. He earned his Ph.D. at FGV EAESP and was a visiting scholar at the University of Sydney, Australia. His current research focuses on decision-making process and cognitive bias, especially in Brazilian family business contexts and innovation. He is also involved in teaching and research projects with startups, scale-ups and small and medium companies. He has a relevant actuation on mentoring and consulting on C-level, especially on uncertain contexts.

Daniel do Prado Pagotto is assistant director of the Entrepreneurship and Innovation Research Laboratory where he conducts research focused on entrepreneurship policy, innovative nascent ventures and quantitative methods applied to entrepreneurship research. He obtained his master's degree at the Federal University of Goiás.

Cândido Vieira Borges Júnior is Professor of entrepreneurship at the Universidade Federal de Goiás, Goiânia, Brazil, where he is also Director of the Entrepreneurship and Innovation Research Laboratory. He obtained his Ph.D. at HEC Montréal. His current research focuses on new ventures, entrepreneurship policy and social capital.

Marcus Alexandre Yshikawa Salusse is an Assistant Professor at the FGV EAESP in São Paulo, Brazil. He is also a project coordinator at the Center for Entrepreneurship and Business Venturing Research, the FGVCenn, where he has co-authored the Global Entrepreneurship Monitor (GEM) — Brazil edition and been involved in teaching and research projects for organizations such as Goldman Sach, Facebook and Social Entrepreneurship Initiatives. He earned his Ph.D. at FGV EAESP, and he was a Visiting Scholar at the Australian Center for Entrepreneurship Research (ACE), Queensland University of Technology (QUT), Australia in 2018. His current research focuses on new ventures, entrepreneurial identity and social entrepreneurship.

Entrepreneurship in Chile

Patricio Duran

Abstract

Over the last decades, the Chilean economy and institutions have experienced substantial growth and development, respectively. Moreover, the country's government has launched programs to support Chilean and foreign start-ups. This scenario has created an ideal business environment for entrepreneurship. However, recent political instability and the discussion of a new Constitution raise questions about the country's future of entrepreneurship. This chapter begins by describing the historical context of Chile from its establishment until 2018. Then, it discusses the environment of entrepreneurship in Chile by highlighting its strengths and weaknesses. This is followed by a close inspection of recent political challenges that the country faces and can affect the future of entrepreneurship. Finally, the chapter presents the case of NotCo, an example of a highly innovative start-up from Chile that, amidst the political and health challenges, can become a leading actor in the global plant-based protein market.

1 Introduction

The Republic of Chile locates in the southern part of South America. It takes around 11 hours of flying from New York City to Santiago, the capital city, 17 hours from London, and 28 hours from Hong Kong. It borders Bolivia and Peru in the north and Argentina in the east. The land area is 743,812 km^2, but most of Chile's population (almost 19 million people) concentrates in the country's center, around Santiago. Chile has a coastline of 6435 km in the west. The Chilean territory also includes

P. Duran
Boeing Institute of International Business, Chaifetz School of Business, Saint Louis University, St. Louis, MO, USA
e-mail: patricio.duran@slu.edu

L.-P. Dana et al. (eds.), *Entrepreneurship in South America*, Springer Texts in Business and Economics, https://doi.org/10.1007/978-3-030-97060-4_5

Fig. 1 Easter Island, Chile; photo © 2020 Patricio Duran

Easter Island in the southeastern Pacific Ocean (Fig. 1). Most of northern (Fig. 2) and southern Chile (Fig. 3) is uninhabited. This country enjoys diverse climates due to its length, including the Atacama Desert in the north, the Mediterranean climate in the central region, and the rainy and cold weather in Chile's southern part.

Spanish is the official language in Chile. Only a very few percentages of the population are proficient in English, but the indicators have improved in the last years (Ferrer, 2020). Most of the people consider themselves as white and non-indigenous. About 9% of the population in Chile belongs to an indigenous group (IWGIA, 2020). Mapuche is the predominant indigenous group, followed by the Aymara, the Diaguita, the Lickanantay, and the Quechua peoples (Dana, 2006; IWGIA, 2020). The main religion in Chile is Roman Catholicism. Evangelism is the second more prevalent religion in the country. Virtually all population in Chile is literate. Chile is a high-income country and one of the wealthiest countries in Latin America, with relatively low poverty levels. In 2019, Chile had the 45th highest real GDP per capita between Panama and Poland (International Monetary Fund, 2020). Over the last decades, the country has experienced a solid commitment to democracy and pro-market policies (Duran et al., 2017) that have positioned the country as one of Latin America's most stable countries, both politically and economically. However, Chile started to suffer from political tension and social conflict due to recent historical events. Additionally, the COVID-19 pandemic contributed to people's concerns about health and social security and the country's future economic situation (Statista, 2020).

Fig. 2 San Pedro de Atacama, north of Chile; photo © 2020 Patricio Duran

Fig. 3 Patagonia, south of Chile; photo © 2020 Cristobal Barra, used with permission

2 Historical Context

The Spanish crown conquested Chile in 1540. One year later, Pedro de Valdivia founded Santiago. Since then, the country was part of the Spanish empire for more than two centuries. In 1808, Napoleon Bonaparte, the French statesman and military leader, took control of Spain. This event triggered independent movements in Chile, including Chile's Government Junta, on September 18, 1810. The Junta proclaimed Chile as an autonomous republic within the Spanish monarchy. After some Spanish crown attempts to reconquer Chile, this country was proclaimed a fully independent republic on February 12, 1818. Between 1818 and 1891, the country's elite and authorities aimed to consolidate its political institutions and strengthen government sovereignty over inhabited territories (Collier & Sater, 1996).

From 1891 onwards, Chile has experienced different political eras characterized by continuous political regime changes and periods of substantial economic reforms (Gazmuri, 2014). The Parliamentary era (1891–1925) began with a civil war between the Chilean presidency and its congress. The conflict ended in the establishment of a parliamentary republic that lasted for almost three decades. During this period, the state largely benefitted from taxes collected from foreign investors' sodium nitrate production (Collier & Sater, 1996). The government's authorities used such resources to invest in infrastructure.

The Presidential era followed up the Parliamentary era. It started in 1925 with the approval of a new Constitution after 1 year of political crisis, including a military coup by the conservative military elite to take the pro-reformist President out of power. The Presidential era ended in 1973 with another military coup led by General Augusto Pinochet against Salvador Allende's socialist government.

During the Presidential era, Chile experienced profound political, social, and economic changes (Barr-Melej, 2002). First, Chile enjoyed the surge of a robust middle class that gained power and influence over this period. Second, the state had an active role in the country's industrialization by creating companies in the oil and gas, energy, and agribusiness sectors. Finally, many governments led significant educational reforms to reduce illiteracy, extend university coverage, and educate technicians to support national industrialization. From the 1960s, Chile experienced more radical socio-economic reforms, including a land ownership restructuring and the nationalization of copper (Lagos, 2018). In 1970, Chile elected the socialist Salvador Allende as President of the Republic. This government deepened several reforms to nationalize the economy and redistribute resources to less favored sectors (Winn & Kay, 1974). However, during this period, Chile experienced a substantial political and economic crisis (Goldberg, 1975) that triggered a military coup led by General Augusto Pinochet on September 11, 1973.

During Chile's military dictatorship (1973–1990), the government executed multiple economic policies of free-market reforms (Ffrench-Davis, 2002) to solve the economic collapse that originated in the socialist government. These reforms included the privatization of the Chilean pension system, healthcare, and higher education. Additionally, the military government deregulated the bank system, privatized public utility companies, and reduced corporate taxes. In 1988, the

Fig. 4 Titanium La Portada under construction, Santiago, Chile; photo © 2020 Cristobal Barra, used with permission

military government called for national elections to vote on a new eight-year presidential term for general Augusto Pinochet, according to the Chilean Constitution approved in 1980. About 54% of voters rejected the extension of the military government (Biblioteca del Congreso Nacional de Chile, 2021).

Since the returns to democracy, Chile experienced a consolidation of its economic growth and institutional development, illustrated by rapid infrastructure growth (Fig. 4). In December 1989, Chile experienced a new presidential election after 17 years of military dictatorship. Patricio Aylwin, a Christian Democrat representing the left-center political coalition, won the election in 1989. In addition to the efforts to consolidate Chile's democracy, the Aylwin government (1990–1994) aimed to reduce poverty and inequality (Navia, 2010). In 1994, Eduardo Frei Ruiz-Tagle (Christian Democrat) became the President of Chile for 8 years. His government continued Aylwin's policies to reduce poverty and improve health and education (Espinoza, 2008). In 2000, the socialist Ricardo Lagos initiated his mandate as President of the Republic. Over his government, Chile signed several Free Trade

Fig. 5 Concepcion, Chile, after the earthquake in 2010; photo © 2020 Patricio Duran

Agreements with Brunei, China, the European Community, New Zealand, Singapore, South Korea, the USA, consolidating Chile as an open economy (The Economist, 2004). In 2006, the socialist Michelle Bachelet, the first female President of Chile, succeeded Ricardo Lagos. Bachelet's government aimed to increase the minimum wage salary and reduce poverty (Sehnbruch, 2009). After 20 years of left-center governments, Sebastian Piñera, businessman and right-center politician, was elected as the President of Chile (2010–2014). His government focused on rebuilding Chile after the 8.8-moment magnitude scale earthquake and tsunami that the country suffered at the beginning of 2010 (Polanco, 2012; see Figs. 5 and 6). In 2014, Chile re-elected Michelle Bachelet as President. During her second mandate, Bachelet developed substantial reforms in education, taxation, and the environment, such as introducing free university education for the nation's neediest students and ending up profit-making educational institutions (Waylen, 2016). In 2018, Sebastian Piñera was re-elected as the President of Chile. Piñera's second presidency has faced dual shock from the social unrest in 2019 and the coronavirus pandemic (COVID-19) in 2020. These two shocks combined have increased political and economic uncertainty (Economic Policy Uncertainty, 2020), generating challenges and opportunities for entrepreneurship in Chile.

Fig. 6 Talcahuano, Chile, after the tsunami in 2010; photo © 2020 Patricio Duran

3 The Environment of Entrepreneurship in Chile

Over the last decades, Chile has gained the title of being one of the most stable countries in the Latin American region (BBC, 2020). For example, the World Economic Forum's Global Competitiveness Index ranks Chile as the most competitive economy in Latin America (Schwab, 2019). More specifically, Chile ranked in 33rd place, between the Czech Republic and Portugal. The most notable strengths that Chile exhibits concern its macro-economic stability and well-developed financial system. However, the Global Competitiveness Index highlights some of Chile's weaknesses, such as the relatively low adoption of information and communication technology. Additionally, Chile exhibits a relatively low-developed labor market given high redundancy costs and low cooperation in labor-employer relations, a small market size to attract imports of goods and services, low-developed innovation capabilities due to the low R & D expenditures (as % of GDP), and lack of diversity of the workforce (Schwab, 2019). These are some of the macro-level challenges that any entrepreneur would face when doing business in Chile.

The World Bank (2020)'s Doing Business Ranking classifies Chile as one of the easiest countries in Latin America to do business. In 2020, Chile ranked in 59th place, between Italy and Mexico. It takes around 4 days to start a business in Chile. The Doing Business Ranking highlights the efficiency of getting electricity connection in the country and the reliability of electricity supply, and the transparency of tariffs. Additionally, Chile has a relatively high efficiency of construction permits regarding the number of procedures, time, and cost. Finally, Chile also has well-developed governance institutions oriented to protect minority investors from conflicts of interest between controllers and minority shareholders.

The World Bank's Doing Business Ranking point out two issues that Chile has and may constraint the development of new business initiatives. The first issue concerns the Chilean credit system. This country lacks well-developed legal rights to protect the rights of borrowers and lenders. Further, credit information is not widely available, making it difficult for lenders to assess credit risks. The second issue that Chile faces relates to inefficiencies in paying taxes in terms of time, total tax and contribution rate, and the number of payments needed for a company to pay all taxes, including sales tax, profit tax, and labor taxes contributions. As aforementioned, over the last decade, past governments in Chile have executed several tax reforms oriented to sustain more fiscal expenditures to tackle social issues. However, this has brought higher complexity to the Chilean taxation system.

The aforementioned macro-institutional environment in Chile has created some favorable conditions for entrepreneurial initiatives. According to Bosna et al. (2020)'s Global Entrepreneurship Monitor, Chile enjoys adequate physical infrastructure, government entrepreneurship programs, and cultural and social norms that motivate entrepreneurship. Seventy-one percent of adults in Chile know someone who has started a new business, and about 76% believe they have the skills and knowledge to start a business. However, about 58% of adults in Chile have fears of failure. The lack of institutional support that the country offers to entrepreneurs that fail, such as well-developed bankruptcy laws, could explain Chileans' fears of creating a business.

Global Entrepreneurship Monitor also identifies some weaknesses in the entrepreneurial environment, including the school stage's lack of entrepreneurial education. Although Chile enjoys relatively strong and sophisticated educations institutions, they are mainly oriented to develop human talent that is useful for current companies and government instead of developing innovation and entrepreneurial capabilities. The second shortage that entrepreneurs face in Chile refers to the low availability of entrepreneurial finance. It is prevalent in Chile that entrepreneurship is informally financed. The informal investment rate is at least 10%, eight percentage points more than the world average (Bosna et al., 2020). Such investment comes from the entrepreneur's family and close friends, which coincides with the literature that suggests that Chile is a family-based economy (Berrone et al., 2020; Duran & Ortiz, 2020). Entrepreneurs aiming to raise capital from Chilean venture capitalists complain about the lack of actors in the venture capital industry, investors' short-term perspective, high risk-aversion, and complexity in raising the capital, including the time invested in preparing business plans (Neumann & Villalobos, 2018).

4 Government Initiatives to Incentive Entrepreneurship in Chile

To improve entrepreneurs' financial support and create an entrepreneurship ecosystem, Chile has implemented numerous initiatives since the new millennium. Such government initiatives include (1) specific regulations to increase the protection of investors and deepen the capital market, (2) royalty laws to mining companies to subsidize technological innovation, (3) seed capital for start-ups and incentives to promote early-stage investments, (4) public-private cooperation in recommending entrepreneurship policies, and (5) lower barriers and bureaucracy for entrepreneurs (Bustamante et al., 2021). As part of the initiatives to provide capital for start-ups, the program "Start-Up Chile" has captured international recognition given its global scope (The Economist, 2012).

Start-Up Chile was launched in 2010 by CORFO (the Chilean Economic Development Agency). The main objective of Start-Up Chile is to encourage entrepreneurship and innovation to improve productivity in the country. Start-Up Chile offers three programs. The first, "S Factory," concerns a 4-month pre-acceleration program for start-ups led by female founders. It orientates to early-stage projects that are technology-related to global impact. S Factory funds up to USD 19,000. The second program, "Seed," is a 6-month acceleration program for companies with a functional product and early validation. It funds up to USD 65,000. The third Start-up's program, "Growth," supports the expansion of innovative tech-based businesses. This 12-month program attracts global tech-based businesses looking to scale their sales and expand to new markets using Chile as a platform. Start-Up Chile participates as a co-funding up to USD 78,000. By 2020, Start-Up Chile has helped 1960 start-ups with a valuation of USD 2.1 billion. It currently manages a portfolio of 793 start-ups.

5 Toward the Future

Over the last three decades, Chile enjoyed political stability and sustained economic growth. However, recent political events may impact the Chilean macro-environment, affecting future entrepreneurship. In October 2019, Chile experienced a social outbreak characterized by massive protests and open confrontations with the national police force. It has been suggested that the outbreak responds to the Chilean society's discontent regarding the malfeasance of the elites and inequality in the country (Jadresic, 2019). The surged of the COVID-19 pandemic interrupted the political turmoil in Chile, given the government-imposed lockdowns.

To respond to the protests, Chile's National Congress signed an agreement to hold a referendum that would rewrite the national Constitution. Several political groups in Chile have questioned the illegitimacy of the current Chilean Constitution, given it was initially formulated and proclaimed during the Military Government in 1980. Moreover, left-wing politicians sustain that the Constitution harbors social inequalities in the country since it supports a deep free-market society with a minimum participation of the state in tackling social needs and security.

On October 25, 2020, a year after the social outbreak, Chile carried out a national referendum asking citizens whether the country should rewrite a new Constitution. About 78% of voters favored a new constitution (Servicio Electoral de Chile, 2020). Therefore, over the first half of 2021, Chile will hold a national election to choose the 155 constituents, who will have a term of up to 1 year to write the new Constitution.

Later, Chilean citizens will participate in new elections to accept or reject the constituents' new Constitution. In case voters approved the proposal, the new Constitution would be enacted in 2022. The Chilean society expects that the new Constitution will help to mitigate the political uncertainty the country has experienced since October 2019. For example, the Economic Policy Uncertainty Index (2020) shows that since October 2019, Chile's political uncertainty has been up to three times higher than the average political uncertainty the country exhibited between January 1993 and September 2019.

The effects of the social outbreak on entrepreneurs in Chile have been relevant. According to Manuel Melero, the President of the National Chamber of Commerce Services and Tourism of Chile, the social outbreak has been the "biggest crisis ever suffered our activity in history" (CNC, 2020; p. 15). Consequently, many entrepreneurs have decided to close their doors given the uncertainty of not knowing when the country could back to normal. COVID-19 has extended and sharpened the crisis that entrepreneurs face in the country.

Despite the uncertain political and economic environment in Chile, recent innovative entrepreneurship has seen opportunities to strengthen its position locally and also find a way to expand its business internationally. For example, start-ups such as Cornershop and the Not Company are opening new paths for other Chilean and Latin American entrepreneurs to follow. The following section provides the case of the Not Company.

6 Case Study: The Not Company

The Not Company (NotCo) is a food science company founded in Chile in November 2015. One of the notable characteristics of NotCo is that the firm employs artificial intelligence to create novel plant-based meat and dairy alternatives. Its current products include Not Mayo (Fig. 7), Not Milk (Fig. 8), Not Yogurt, Not Burger (Fig. 9), and Not Cheese. NotCo aims to reinvent the food people like to eat, using plants to replicate animal-based products and make them taste even better. Its mission is "to take animals out of food production while never, ever compromising on taste" (Notco, 2020). NotCo aims to be a leading competitor in the global plant-based protein market. A market of USD 18.5 billion in revenues in 2019 (Yu, 2020).

NotCo's founders are Matias Muchnick, Pablo Zamora, and Karim Pichara. Matias Muchnick is a commercial engineer who graduated from the University of Chile in Santiago. He also participated in business academic programs at the University of California, Berkeley, Stanford University, and Harvard Business School. Before founding NotCo, Matias worked in JP Morgan and Larrain Vial, a Chilean financial firm. After some experience as the founder of Chooz, a mobile app that aims to incentivize healthy living, Matias went to the University of California at Berkeley, intending to develop a project that combines food with technology. Later he met Karim Pichara, Ph.D. in computer science from the Pontifical Catholic of Chile, with a postdoc in applied computer science from Harvard University. Karim is an expert in machine learning and data science. While Karim was working as a

Fig. 7 Not Mayo exhibited in a supermarket in Santiago, Chile; photo © 2020 Carolina Martinez, used with permission

researcher in astrophysics at Harvard University, Matias approached him to convince him to join NotCo to analyze plants' molecular structure. Later, Pablo Zamora joined the co-founder team. Pablo has a Ph.D. in Biotechnology from the University of Santiago in Chile. He worked as associate director of the Life Science Innovation Center at UC David Chile before joining NotCo.

With an initial capital of USD 250,000, the three co-founders developed "Giuseppe," a machine learning software technology that learns infinite combinations of plants to predict how to make plant-based ingredients taste like animal-based products (Brodwin, 2017). NotCo's first product, Not Mayo, is an eggless and soyless mayonnaise with zero cholesterol and gluten. This product rapidly disrupted the mayonnaise market in Chile. After 9 months of being introduced to supermarkets, Not Mayo achieved 8% of the market share (Comieles, 2019).

One of the main reasons to install the company factory in Chile is the wide variety of products that the region offers and its human capital (Del Real, 2018). The

Fig. 8 Not Milk exhibited in a supermarket in Santiago, Chile; photo © 2020 Carolina Martinez, used with permission

ingredients available in Chile and Latin America help NotCo explore infinite combinations of raw materials to achieve the desired flavor. Additionally, NotCo can rely on the highly skilled human capital in biochemistry and informatics that Chile offers.

NotCo has been very successful in raising capital from foreign investors. In 2018, NotCo raised USD three million from venture capitalists such as Kaszek Ventures and IndieBio, one of the most important biotechnology accelerators from Silicon Valley. Two years later, amidst the COVID-19 pandemic, NotCo raised USD 85 million more from investors. This amount of capital has been the highest foreign investment ever received by a Chilean start-up (Reyes, 2020). The funding came from several investors, including the consumer-focused private equity firm L Catterton Partners, Twitter co-founder Biz Stone's Future Positive investment firm, the giant venture capital firm General Catalyst, Kaskek Ventures, The Craftory, Bezos Expeditions (Jeff Bezos' venture capital firm), Endeavor Catalyst, IndieBio, Humboldt Capital, and Maya Capital (Shieber, 2020). Together with prior investment rounds, NotCo has raised USD 118 million in risk capital (Fajardo et al., 2020). By 2020, TechCrunch values NotCo in USD 300 million (Shieber, 2020).

Fig. 9 Not Burger; photo © 2020 Patricio Duran

NotCo expects that the fresh capital raised will help the company consolidate its position as the number one company in the food-tech category, locally and internationally. To do so, NotCo plans to invest in new products, widen the current distribution channels, and add new business partners to its current portfolio of associated firms in Chile, such as the fast-food chain Burger King and the pizza restaurants Papa John's (Yu, 2020). Also, NotCo plans to expand the business internationally within the Latin American region and the USA. In addition to Chile, Argentina, and Brazil's current presence, NotCO plans to expand to Peru, Colombia, and Mexico (Fajardo et al., 2020). In the USA, NotCo plans to install a subsidiary in Silicon Valley to introduce NotCo's products to the American market. NotCo expects that by 2024, the USA will account for 70% of its total revenues by strengthening its current technology, developing new laboratories, and hiring new talent (Fajardo et al., 2020).

In 2020, the World Economic Forum named NotCo as one of the top 100 most innovative start-ups worldwide, being the only Chilean start-up to achieve this recognition and one of the four Latin American firms that were part of the list. According to Nicolas Szekasy, the Kaskek Ventures' managing partners, "we continue to actively support the company since its early days with a strong conviction of the potential that NotCo has to be the leading global player in the food-tech space. In this uncertain time, consumers have amplified their appetite for the plant-based world. In parallel, COVID has allowed us to see that meat production is not only environmentally harmful and inefficient but also that its supply chain is fragile. So we are happy to witness an inflection point where plant-based products are becoming an increasing proportion of a new normal, once they can actually taste amazing like we see NotCo crafting." (Shieber, 2020).

NotCo is an example of a highly innovative start-up from Chile that can become a leading actor in the US plant-based protein market amidst the political and health challenges. This will not be an easy task for the company. According to Lucho Lopez-May, CEO of NotCo in the US: "we know that 33% of plant-based milk consumers in the US turn to dairy products because they do not meet expectations regarding taste. We are here to change that trend." (EconoSus, 2020). How will NotCo be able to change such a trend? In the USA, the company signed an alliance with Whole Foods to distribute NotCo products (EconoSus, 2020). However, the company needs to target the mass market to sustain its expected growth (Watson, 2020). NotCo believes that NotBurger could be a high-potential product in the USA. Today, Impossible Burger remains the main actor in the plant-based burger sector in this country. According to Matias Muchnick, NotBurger "is on taste parity with the Impossible Burger in consumer taste tests" (Watson, 2020). One way to achieve success in the US is creating alliances with US restaurant chains like the one that NotCo has with Burger King in Chile. Flavia Buchmann (Chief Marketing Officer at NotCo) sustains that "NotCo has not only created a 100% plant-based hamburger, but it's a Whopper. It's a big step in what is the reason for NotCo's existence: enable people to eat delicious food in a sustainable way" (Vegconomist, 2020). She also challenges customers to notice the difference between a traditional Whopper and the Rebel Whopper, the Whopper's plant-based version. How open is the American consumer to try the plant-based version of their favorite burgers? How likely is that NotCo and other similar companies change the US fast-food consumer habits?

References

Barr-Melej, P. (2002). *Reforming Chile: Cultural politics, nationalism, and the rise of the middle class*. Univ of North Carolina Press.

BBC. (2020). *Chile country profile*. Retrieved December 17, 2020, from https://www.bbc.com/news/world-latin-america-19357497

Berrone, P., Duran, P., Gómez-Mejía, L., Heugens, P., Kostova, T., & van Essen, M. (2020). Impact of informal institutions on the prevalence, strategy, and performance of family firms: A meta-analysis. *Journal of International Business Studies*. https://doi.org/10.1057/s41267-020-00362-6

Biblioteca del Congreso Nacional de Chile (2021) *Plebicito de 1988 marca el fin del régimen militar*. Retrieved April 16, 2021, from https://www.bcn.cl/historiapolitica/elecciones/detalle_eleccion?handle=10221.1/63196&periodo=1973-1990

Bosna, N., Hill, S., Ionescu-Somers, A., Kelley, D., Levie, J., & Tarnawa, A. 2020. Global entrepreneurship monitor 2019/2020 global report.

Brodwin, E. (2017). An eggless mayo start-up is out to beat Hampton Creek–here's the verdict. *Business Insider*.

Bustamante, C. V., Mingo, S., & Matusik, S. F. (2021). Institutions and venture capital market creation: The case of an emerging market. *Journal of Business Research, 127*, 1–12.

CNC. (2020). *Estallido social y Covid-19: Impacto de una crisis sin precedentes para el sector en la voz de sus protagonistas*. Retrieved March 29, from https://www.cnc.cl/wp-content/uploads/2020/06/30.06.20-Revista-Enlaces-N%C2%BA19.pdf

Collier, S., & Sater, W. F. (1996). *A history of Chile, 1808–1994*. Cambridge University Press.

Comieles, P. (2019). *Chile: NotCo, el nuevo algoritmo de la comida*. Retrieved Dec 18, from https://ia-latam.com/2019/01/10/chile-notco-el-nuevo-algoritmo-de-la-comida/

Dana, L.-P. (2006). Indigenous peoples in Chile. *International Journal of Entrepreneurship and Small Businesses, 3*(6), 779–786.

Del Real, J. (2018) *The not company, una compañía innovadora que desafía a la tecnología*. Retrieved Dec 6, 2020, from https://www.expoknews.com/the-not-company-una-compania-innovadora-que-desafia-a-la-tecnologia/

Duran, P., Kostova, T., & van Essen. (2017). Political ideologies and the internationalization of family-controlled firms. *Journal of World Business, 52*(4), 474–488.

Duran, P., & Ortiz, M. (2020). When more is better: Multifamily firms and firm performance. *Entrepreneurship Theory and Practice, 44*(4), 761–783.

Economic Policy Uncertainty. (2020). *Chile monthly index*. Retrieved December 10, 2020, from https://www.policyuncertainty.com/chile_monthly.html

EconoSus. (2020). *NotCo da el "gran salto": ¿A qué mercado llega la empresa de alimentos 4.0 cautivó a Jeff Bezos? Economía Sustentable*. Retrieved Dec 23, 2020, from https://economiasustentable.com/noticias/notco-da-el-gran-salto-a-que-mercado-llega-la-empresa-de-alimentos-4-0-cautivo-a-jeff-bezos

Espinoza, O. (2008). Creating (in) equalities in access to higher education in the context of structural adjustment and post-adjustment policies: The case of Chile. *Higher Education, 55*(3), 269–284.

Fajardo, D., Guerrero, F., & Nogales, D. (2020). La startup de NotFronteras: cómo The NotCompany está conquistando al epicentro mundial de capital de riesgo y a los consumidores. *La Tercera*. Retrieved Dec 11, 2020, from https://www.latercera.com/pulso/noticia/la-startup-de-notfronteras-como-the-not-company-esta-conquistando-al-epicentro-mundial-de-capital-de-riesgo-y-a-los-consumidores/BELSHAPJGZCGBEQMIJHDNVFNAI/

Ferrer, C. (2020*) Nivel de inglés en Chile pasa de "bajo" a "medio."* EMOL. Retrieved April 2, 2021, from https://www.emol.com/noticias/Nacional/2020/11/24/1004751/Ranking-ingles-nivel-medio-Chile.html

Ffrench-Davis, R. (2002). *Economic reforms in Chile*. From Dictatorship to Democracy.

Gazmuri, C. (2014). Historia de Chile 1891–1994: política, economía, sociedad, cultura, vida privada, episodios.. RIL editores.

Goldberg, P. A. (1975). The politics of the Allende overthrow in Chile. *Political Science Quarterly, 90*(1), 93–116.

Jadresic, E. (2019). The roots of Chile's social discontent. *Financial Times*. Retrieved April 16, 2021, from https://www.ft.com/content/45dc28b8-9247-4d4b-8fcc-e90691d1a1d6

IGWIA. (2020). *El Mundo Indigena 2020*. Retrieved April 4, 2021, from https://www.iwgia.org/es/recursos/mundo-indigena.html

International Monetary Fund. (2020). *Chile*. Retrieved December 17, 2020, from https://www.imf.org/en/Countries/CHL

Lagos, G. (2018). Mining nationalization and privatization in Peru and in Chile. *Mineral Economics, 31*(1), 127–139.

Navia, P. (2010). Living in actually existing democracies: Democracy to the extent possible in Chile. *Latin American Research Review*, 298–328.

Neumann, S., & Villalobos, G. (2018). El fundador de NotCo detalla los desafíos de levantar capital en Chile. *Revista Pauta*. Retrieved Dec 23, 2020, from https://www.pauta.cl/negocios/el-fundador-de-notco-detalla-los-desafios-de-levantar-capital-en-chile

NotCo. (2020). *Our manifest.* Retrieved December 8, 2020, from https://notco.com/us/about-us

Polanco, M. M. (2012). Efectos sociales del terremoto en chile y gestión política de la reconstrucción durante el gobierno de Sebastián Piñera (2010-2011). *Revista Enfoques: Ciencia Política y Administración Pública, 10*(16), 19–46.

Reyes, V. (2020). *NotCo recaudó nuevo capital y queda como la startup chilena con mayor inversión extranjera. Biobiochile.* Retrieved Dec 2, 2020, from https://www.biobiochile.cl/noticias/economia/negocios-y-empresas/2020/09/09/notco-recauda-nuevo-capital-y-se-convierte-en-la-startup-chilena-con-mayor-inversion-extranjera.shtml

Schwab, K. (2019). *Global competitiveness report 2019*. World Economic Forum.

Sehnbruch, K. (2009). *A record number of conflicts? Michelle Bachelet's inheritance of unresolved employment issues*. Working Paper. Regents of the University of California.

Shieber, J. (2020). *Competing with both Perfect Day and Beyond Meat, Chile's NotCo raises $85 million to expand to the US. Techcrunch*. Retrieved December 1, 2020, from https://techcrunch.com/2020/09/09/competing-with-both-perfect-day-and-beyond-meat-chiles-notco-raises-85-million-to-expand-to-the-us/

Servicio Electoral de Chile. (2020). *Votación constitución política 2020*. Retrieved April 16, 2021, from https://pv.servelelecciones.cl/

Statista. (2020). *Global consumer survey*. Retrieved December 17, 2020, from https://www.statista.com/global-consumer-survey

The Economist. (2004). *Chile's foreign policy: You're my best friends*. Retrieved Aprl 16, 2021, from https://www.economist.com/the-americas/2004/03/11/youre-my-best-friends

The Economist. (2012). *Entrepreneurs in Latin America: The lure of Chilecon valley*. Retrieved April 2, 2021, from https://www.economist.com/business/2012/10/13/the-lure-of-chilecon-valley

Vegconomist. (2020). *Jeff Bezos funded start-up NotCo to produce plantbased Rebel Whopper for Burger King*. Retrieved December 23, 2020, from https://vegconomist.com/food-and-beverage/jeff-bezos-funded-startup-notco-to-produce-plantbased-rebel-whopper-for-burger-king/

Watson, E. (2020). *To boldly go... NotCo raises $85m to expand plant-based empire, gears up for US market entry. Food Navigator-USA.com.* Retrieved December 23, 2020, from https://www.foodnavigator-usa.com/Article/2020/09/09/NotCo-raises-85m-to-expand-plant-based-empire-gears-up-for-US-market-entry

Waylen, G. (2016). *Gender, institutions, and change in Bachelet's Chile*. Palgrave Macmillan.

Winn, P., & Kay, C. (1974). Agrarian reform and rural revolution in Allende's Chile. *Journal of Latin American Studies, 6*(1), 135–159.

World Bank. (2020). *Doing business report 2020*. The International Bank for Reconstruction and Development/The World Bank.

Yu, D. (2020). *Latin American plant-based company NotCo closes $85 million series C round upon US entry*. Retrieved on December 18, 2020, from https://www.forbes.com/sites/douglasyu/2020/09/09/latin-american-plant-based-company-notco-closes-85-million-series-c-round-upon-us-entry/?sh=bfd07477 69be

Patricio Duran (Ph.D., University of South Carolina) is an Assistant Professor of International Business at the Boeing Institute of International Business, Chaifetz School of Business, Saint Louis University. His research focuses on family firms, institutions, non-market strategy, international business, and politics. Patricio has published in *Academy of Management Journal, Journal of International Business Studies, Journal of Management, Entrepreneurship Theory and Practice, Journal of Management Studies, Journal of World Business, Global Strategy Journal, among others.*

Entrepreneurship in Colombia

Santiago Garcia Carvajal

Abstract

The chapter refers to the strategic adaptations made by Colombian entrepreneurs, throughout their business life cycle, and the importance they give to their social relationships in the process of evolution of their business activity, aspects of its idiosyncrasy, and the door is opened to interpret the microenterprise as a complex organism that reacts to its environment.

1 Introduction

In Colombia, an Entrepreneur's creativity for survival is synonym to Innovation. It occurs in response to an excess of society's individualism and lack of collective consciousness that impedes the reach of collective agreements. Thus, social agreements achieve maximum individual benefit at the expense of collective wellness (Gómez, 1999). In other words, Colombia accounts for a remarkable individual creativeness married to an equally remarkable social indiscipline. That scenario offers various advantages such as individual creativity and a great social mobility that allows coexistence of an enormous regional diversity and plurality that impedes the rise of a dictatorship. In contrast, complexity to achieve mutual objectives brings the appearance of patronizing systems, corruption, and drug trafficking among other consequences.

It is true that entrepreneur's excessive individualism has an effect on teamwork efficiency. Pereira (2003, as cited in Gómez, 1999) said; "A Japanese professor in Colombia used to say: Colombians are smarter than Japanese, but two Japanese can do we work of many Colombians." However, based upon the Global

S. G. Carvajal (✉)
Universidad Militar Nueva Granada, Bogotá, Colombia
e-mail: santiago.garcia@unimilitar.edu.co

L.-P. Dana et al. (eds.), *Entrepreneurship in South America*, Springer Texts in Business and Economics, https://doi.org/10.1007/978-3-030-97060-4_6

Competitiveness Report (Porter & Schwab, 2008) on the Colombian competitive position chapter, it is clear that the quality of management performance is within Latin-American standards (74th position in the world rank).

According to Baumol (1968), Entrepreneur's management performance implies a resourceful attitude and customized Marketing implementations as indispensable activities to engage. Limited capital and risk money market available in the banking industry for startups; are two major factors that compel entrepreneurs to innovate means to attain resources. On the other hand, entrepreneurs make additional efforts aside from those necessary to maintain core business regular operations in reaction to discontinuous production mechanisms at connected industries (Leibenstein, 1968).

2 Historical Context

Leach (2002), in Bañegil Palacios et al. (2011), define the family business as a highly complex social organization, where the company and the family coexist, entities that function as two superimposed subsystems, interdependent and generators of conflict. The family business is a type of business unit that usually operates from the availability of capital and work of family or domestic origin (Lozano Posso, 2000), and in which labor relations present differentiating elements with respect to other types of organizations' business. In this sense, the family business is a cell of the economy, made up of a microorganism full of opposite intentions, depending on mutual and limited resources whose control is in the hands of a family leader who intends to inherit the company to his descendants (Soto Maciel, 2013), forcing them to conserve the roots and values that allow maintaining the family unit through heritage (Steckerl, 2006).

The model of the three circles of Tagiuri and Davis (1996), conditions the existence of the family business to the interconnection of three subsystems: the property, the family, and the company. According to Croutsche and Ganidis (2008), this conceptual heterogeneity is mainly related to the difficulty in setting the border limits between the family bond, the level of control, and the time of ownership of the company (Soto Maciel, 2013).

This is interpreted from the need to incorporate continuous learning about the business, to all members of the family, in order to create knowledge as an intangible asset and the creation of a family protocol in the company to establish those border limits that ensure the sustainability of the business in the long term.

According to the organizing principle of knowledge by Edgar Morin (1990) "what is vital today is not only learning, not only relearning, not only unlearning; but to organize our mental system to relearn to learn "and also says what teaches to learn is not the method, but" I do not contribute the method, I start in search of the method" (Morin, 1982, p. 35).

Each family is different and each company is different, the search for the method must be that family consensus on the formation of family values around the company, articulated with cutting-edge techniques that help transition the company, identifying the turning points where for natural reasons of the evolution of the times, the descendants form a different vision than the founders had on the business.

In the words of Edgar Morin "complexity is the challenge, not the answer" (2001, p. 143) or in other words "Complexity is a problem word, and not a solution word" (2001, p. 22). Complexity must handle what can be rationalized and what cannot, since "rationality aims to dialogue with the irrational."

Morin asserts that what is required is complex thinking that must not be justified; rather, it has to be imposed progressively along a path, in which the limits, insufficiencies, and deficiencies of simplifying thinking will appear, above all, that is, the conditions in which it is not possible to avoid complex thinking (2006, p. 22); "It includes imperfection because it includes uncertainty, and the recognition of the irreducible" (2006, p. 143).

Like the vision of the hard sciences, Morin also does not stop observing the existence of interactions that give rise to nonlinearity and chaos: "What is complexity? At first glance, it is a quantitative phenomenon, an extreme amount of interactions and interferences, between a very large number of units (2006, p. 59) and the complexity is effectively the fabric of events, actions, interactions, feedbacks, determinations, hazards that constitute our phenomenal world" (2006, p. 32).

Ray Kurzweil affirms that "the imminent fusion of our biological thought with the non-biological intelligence that we are creating" (2005, p. 4) will allow the creation of computers, the re-creation of humans, and the interaction between one and the other, it will make it possible, technically at least, to solve problems of a planetary scope, or even greater ones. In the words of this author: "Ultimately, the entire universe will be saturated with our intelligence: This is the destiny of the universe" (Kurzweil, 2005. p. 29).

The analysis of organizational theories leads to complex adaptive systems (CAS, from the English Complex Adaptive System) because it is diverse and made up of multiple interconnected elements, because it has the ability to change and learn from experience. Training in managerial strategy under complex environments overcomes the obstacle of ambivalence and disorientation by encouraging the learning of a third person, willing to discard acquired beliefs, in favor of consolidated statements that explain all the nuances. The training of neural networks for social environments, together with the methodology of competitive hypotheses, allows the formation of that third person (in this case a digital person) that acts as a projection technique in the transactional analysis between individuals and allows accumulating experience in one place tangible and available in the organization.

Human Capital refers to the capacities and commitments that are part of people's knowledge; Competencies, the ability to innovate and improve motivation, and commitment are articulated there. For some authors, such as Diaz and Raúl (2001) this type of capital describes personal experience and integrated knowledge, both explicit and tacit knowledge, then, the ability to learn is the basis of the other two types of Intellectual Capital.

Structural Capital is related to the accumulation of knowledge of the organization; therefore, they must be kept within it, despite the fact that the workers leave the companies, because to a certain extent it is independent, despite being generated by Human Capital; the culture, technology, and knowledge of the organization would be included there. Authors such as Inche and Chung and Zhao (2004) recognize this capital as an assessment of packaged, disseminated, and accessible knowledge through infostructures, technologies, and technological systems that allow the human being to value themselves much more; Now, for Diaz and Raúl (2001) it is that type of knowledge that arises, over time, in the company and, little by little, is internalized, either in people or in teams; then, the company becomes its sole owner. In this vein, a relevant meaning to this analysis is the one presented by Bueno (2001) for whom Structural Capital is the organization's own knowledge, and it arises to the extent that it is possessed by people and teams. That the entity has made explicit, codified, systematized, and internalized through a formal process that operates through the creation of routines (p. 18).

Relational Capital. As the name implies, it is the set of relationships that the organization has with clients and the value that it has managed to develop through political, social, economic and environmental compliance with the State and society itself. With which a brand value is generated that enhances the achievement of new customers.

The former capital, in turn, is subdivided into Communication Capital and Commercial Capital. In the first case, there are relationships with clients, suppliers, and their degree of satisfaction. While, for the second, communication activities are located in terms of marketing such as Websites and extranets.

3 The Environment for Entrepreneurship

Globalization in the face of the needs of relations between nations, in the face of the liberation of trade, and in the face of information and communication technologies, has acquired significant notoriety in all aspects of society. This notoriety is evidenced by the new virtual environments and electronic commerce platforms that encompass a disruptive process for economic development and the future of the world. It is easy to see globalization as a threat if we highlight the educational and opportunity gaps between diverse sociocultural groups, where technology, due to its competitive nature, sophisticated development, vicarious learning and high cost of implementation, can further unbalance the balance between poverty, unemployment, living conditions, and precarious social integration; In contrast, the robotization and systematization of many conventional jobs emerge as better solutions for organizations, facilitating access to educational means, opportunities to strengthen social capital, by virtue of the improvement of relations between the State and its citizens or through the development of business networking, which integrates people dedicated to the same business activity or complementary activities, generates the proliferation of social networks that bring together communities dissolved by the distance or diversity of occupations, the transfer, integration, and incorporation of specialized knowledge and in general the use of new technologies that have given us better types of communication and exchange of goods and services.

The result of the articulation and contrasts between these phenomena will bring us benefits and lights to contribute to better social development, learning to be able to innovate and meet objectives. These new tools place us in a better situation to remain at the forefront of events, and adapt to constant changes, through knowledge of the cause of the transformation of things, of why? and what for? How we have benefited throughout this time through technological networks, in the same way that past generations have experienced a change in sociocultural paradigms with the advent of new inventions such as radio, television, and the telephone. This new perspective and horizon that arises, must be seen not as a threat but as an opportunity that we must take advantage of in our lives.

The subject of study of this chapter converges in the research case: It is the Colombian entrepreneur. What is the way for it to take a quantum leap? The conversion of the conventional business to the digital business, which incorporates knowledge as an asset, and its intellectual property, the investigation of its internal operations, logistics, the recognition of weaknesses and threats when facing global competition. The environment faced by the entrepreneur in the face of the rise of free trade generated by the new paradigms of economic integration, which have had an effect on geography and have made the space-time dimension become irrelevant. That is, how an MSME or family business can be inserted into the global environment. What are some skills and behaviors that the global entrepreneur should adopt in this new millennium?

In his two seminal works The Theory of Economic Development and Business Cycles, Schumpeter (1912) developed a path analysis on the role of the entrepreneur in economic development. To this day, the entire body of his developed literature on entrepreneurship represents the greatest authority in the field. According to Orati and Dahiya (2001), along the same lines as Shumpeter, argue that innovation is what determines the value of entrepreneurship in economic societies. Shumpeter addresses that it is the principle of innovation that precipitates a change in the production function, and only the entrepreneur is the catalyst for this change. In this context, entrepreneurship takes on significance as an engine of growth and contributes to the wealth of nations (Schumpeter, 1939).

4 Toward the Future

Colombia has experienced the effects of globalizacion for some decades, as stated by Rojas (2017) that since the 1990s, thanks to the economic openings that were taking place, it was imperative to also change the political system of Colombia, giving rise to the Political Constitution of Colombia as the norm of norms where there was a democratic structure oriented to articulate within a structuring process at the world level in the trade of goods and services that shows as a result, two sides of the same coin as can be seen in Table 1.

In terms of economy, this puts Colombia at a disadvantage in relation to other industrialized countries because Colombian companies that seek rapid adaptation in the international market are forced to generate added value in the country both at the

Table 1 The two sides of the coin for the effect of Globalization in Colombia

Positive effects	Negative effects
Opportunity for companies to open markets in other countries.	Small producers lose their ability to compete.
Work and academic mobility.	Loss of jobs.
Foreign investment.	Monopolies are generated.
Greater offer of products, goods, and services, which improve the quality of life.	GDP decline.
Large-scale technological development, greater coverage in telecommunications.	Internal conflicts are generated, loss of citizen security.
The state initiates processes of decentralization of power and the modernization of administrative processes in public entities.	Increase the power of the World Bank. International Monetary Fund.

Source: Effects of Globalization on the Economic Development of Colombia in the 2010-2015 Period. Digital Repository, Nueva Granada Military University

production and the level of production. Generation of jobs and industrialization of the company. The reality is that we still do not meet the necessary conditions to position ourselves as one of the countries benefiting from globalization, since at an educational level we do not reach the standards, and additionally there is no culture of scientific research because the incentives are not enough to motivate these aspects (Portafolio, 2009). However, their international counterparts have an industrial and technological power far superior to national companies when competing in the global market and they do not have to bear the burden of facing the discontinuity in the production of inputs to achieve the final production; on the contrary, they are benefited by the economies of scale offered by global distribution, complying with the required standards and continuously.

The economic opening of economic blocks with different countries has opened Colombian companies to a world market, which, being more competitive, has led companies to face a market for which they are not adapted.

Globalization has generated a new world order economically, politically, and socially. It also allows the local dimension to have a meaning globally. This makes the so-called "glocal" spaces current.

Faced with an economistic conception of the relations between societies and nations, other development models emerge with force, among which sustainable development is beginning to stand out.

In a modern digital age of globalization, a transformation on demand is inherent. Suppliers must be at the forefront of changes, most companies have innovation as their mantra, since that is the market demand. This implies the incursion into value co-creation activities through technological platforms either in traditional markets with the use of modern or conventional technologies. The competitiveness of nations is a macroeconomic concept; however, this concept must begin with business competitiveness, developing knowledge about the structure of industries, knowing our idiosyncrasies and the importance that the employer gives to the people he/she values.

5 Case Study

Next, a data mining proposal is presented on the field work carried out on the capture of 273 surveys, 73% of them in the city of Bogotá, between November 25, 2017, and June 5, 2018, previously. They were trained on the validity and reliability of data collection, when verifying each code of the businessmen's chamber of commerce, against the online database of the Unified Business Registry. The research form was loaded into a file of forms in Google forms and linked in the virtual classrooms of the Business Direction & Strategy and Market Management subject, as a cross-sectional research project for the research line of the academic program (Fig. 1).

Family entrepreneurship is difficult to sustain over time, due to the so-called generational crises, the family business (EF) tends to be perceived as part of the past, as it is conceived as a form of business organization that has little to do with the era of globalization; but nothing could be further from the truth. Data from the International Financial Cooperation of the World Bank (IFC, World Bank, 2011) show that in the United States there are 12 million family businesses that provide 59% of jobs and generate 78% of new jobs. In Spain, on the other hand, family businesses represent 71% of all businesses. This trend is the constant worldwide (Garcia, 2019) (Fig. 2).

Human Capital: Family entrepreneurship forms an intricate relationship between human formation, transfer of roots and family values, and business skills. This is transmitted from parents to children, communication between family members does not establish clear differences on business and family issues, knowledge is shared. The councils educate the successors and warn about the risks that different alternatives offer. The education and training of the entrepreneur passes through the filter of their family training. The variable questions used in the research

Fig. 1 Local pastry shops in neighborhoods in Bogota. Source: © Author

Fig. 2 Martial arts academy in Bogota. Source: © Author

instrument that measure human capital through the ability to form family networks are the following (Garcia, 2019) (Fig. 3):

Have my parents been a great influence on my business life?
I do not trust advice I receive from members outside the family?
Is the advice I receive from non-family members better than that of the family?
Do I share my business tips with other people?
Do I have a high tolerance for risk?
Am I a competitive person?
Do many people seek my advice on business matters?
Don't I compare business practices to see how I can improve mine?
Does my family play an important role in the success of my business?
Do I trust the advice my family gives me?

Structural Capital: For family entrepreneurship, what can be identified as routine is the usual decision-making process, in relation to the importance that is given so much to the individualism of the entrepreneur to embark on new challenges without the help of other people. As is the custom of relying on its network of providers and experts who are the source of information and resources for the formation of teams, in this sense the time factor helps to determine these routines and customs. Organizational knowledge is transferred and accumulated in relation to the confidence that the entrepreneur has to communicate his strategies and purposes with members of both his family, if he cares about the success of the entrepreneur and has a shared vision of the business, such as from people outside the organization, at the expense of running the risk of valuable information falling into the hands of competitors. The variable questions used in the research instrument that measured structural capital

Fig. 3 Local Miselania in Bogota. Source: © Author

through the ability to form communication networks are the following (Garcia, 2019) (Fig. 4):

Looking for business advice from different people?
Does my family really care about the success of my business?
Am I often in conflict with my family regarding my business?
Am I very reserved in matters of strategy of my business so that the competitors do not know what I do?
Do I have a strong network of providers who help me make decisions?
Do I have a strong network of experts who help me make decisions?
Would others describe me as a person who works well in a team?
I don't like working in a team?
Do others like to work with me?
Do I spend a lot of time developing a strong network of business relationships?

Relational Capital: In family entrepreneurship, market orientation and business decision-making goes through the filter of approval of family members, the trust generated by the network of contacts that led to a potential client and the family unit in decision-making against the criteria of choosing new business opportunities for the company. In other words, it is the business development policy that the company has, the means it uses to increase its customer base compared to the family view of the business. The variable questions used in the research instrument that measured structural capital through the capacity of formation of exchange networks are the following (Garcia, 2019):

Fig. 4 Single mom liquor Store in Bogota. Source: © Author

Does my family agree with my business decisions?
Do my friends often give me bad advice?
Do I have a strong network of business acquaintances?
Do business organizations offer the benefit of sharing ideas?
Do I have extensive communications with members of other business communities?
Am I often in conflict with members of my network of business relationships?

A model is an abstraction of reality, it is a simplified representation of some phenomenon in the real world. A mannequin in a store is a model. Also, the accounting formula: Credit – Debt = Capital of the company. The dependent variables are the fundamental factors to be explained or predicted and which are influenced by some other factor. What are the main variables in the valuation of intellectual capital? Scholars of knowledge management have always been inclined to highlight the formula: INTELLECTUAL CAPITAL = HUMAN CAPITAL + RELATIONAL CAPITAL + STRUCTURAL CAPITAL. More recently, thanks to the need to value intangible assets, a fifth variable, intellectual property, was added to the list (Fig. 5).

Fig. 5 Baby clothing boutique. Source: © Author

6 Conclusion

Technology goes beyond the use of mobile devices and computers, technology must be understood as the systematic process of generating well-being for societies, integrating business conglomerates that stimulate economies of scope and knowledge in all areas of life, for example, in the continuous improvement of the provision of public services such as water, sewerage, transportation, but also improve the power of negotiation with suppliers and customers, etc. It is thinking beyond how to generate economic resources that allow a country to provide services to its inhabitants. It is the incorporation of systematized means of logistics, communication, and education in the inclusion of marginal societies in the opportunities of the twenty-first century, being economically and technologically capable of maintaining, repairing, and updating it.

Nowadays, people spend a large part of their time on social networks and text messages, to the point of producing a cultural revolution of the utmost importance, people feel threatened and favored by new technologies that force changes in their lives, but they also facilitate and automate many everyday processes. The new participatory sciences are modifying both the transmission of their content and their content itself: in engineering, genetics, social studies, etc.

The Microenterprise is the door to the Globalization of the economy in a country, the force with which they are initiated and the great opportunity that they offer in the popular sectors, in the young people, in the innovative ideas, is of vital importance; Teachers and parents as leaders of the basic cell of societies, must educate their children and students for innovation and entrepreneurship, in order to sow in children, who are the future of the community, the infinite desire to emerge Thanks to the ability to convene that audiovisual media have, values and discipline must be stimulated so that they lose the fear of proposing new things in every aspect of their life; If children manage to positively modify their behavior and innovate in personal life, they will be able to generate value for societies, and in their productive lives they will generate much more sustainable business ideas over time, competitive and above all global.

References

Bañegil Palacios, T. M., Barroso Martínez, A., & Tato Jiménez, J. L. (2011). Profesionalizarse, emprender y aliarse para que la empresa familiar continúe. *Revista de Empresa Familiar, 1*(2), 27–41.

Baumol, W. J. (1968). Entrepreneurship in economic theory. *American Economic Review, 58*(2), 64–71.

Bueno, C. E. (2001). *Gestión del conocimiento en universidades y organismos públicos de Investigación, El capital intelectual como marco de análisis. España: Universidad Autónoma de Madrid*. Recuperado el 18 noviembre de 2020, de http://www.madrimasd.org/informacionidi/biblioteca/publicacion/doc/16_GestionConocimientoUniversidad-desOPIS.pdf

Croutsche, J. J., & Ganidis, B. (2008). Diversité des entreprises familiales. *La Revue des Sciences de Gestion, 2*, 93–98.

Chung, K. H., & Zhao, X. (2004). Making a market with spreads and depths. *Journal of Business Finance & Accounting, 31*(7–8), 1069–1097.

Diaz, M., & Raúl, J. (2001). *Modelo de Gestión (gc) aplicado a la universidad pública en el Perú*. http://sisbib.unmsm.edu.pe/bibvirtual/tesis/Basic/DiazMJ.Contenido.htm.

Effects of Globalization on the Economic Development of Colombia in the 2010–2015 Period. *Digital Repository, Nueva Granada Military University*.

Garcia, S. (2019). La identificación de recursos estratégicos orientados al sostenimiento de la empresa familiar en Bogotá: una simulación del comportamiento social y empresarial del sujeto. *Revista Internacional Administración & Finanzas, 12*(2), 1–22.

Gómez, B. H. (1999). *El Almendrón. Comentario de ¿Para dónde va Colombia?* Tercer Mundo Editores. http://www.eltiempo.com/archivo/documento/MAM-863820

Kurzweil, R. (2005). *The singularity is near: When humans transend biology*. Penguin books.

Leach, P. (2002). *La Empresa Familiar*. Ediciones Granica.

Leibenstein, H. (1968). Entrepreneurship and development. *American Economic Review, 58*(2), 72–83.

Lozano Posso, M. (2000). El protocolo en las empresas de propiedad familiar. *Estudios Gerenciales, 16*(74), 49–67.

Morin, E. (2006). *El Método 6*. Ediciones Cátedra.

Morín, E. (2001). *Los siete saberes necesarios para la educación del futuro*. Dower.

Morin, E. (1990). *Introducción al pensamiento complejo*. Gedisa.

Morin, E. (1982). *Para salir del siglo XX*. Kairós.

Orati, V., & Dahiya, S. B. (2001). *Economic theory in the light of Schumpeter's scientific heritage*. Spellbound Publications.

Pereira, F. (2003). Reflexion sobre algunas características del espíritu emprendedor Colombiano. *Economia Gestión y Desarrollo, 1*, 9–26.

Portafolio. (2009). *Colombia no reúne las condiciones para beneficiarse de la globalización.* Recuperado de http://www.portafolio.co/economia/finanzas/colombia-reune-condiciones-beneficiarse-globalizacion-estudio-contraloria-179572

Porter, M. E., & Schwab, K. (Eds.). (2008). *The global competitiveness report 2008–2009*. World Economic Forum.

Rojas (2017). *Enfoques económicos*. Recuperado de https://repository.unimilitar.edu.co/bitstream/10654/16684/3/RojasCarrascalAuraCristina2017.pdf

Soto Maciel, A. (2013). La empresa familiar en México situación actual de la investigación. *Contaduría y administración, 58*(2), 135–171.

Steckerl, V. (2006). Modelo explicativo de una empresa familiar que relaciona valores del fundador, cultura organizacional y orientación al mercado. *Pensamiento y Gestión, 20*, 194–215.

Tagiuri, R., & Davis, J. (1996). Bivalent attributes of the family firm. *Family Business Review, 9*(2), 199–208.

Schumpeter, J. A. (1912). *1949. The theory of economic development: An inquiry into profits, capital, credit, interest and the business cycle*. Harvard University Press.

Schumpeter, J. A. (1939). *Business cycles: A theoretical, historical and statistical analysis of the capitalist process*. McGraw Hill.

World Development Report. (2011). *Conflict, security, and development, paperback*. (ISBN 978–0–8213-8439-8) SKU 18439.

Santiago Garcia Carvajal, Master's in Business Administration, Southern New Hampshire University, Minor Marketing Management. Professional experience in market research, consumer product management, software marketing, and journalism. Experience in internationalization plans and holding academic and business events. Currently, Professor of the in the online Higher Management Specialization, Nueva Granada Military University, Bogota, Colombia.

Entrepreneurship in Ecuador

Sara A. Wong

Abstract

In Ecuador, as in many countries worldwide, entrepreneurship has gained a great deal of importance in the past decade, both as an economic and as scholarly activities, and as the focus of public policy. However, entrepreneurial activities are not new in this small, open economy, located by the Pacific Ocean in the northern part of South America. Throughout its history, the primary export productive specialization of Ecuador has been accompanied by a succession of boom-and-bust cycles usually linked to the production of a single commodity. In the latest cycle, between 2004 and 2014, there was an unprecedented inflow of foreign currency due to the boom of commodity prices, in particular oil, whose revenues contributed to financing the government's social and infrastructural plans in that decade. This abruptly ended after the collapse in the price of oil in 2014, and the recovery was still underway when the pandemic hit this economy. In times of crisis, entrepreneurial activities are a necessity, and this country has long been continuously experiencing events that have challenged the entrepreneurial spirit of the Ecuadorian people.

1 Introduction

This chapter contributes to the objectives of this book by exploring the characteristics, challenges, opportunities, and idiosyncrasies of the entrepreneurial environment and entrepreneurship in Ecuador. According to the World Economic Forum's (WEF) Global Entrepreneurship Monitor (GEM), this country ranked

S. A. Wong (✉)
ESPAE-Business School & Center for Asia-Pacific Studies, ESPOL Polytechnic University, Guayaquil, Ecuador
e-mail: sawong@espol.edu.ec

L.-P. Dana et al. (eds.), *Entrepreneurship in South America*, Springer Texts in Business and Economics, https://doi.org/10.1007/978-3-030-97060-4_7

No. 1 in Total early-stage Entrepreneurial Activity (TEA) in 2017—and has been among the top 4 for several years (2004, 2013–2016, and 2019; see WEF's GEM database n.d.-b). This can be explained by Ecuador's level of development, although, as the relevant literature has pointed out, the relationship between economic development and entrepreneurship is rather complex, and context and population entrepreneurial attitudes also matter.[1] Moreover, policy discussion about what is relevant for economic growth and welfare in a developing country has addressed how entrepreneurship can help alleviate poverty and how it can propel growth and maintain/create jobs in a crisis and as a way to formalize businesses. The latter is key for the Ecuadorian economy, badly hit by the COVID-19 pandemic, where informal employment comprises 50%, or more, of total employment. Thus, Ecuador makes for an interesting case to explore entrepreneurship issues.

This chapter characterizes the evolution of entrepreneurship in Ecuador from various angles. It starts with the obvious one: entrepreneurship as an economic activity at the individual level. Then, it considers the cultural background of Ecuadorian society, highlighting Ecuador's current policies—or the lack thereof—and compares Ecuador's entrepreneurship performance with that of its regional peers.

By means of a case study, described in Sect. 5, this chapter illustrates the challenges of entrepreneurs in Ecuador, the most relevant aspects of doing business, key success factors, and strategies for staying in business. Finally, the chapter draws lessons for successful entrepreneurship in Ecuador and poses questions about the future of entrepreneurship in this country.

The chapter uses secondary data and interviews from the case study. It applies document and statistical analyses. The latter uses quantitative and qualitative data tabulated from the World Bank's Ease of Doing Business Reports and both the GEM online dataset and the Executive Opinion Survey (EOS) dataset of the Global Competitiveness Report (GCR) from the WEF (n.d.-a).

As explained in Sect. 3, various measures suggest improvements in Ecuador's entrepreneurship environment. Yet, challenges remain. Moreover, there have been

[1]There is a vast literature on the underpinnings of entrepreneurship, entrepreneurial activities, and the entrepreneurs. From the views that stress on the risk of such activity (Cantillon, 1756; Knight, 1921, among the most widely cited), to those that focus on its cultural aspects (e.g., Leighton, 1988; Dana, 2002, 1990), to the ones that stress innovation (Schumpeter, 1939, 1934)—widely cited in development—to others that highlight entrepreneurship as the need for achievement (McClelland, 1961) or the recognition in compensation for social marginality (Hagen, 1962), or that rather stress certain traits and behaviors of the entrepreneur, e.g., a social agent for change, as innate, as learned, her desire for independence, her need for autonomy in the workplace, and her desire to develop skills and acquire social status (Barth, 1967; Kets de Vries, 1977; Sexton & Upton, 1990; Gibb, 1986; Knight, 1987; Creedy & Johnson, 1983; Evans & Leighton, 1990; Vivarelli, 2004, 1991; Blanchflower & Oswald, 1998) to those that search for the reasons why entrepreneurs pursue such activity (for instance, Lazear, 2005; Poschke, 2013; Lederman et al., 2014); among others. The reader is invited to discover these and many more, as these references discuss the concepts and theories on which the measurement of entrepreneurship, entrepreneurial activities, and the entrepreneurs are based.

setbacks in the past six years, particularly on governmental support and policies and programs, physical and services infrastructure, post-school entrepreneurial education and training, and commercial and professional infrastructure. These aspects do not account for the COVID-19 pandemic which brings in both opportunities and more challenges.

The behavior and attitudes of entrepreneurs in Ecuador reflect high entrepreneurial intentions, as well as high perceived entrepreneurial capabilities, but low perceived entrepreneurial opportunities, with a falling fear of failure, and low expectations of high job creation (GEM database, see Sect. 3). These data also show one of the highest TEA of female/male ratios; however, with low ratios for the female/male opportunity-driven TEA, which suggests a TEA driven to a great extent by early-stage female entrepreneurs by necessity, rather than by the desire to become independent or increase their income.

Two applicable measures of cultural and social support are the prevalence of informal investors and the emphasis on traditional rather than secular-rational values.

On the way forward, Ecuador aspires that the new, and first, law of entrepreneurship ("Ley Orgánica de Emprendimiento e Innovación," Supplement to the Official Registry No. 151, February 28, 2020), helps create a better environment for entrepreneurship in this country.

2 Historical Context

In the past 50 years, the Ecuadorian economy has been marked by its dependence on commodity prices. While this has allowed the government to finance both capital and social investments, it may have also sowed the seeds of its own lackluster economic performance in that period (Fig. 1).

According to the data in Díaz (2018), between 1972 and 2015, the Ecuadorian gross domestic product (GDP) grew at an average rate close to 4% per year; however, in per capita terms, GDP grew at a disappointing average rate of 1.7% per year. Disappointing, because comparing Ecuador and Latin America's indexes of real GDP per capita, that of Ecuador is below the regional one throughout the period, and the gap has widened in recent years. Díaz notes that the performance of the Ecuadorian economy surpassed that of Latin America only during two periods. The first was during the 1972–1981 oil boom when Ecuador went from being an agricultural economy to one that exports oil. The second period began in 2000 when the Ecuadorian government officially dollarized the economy, abandoning Ecuador's national currency (the Sucre) and replacing it with the US dollar, as a way out of its serious economic crisis in the late 1990s. Dollarization has served to eliminate the high inflation rates present since the 1970s, which averaged 32% per year between 1972 and 2000. By 2000, the inflation rate returned to single-digit levels, registering an average of close to 4% per year between 2004 and 2015 (Díaz, 2018).

Fig. 1 The new and "old" Guayaquil, main port city of Ecuador, perhaps best describes the complex entrepreneurship environment in Ecuador. A new vibrant commercial area. Behind, the traditional neighborhood "Las Peñas," known as the place where the city was founded. *Source:* ©SaraA.Wong

The openness index (sum of exports and imports) of Ecuador has increased from an average of 21% of GDP in the 1960s to 32.7% during the 1970s (the first oil boom decade), to 55.6% during the second oil boom in the 2000s, to the 52.3% in the 2010s (own calculations using the World Bank's World Development Indicators, WDI, database). Ecuador moved slowly away from the import substitution policy—although some temporary protectionist measures were adopted in the late 2000s and early 2010s—and has become an economy with greater participation in international markets and where the government plays a more prominent role.

However, increased trade has not come with increased trade diversification: Ecuador's exports are still concentrated in a few products such as oil, bananas, cocoa, tuna and fish, shrimp, and flowers—representing around 90% of total exports, with low value added or based in natural resources (World Bank Group, 2018). This trade concentration makes Ecuador vulnerable to international price fluctuations—as recently seen with the end of the super-cycle of high commodity prices and the ensuing economic crisis. Nor is its trade well connected to regional or global value chains (GVCs). According to a World Bank report, the degree of Ecuador's participation in GVCs is below that of Chile, Peru, and Mexico, and Ecuador's participation is now located upstream in the GVCs which agrees with its specialization in primary products with low value added (World Bank Group, 2019).

Despite the large increase in government revenues during the two oil price booms, no balance was achieved in its fiscal accounts (imperative during the dollarization period). Average deficits increased during these oil boom periods, which ended up being financed with greater, especially external, public debt. This currently may represent a threat to the sustainability of dollarization.

According to data from the World Bank's WDI, throughout the past 5 decades there has been gains in social indicators such as an increase in life expectancy (from 58 in 1970 to 77 in 2018), a decrease in infant mortality rate (from 95.4 per 1000 live births in 1970 to 12 in 2019), and a reduction in poverty incidence from 36.7% in 2007 to 25% in 2019 (using national poverty lines). However, the current COVID-19 pandemic, with the deep economic setbacks that have brought in, is expected to reverse decades of gains in several social indicators.

Ecuador was recently facing a crisis with the end of the super-cycle of high commodity prices in 2014. From the latter, Ecuador had not yet recovered when it had to face a series of challenges such as the 2016 earthquake, manifestations of social discontent at the end of 2019, and the current pandemic. All these factors pose challenges for entrepreneurship and entrepreneurs. However, simultaneously, they emphasize entrepreneurship as a way to improve the economy of households and the country when formal work is scarce (Ács, 2007).

When it comes to entrepreneurship, micro and small and medium enterprises (MSME) play an essential role in Latin America. Yet, they tend to remain small or slowly grow. One key reason behind such slow growth is the lack of innovation (Lederman et al., 2014). In Ecuador, around 20% of all sales come from MSMEs (Camino-Mogrovejo et al., 2018) (Fig. 2). Furthermore, nascent entrepreneurs or owner-managers of "new business" display low rates of innovation (GEM, various

Fig. 2 A dragon fruit ("Pitahaya") farm. This fruit has seen a surge in export activity in recent years, in several cases undertaken by new SMEs. *Source:* ©SaraA.Wong

issues). However, in Ecuador, firms are small also due to poor business capacity, poor access to credit, and poor credit conditions (World Bank, 2012).

Studies on opportunity and necessity entrepreneurs have stressed cultural norms and national values (e.g., Hechavarría & Reynolds, 2009), which offers an interesting path to explain the prevalence of entrepreneurship by necessity in Ecuador according to data from the GEM. Such norms and values are established by people and their social and human capital. In Ecuador, for instance, informality permeates across economic activities and individual behaviors (World Bank, 2012).

The next section presents data on the business environment, reflecting on the difficulties and challenges for entrepreneurs. The prevalence, throughout the years, of dragging factors for entrepreneurship and doing business, in general, can be seen as the result of the lack of coordination between the goal of promoting entrepreneurship—emphasized by the government in the last decade—and public policy, an issue that has been studied in the literature (e.g., Schott & Wickstrom Jensen, 2008).

3 The Environment for Entrepreneurship

This section discusses available measurements regarding the environment for entrepreneurship in Ecuador. When deemed relevant, measurements for regional partners are also presented as a benchmark.

A variety of measures and discussions on measurement issues can be found in the literature (e.g., Ács et al., 2014, 2018; Coduras & Autio, 2013). Ács et al. (2014) summarize the approaches to measuring entrepreneurship in three categories:

- *Framework* indicators (reflecting entrepreneurial framework conditions, comparing the national regulatory framework for new business entry, or distinguishing between framework conditions, entrepreneurship performance, and economic impact).
- *Output* indicators (tracking the creation of a new business or entry into self-employment, using survey or registry data).
- *Attitudes* (tracking opinions, values, and attitudes relevant for entrepreneurship).

This section utilizes these approaches without discussing their advantages or drawbacks, by presenting data from the widely used GEM's output indicator, its survey, and its National Experts Survey (NES). The World Bank's Ease of Doing Business Reports provides further insights on entrepreneurial frameworks for Ecuador and fellow Andean countries. Finally, data from the Executive Opinion Survey of the Global Competitiveness Report gives context on the most difficult aspects of doing business in Ecuador.

3.1 Framework for Entrepreneurship in Ecuador

The NES provides information on nine factors believed by the GEM to have a significant impact on entrepreneurship, known as the Entrepreneurial Framework Conditions (EFCs). Figure 3 shows three panels, each with a point in time, to convey the evolution of the EFCs for Ecuador and fellow Andean countries Chile, Colombia, and Peru. This Likert scale (very bad (1) to very good (5)) shows that, for Ecuador, conditions that enhance (or hinder) new business creation have improved since 2004 when the country first appeared on the GEM.[2] It also shows that among the fellow Andean countries, Chile has the best EFCs, closely followed by Colombia.

Despite this positive evolution, Ecuador experienced setbacks in the past 6 years on several of its EFCs such as governmental support and policies, governmental programs, physical and services infrastructure, post-school entrepreneurial education and training, and commercial and professional infrastructure. These setbacks do not account for the challenges (and opportunities) that the COVID-19 pandemic brought to Ecuador's EFCs in 2020 and 2021.

Reynolds (2012) assesses the national factors that affect the creation of new businesses. Two national factors presented in several of his models are relevant for the case of Ecuador: (i) the prevalence of informal investors, which is an indicator of the expected support from the local community for business creation, whereby "more informal investors are associated with more participation by nascent entrepreneurs" (Reynolds, 2012, p. 215); and (ii) the emphasis on traditional rather than secular-rational values. The traditional values emphasize work, a strong sense of responsibility for one's family, self-reliance, and a reluctance to approach national agencies or government leaders to seek help with personal or family issues. On the contrary, secular-rational values are associated with reliance on government programs. These two are also key measures of cultural and social support.

Besides the cultural and regulatory context, this chapter also examines constraints and opportunities; thus, we summarize the main prevailing factors identified as bottlenecks for conducting new and established business in Ecuador, in three reports, cited earlier in this chapter: the GEM, the Ease of Doing Business, and the GCR.

The GEM highlights the low accessibility to financing for entrepreneurs in Ecuador. There is a shortage of funds for seed and venture capital. Furthermore, it is difficult to access credit in the financial system under preferential conditions for entrepreneurs. Needless to say, it is important to create a favorable business environment to attract foreign and domestic investors (Hisrich et al., 2016). In fact, the literature has identified financial constraint as one of the main obstacles for individuals to start their own business (Demirgüc-Kunt et al., 2009).

[2] Care should be taken when comparing countries and factors over time, due to changes in questions and the conceptual framework for entrepreneurship. Nonetheless, the GEM strives to ensure procedures that render their figures comparable across countries. When some definitions change, as with the conceptual framework for entrepreneurship, the GEM discloses the relevant information on the consortium website (http://gem-consortium.ns-client.xyz/about/wiki)

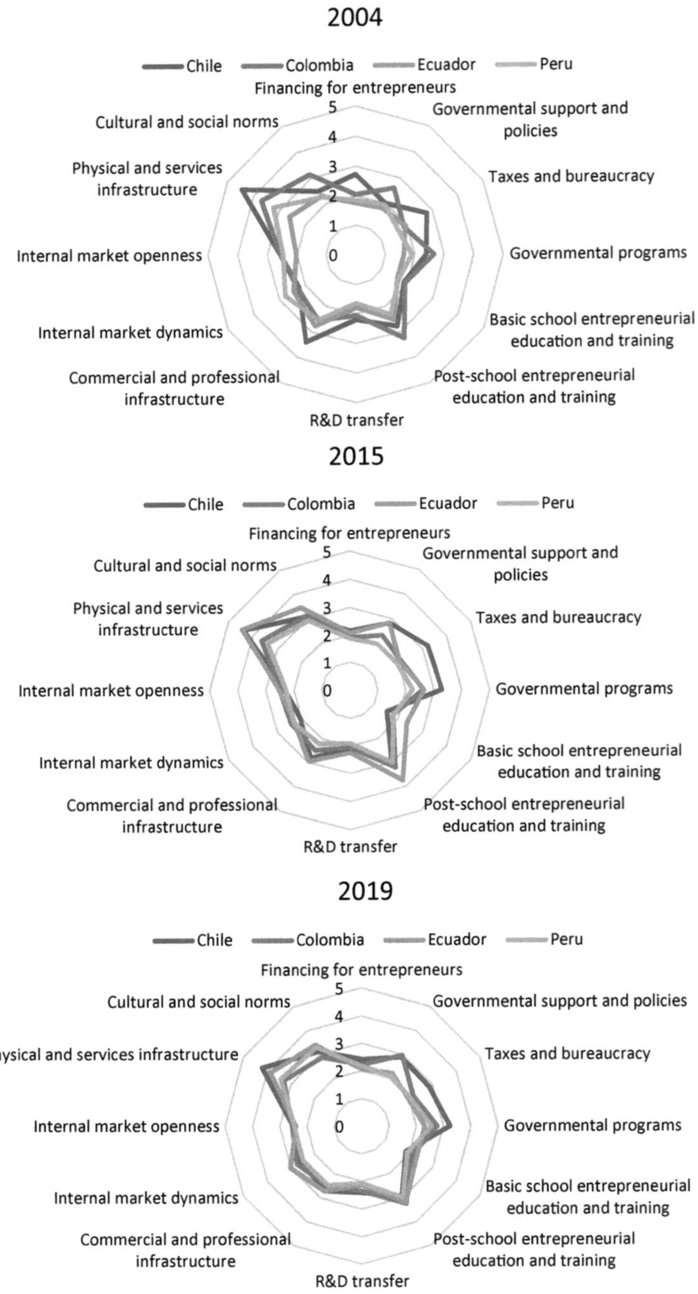

Fig. 3 Entrepreneurial framework conditions for Ecuador, Chile, Colombia, and Peru. Selected years. Likert scales. Source: Global Entrepreneurship Monitor database, Entrepreneurial Framework Conditions. Available at https://www.gemconsortium.org/data/key-nes. Notes: In exhibit "2004" data for Chile and Colombia correspond to year 2005 and 2006, respectively. In exhibit "2019" data for Peru is for the year 2018

From the Ease of Doing Business Reports, we summarize four constraints for businesses in Ecuador:

1. Excessive tax burden for companies, especially regarding the number of hours devoted to filing taxes.
2. Excessive delay in the resolution of insolvencies. The Ease of Doing Business Report (World Bank, 2017) identified Ecuador as the Latin American country in which business closing procedures take the longest (5.3 years). This processing time has not changed in the most recent reports. On average, in Latin American and Caribbean countries, this procedure is resolved in 2.8 years (World Bank, 2017).
3. The low index of strength of legal rights. "The Strength of Legal Rights Index measures the degree to which collateral and bankruptcy laws protect the rights of borrowers and lenders and thereby facilitate loan provision. The index covers a range from 0 to 12; higher scores indicate that laws are better designed to expand access to credit" (World Bank, 2016). Ecuador consistently scored 1 out of 12 on this index in the past few years (World Bank, Ease of Doing Business Report, various issues).
4. Lengthy procedures for opening a company. In Ecuador, from 2007 to 2017, the number of procedures and number of days to open a business have been reduced from 14 to 11 and from 65 to 48.5, respectively. These indicators remain the same in 2020. Ecuador still requires the most formalities for opening a company among Latin American countries such as Chile, Colombia, and Peru. The cost of such government inaction or excessive regulations might discourage formal businesses or new entrepreneurial initiatives.

According to the GCR, labor rigidity is one of the main bottlenecks of doing business in Ecuador. This country has restrictive labor regulations framed, especially in the high costs of hiring and firing. Restrictive labor regulations have been a constant concern for entrepreneurs.

Another difficulty highlighted in the GCR is regulatory instability for the business sector. Entrepreneurs emphasize that constant changes in regulations (e.g., taxes) create uncertainty and impose increasing costs.

Moreover, certain taxes, such as the tax on the exit of foreign currency and the advance on income tax, and nontariff barriers constitute further restrictions. Businesspersons have asked the government to eliminate these taxes and the safeguards that render inputs more expensive.

Chapter 3 of the 2020 Ease of Doing Business Report (World Bank, 2020) suggests ways to remove obstacles to entrepreneurship that come from lengthy insolvency procedures, taxes, and lack of access to credit.

3.2 Behaviors and Attitudes

The GEM also presents Ecuador's measures of entrepreneurship output and attitudes of entrepreneurs. The GEM's Adult Population Survey (APS) examines the characteristics, motivations, and ambitions of individuals starting businesses, as well as social attitudes toward entrepreneurship, summarized in 15 indicators (see https://www.gemconsortium.org/data/key-aps for their definitions). Below, we summarize relevant results for Ecuador, using data from the GEM, obtained from the World Statistics website (http://world-statistics.org/).

1. Ecuador has one of the lowest Perceived Entrepreneurial Opportunities (PEO) among the Andean Community, and it ranks in mid positions on the global scale.
2. Despite the low PEO, Ecuador has consistently ranked among the top in the world in TEA (recall: Total early-stage Entrepreneurial Activity) whenever the country appears in the GEM database (starting in 2004, no data for Ecuador in 2005, 2006, 2007, 2011, and 2018). In 2019, the latest data currently available, Ecuador ranks second in the world in TEA, with a rate of 36.2, right after Chile (36.71). Its lowest position in the global ranking of TEA was in 2009 (12th with 15.82), and the highest was in 2017 (first with 29.62). Other Andean countries, such as Chile, Colombia, and Peru, usually accompany Ecuador at the top 12 in the global ranking of TEA.
3. Consistent with high TEA rates, Ecuador ranks among the top eight in the world in terms of Perceived Entrepreneurial Capabilities (PEC), steadily climbing up since 2013 and reaching the second position in 2019 with a rate of 78.28.
4. Interestingly, Ecuador's Fear of Failure indicator has been falling down. It was ranked among the top three in 2004 and currently ranks in the lowest quartile. Entrepreneurs have less and less fear of not succeeding in their undertakings. Colombia, Chile, and Peru are also among the countries where entrepreneurs indicate less fear of failure.
5. However, the percentage of the population, aged 18–64 years, who agree with the statement that, in Ecuador, most people consider starting a business as a desirable career choice, has decreased from 81.08 in 2004 (second place at that time) to 59.50 in 2016, and to 72.26 in 2019.
6. In contrast, Ecuador exhibits low rates of entrepreneurial employee activity, that is, the "rate of involvement of employees in entrepreneurial activities, such as developing or launching new goods or services, or setting up a new business unit, a new establishment or subsidiary" (GEM website), placing this country in the lowest quartile. Among the Andean countries, Chile is at the top.
7. In comparison with the other countries in the GEM database, Ecuador in general registers high rates of Established Business Ownership (EBO), placing this country among the top eight. The highest rate was 18.92 in 2012, the lowest was 10.10 in 2004, and the rate was 14.69 in 2019.
8. In terms of Entrepreneurial Intentions (EI) rate, Ecuador ranked second worldwide in 2004 with a rate of 40.6 and has usually remained among the top nine, except in 2016 when ranked 13th with a rate of 36.7 and 12th in 2013 with 39.9. Among the Andean countries, Colombia has been at the top, and Chile's rate has increased over time.

9. In contrast, Ecuador ranks in the last quartile of the Entrepreneurial Motivational (EM) index (percentage of those involved in TEA that is motivated by improvement-driven opportunities, divided by the percentage of those that are necessity motivated). Chile has usually exhibited the highest EM index in the Andean region.
10. Ecuador exhibits a low Business Service Sector (BSS) rate, ranging from 4.77 in 2017 to 9.05% in 2008. Economies in the top ten positions exhibit a BSS of over 30%.
11. Concerning the female/male TEA ratio, Ecuador has ranked among the economies with the highest ratios, with rates of 0.81 in 2004 and 2010, 1.07 in 2012, 1.06 in 2017, and 0.86 in 2019.
12. In contrast, for the female/male opportunity-driven TEA with a ratio of 0.82 in 2013, the first year that this indicator was available, Ecuador ranked in the bottom quartile. With ratios of 0.91, 0.92, and 0.90 in subsequent years, it reached mid positions. This suggests that the relatively higher positions of Ecuador in the female/male TEA rankings are driven, to a great extent, by early-stage female entrepreneurs by necessity, rather than by opportunity or the desire to become independent or increase their income.
13. Compared to other countries, Ecuador shows low expectations of High Job Creation (HJC) coming from nascent entrepreneurs or owner-managers of a "new business." Ecuador is generally positioned in the bottom quartile. The lowest rate was in 2016 with 6.30. In that year, Colombia's HJC expectation rate was 37.9, ranking third. Interestingly, other fellow Andean countries, namely, Chile, Colombia, and Peru, ranked in the top quartile, possibly showing better labor market dynamics than Ecuador.
14. Except for 2004 and 2012, Ecuador's High Status to Successful Entrepreneurs rate indicator ranks in mid positions among all the economies in the GEM database.
15. Finally, Ecuador exhibits low rates of innovation by nascent entrepreneurs or owner-managers of a "new business," positioning this country among the mid or bottom ranks in the rankings by innovation rate. On the contrary, Chile ranks among the top. More worrisome is that this indicator exhibits a decreasing trend for Ecuador.

It is interesting to note that Ecuador exhibited the lowest values (although this did not necessarily translate into the lowest position in the ranking) for all indicators in 2016, a year of crisis, when a strong earthquake hit the coastal region of this country—worsening the damage already caused in investment and infrastructural plans by low oil prices. These low values illustrate how negative shocks may impact the behaviors and attitudes of entrepreneurs.

4 Toward the Future

Two events from 2020 will shape the development of entrepreneurship, entrepreneurial activities, and entrepreneurs in Ecuador in the near future: a newly enacted law and the COVID-19 pandemic. However, besides these events, there are persistent issues related to the culture and context of entrepreneurship in Ecuador, namely, education and the entrepreneurship environment, that should receive more and better attention from government policies and programs. This section summarizes what to expect (or not) from each of them.

As noted in the introduction of this chapter, the first Entrepreneurship Law of Ecuador was enacted in February 2020, and its accompanying rules in August 2020 ("Reglamento General a la Ley Orgánica de Emprendimiento e Innovación," Supplement to the Official Registry No. 260, August 4, 2020). This was a long-overdue aspiration of entrepreneurs. Whether having a legal framework will make any difference in practice remains a question. The law is expected to provide solutions to several challenges for entrepreneurs, for instance, by simplifying the process of starting a formal business,[3] allowing the hire of hourly workers, and providing access to public financial services and funds.

The current COVID-19 pandemic also poses several challenges for entrepreneurs, such as lack of demand, constraints for doing business, accelerated digitization of business, and poor Internet quality. However, it may also create opportunities. In an article published on the World Economic Forum's website, Wong (2020) suggests that using digital tools on the recovery path can leverage greater social mobility and shared value creation and is a must for businesses to survive the ongoing crisis. He indicates that the rise of SMEs and entrepreneurs from emerging markets could accelerate thanks to the ability to build new systems thoroughly and that starting with the basics should be advantageous in the economic recovery post-COVID-19. In Ecuador, issues of informality and inequity, worsened by the pandemic, should also be addressed.

The evidence presented in Fig. 1 suggests a setback on entrepreneurial education and training at all levels in Ecuador in the past six years, which should be addressed by both the government and the private sector. Universities have provided, and must continue to provide, research, resources, incentives, and policies to support entrepreneurs and entrepreneurship. These efforts will need to be scaled up and adjusted to the new demands post-COVID-19.

Finally, in an environment that still holds regulatory constraints for entrepreneurship (as discussed in Sect. 3), the new government that came into office in May 2021 should emphasize changes in the regulatory environment, including stability and ease of the norms, and flexible labor markets without impairing social protection; and, very importantly, facilitate access to financial resources to entrepreneurs and help them to leverage the digital economy and to create solutions to the problems of their communities.

[3]This first law on entrepreneurship allows the implementation of simplified joint stock companies ("Sociedades por Acciones Simplificadas," SAS, by its acronym in Spanish), a new legal figure for businesses. With this figure, sole proprietorships can be formed without minimum capital requirement. Moreover, this can be done with a simple online procedure.

5 Case Study

The MADERO TOSAGUA craft brewery of Julio Valarezo, a young entrepreneur from the province of Manabí, Ecuador, began producing its first craft beer on July 28, 2017, in a 2×2 m space with basic implements. His 2×2 m workspace expanded first to 3×4 m, then to 8×3 m, to finally reach the 10×10 m plant to which the brewery is about to move in. This evolution of his workspace is an evidence of his business' growth. Julio started producing 30 liters of craft beer per month and was processing 800 liters, as of November 2020, when he reached the same production level as that in February 2020, the month before the quarantines started due to the COVID-19 pandemic.

Julio's business model has focused on the development of formulas for niche markets, as well as the customization of packaging and labels (Fig. 4). He processes an average of six styles per month. His business, like other micro or small ventures in Ecuador, has not generated jobs other than for those who started the business.

Fig. 4 MADERO TOSAGUA's best-selling product is beer with passion fruit, called "Passion." In its manufacture, the fermentation technique stands out. It is a product that supports well all transfer and handling. According to its creator, "Passion" stands out among other beers with passion fruit because it is not very bitter and is balanced and has an accentuated and exquisite taste of passion fruit. *Source:* ©JulioErnestoValarezoPita

Julio's major challenge is to position his brand in Ecuador, as a beer company that offers new styles every quarter. His goal is to establish his company as a creative company and continue to win "cups" in the Latin American region. His first gold medal cup was for the "best Ecuadorian freestyle" in February 2019.

However, this venture faces the limitations of an industry that, according to this entrepreneur, is practically new (in the country). The suppliers may not be very formal; for example, they might not deliver on time the products his company needs, and he would have to fight to ensure that they comply with the quality standards that he demands for the inputs used in his productions. Furthermore, new competitors enter the industry every month.

Despite these challenges, he believes that craft beer has great growth prospects in Ecuador and that it offers him the possibility of using his creativity to produce new styles of beer using elements of his province and the country. In fact, MADERO TOSAGUA's slogan is "Pega con Todo" (goes with everything) because it offers different styles for each occasion or target market.

Its expansion strategy has been to generate strategic alliances with other well-known brands in the industry (not necessarily just beer brands), creating formulas and making exclusive presentations for niche markets. These alliances are sealed in a pre-purchase contract that seeks to reduce fixed costs.

In the future, he hopes to produce craft beer for export. He indicates that his company still needs to lower fixed costs, and he hopes to achieve this with higher production volumes.

5.1 Context

This entrepreneur points out an obstacle: the culture of consumers who still think that a low price determines a good purchase and who do not appreciate the quality of the product. A positive aspect of the culture is that Ecuador is a family society, based on recommendation, and those "word of mouth" recommendations have been a fundamental pillar for the growth of this craft brewery.

Too many bureaucratic procedures have been another obstacle for success. For example, filing complicated tax returns and quality controls without advice or support for their application. On the other hand, according to Julio, the Ministry of Foreign Trade constitutes a positive institutional factor, as it aims to internationalize Ecuadorian products.

Julio recognizes the importance of innovation and that there are creative entrepreneurs who seek practical solutions to big problems of society. However, the lack of real-time data on market behavior poses a challenge. He also mentions that although there are research institutions, their studies have not been adequately linked to the needs of companies.

Regarding access to resources, Julio states that access to credit is not based on business plans but only on credit history, which many young entrepreneurs might not have built. In addition, the interest rate for small businesses (microenterprises) is much higher than that for other types of loans, even higher than that for consumer loans. Unfortunately, Julio does not see any positive aspects in terms of access to resources for entrepreneurship in Ecuador.

He considers factors related to entrepreneurship education in the country as a support for establishing a successful commercial company in Ecuador. He mentions as an example that there are entrepreneurship courses or workshops in the curricula of colleges and universities, in addition to entrepreneurship being promoted at the level of government plans and in the press as a way to earn a living and generate new employment (even if it is "only" self-employment). However, he points out that most entrepreneurship educators are not really entrepreneurs and that this generates apathy and ignorance which prevents them from solving real entrepreneurship problems.

Despite all the challenges, Julio remains optimistic about his company's future. This was not his first venture; however, he does expect it to be the one that will "take him to the moon" by paying him the price of a ticket for a trip that Elon Musk would offer.

6 Concluding Remarks

One main lesson of this chapter is that there are aspects of the business environment in Ecuador, which are not conducive to entrepreneurship. A complex process to start a business, lack of seed capital, higher interest rates for microenterprises, perceived lack of support from governmental policies and programs, setbacks on entrepreneurial education and training are among the challenges faced by entrepreneurs in Ecuador. Ecuador's performance in rankings of business environment and entrepreneurship improved in the past decade; however, there have been setbacks in recent years. These challenges that prevent entrepreneurs from thriving in business and entrepreneurship activities should be addressed for good.

Cultural aspects in Ecuador, such as informality, may hinder entrepreneurial activities (as our case study indicates). Yet, they may also spur new enterprises, however, small they may be. Perhaps, for this situation, one can associate entrepreneurship in Ecuador with traditional values based on self-reliance and a reluctance to approach national agencies or government leaders to seek support, as opposed to a view with secular-rational values associated with reliance on government programs.

Despite the difficult outlook and setbacks on both government support and policies, as well as government programs for entrepreneurship and entrepreneurs, new laws create hope for entrepreneurial activities and entrepreneurs. Further, COVID-19 pandemic may also bring both opportunities and challenges. However, active policies including those of labor markets, and investment in the digital economy and digitization of business are required.

References

Ács, Z. J. (2007). How is entrepreneurship good for economic growth? *Innovations, 1*(1), 97–107.

Ács, Z. J., Autio, E., & Szerb, L. (2014). National Systems of entrepreneurship: Measurement issues and policy implications. *Research Policy, 43*(3), 476–494.

Ács, Z. J., Estrin, S., Mickiewicz, T., & Szerb, L. (2018). Entrepreneurship, institutional economics, and economic growth: An ecosystem perspective. *Small Business Economics, 51*, 501–514.

Barth, F. (1967). On the study of social change. *American Anthropologist, 69*, 661–669.

Blanchflower, D. G., & Oswald, A. (1998). What makes an entrepreneur? *Journal of Labor Economics*, 26–60.

Camino-Mogrovejo, S., Bermúdez-Barrezueta, N., Alvarado-Aucaquizhpi, D., & Vite-Vera, F. (2018). *MIPYMES y Grandes Empresas en el Ecuador, Período 2013—2017*, Superintendencia de Compañías del Ecuador.

Cantillon, R. (1756). In R. Gyles (Ed.), *Essai sur la nature du commerce en général*. London and Paris.

Coduras, A., & Autio, E. (2013). Comparing subjective and objective indicators to describe the national entrepreneurial context: The global entrepreneurship monitor and the global competitiveness index contributions. *Investigaciones Regionales, 26*, 47–74.

Creedy, J., & Johnson, P. S. (1983). Firm formation in manufacturing industry. *Applied Economics*, 177–185.

Dana, L. (2002). *When economies change paths: Models of transition in China, the central Asian republics, Myanmar, and the nations of former Indochine Française*. World Scientific.

Dana, L. (1990). Saint Martin/Sint Maarten: A case study of the effects of politics and culture on economic development. *Journal of Small Business Management, 28*, 91–98.

Demirgüc-Kunt, A., Klapper, L. F., & Panos, G. A. (2009). "*Entrepreneurship in post-conflict transition. The role of informality and access to finance*", World Bank policy research working paper No. 4935.

Díaz, J. (2018). "La historia económica contemporánea de Ecuador, 1972–2015", chapter 1, *in Reformas y desarrollo en el Ecuador contemporáneo*, Javier Díaz-Cassou and Marta Ruiz-Arranz, editores. Inter-American Development Bank.

Evans, D., & Leighton, L. (1990). Small business formation by unemployed and employed workers. *Small Business Economics*, 319–330.

Gibb, A. (1986). "Understanding and influencing the business start-up process", *Proceedings of the First Canadian Conference on Entrepreneurial Studies*, Memorial University, St. John's, Newfoundland, 1–35.

Hagen, E. (1962). *On the theory of social change: How economic growth begins*. Homewood.

Hechavarría, D. M., & Reynolds, P. D. (2009). Cultural norms & business start-ups: The impact of national values on opportunity and necessity entrepreneurs. *International Entrepreneurship and Management Journal, 4*(5), 417–437.

Hisrich, R. D., Petković, S., Ramadani, V., & Dana, L. P. (2016). Venture capital funds in transition countries: Insights from Bosnia and Herzegovina and Macedonia. *Journal of Small Business and Enterprise Development, 23*(2), 296–315.

Kets de Vries, M. (1977). The entrepreneurial personality: A person at the crossroads. *The Journal of Management Studies, 14*, 34–57.

Knight, R. (1987). Can business schools produce entrepreneurs? An empirical study. *Journal of Small Business and Entrepreneurship, 5*, 17–26.

Knight, F. (1921). *Risk, uncertainty and profit*. Houghton Mifflin.

Lazear, E. (2005). Entrepreneurship. *Journal of Labor Economics*, 649–680.

Lederman, D., Messina, J., Pienknagura, S., & Rigolini, J. (2014). *Latin American entrepreneurs: Many firms but little innovation*. World Bank.

Leighton, D. (1988). Summary. In R. Peterson & K. Ainslie (Eds.), *Understanding entrepreneurship, Kendall hunt*. Dubuque.

Ley Orgánica de Emprendimiento e Innovación. (2020). Supplement to Official Registry No. 151, February 28, 2020.
McClelland, D. (1961). *The achieving society*. Van Nostrand.
Poschke, M. (2013). *The decision to become an entrepreneur and the firm size distribution: A unifying framework*. McGill University.
Reynolds, P. D. (2012). "Entrepreneurship in Developing Economies: The Bottom Billions and Business Creation." *Foundations and Trends in Entrepreneurship*, January 2012.
Schott, T., & Wickstrom Jensen, K. (2008). The coupling between entrepreneurship and public policy: Tight in developed countries but loose in developing countries. *Estudios de Economia, 35*(2), 195–215.
Schumpeter, J. (1939). *Business cycles: A theoretical, historical and statistical analysis of the capitalist process*. McGraw-Hill.
Schumpeter, J. (1934). *The theory of economic development*. Harvard University Press.
Sexton, D., & Upton, N. (1990). Female and male entrepreneurs: Psychological characteristics. *Journal of Business Venturing, 5*, 29–36.
Vivarelli, M. (2004). Are all the potential entrepreneurs so good? *Small Business Economics*, 41–49.
Vivarelli, M. (1991). The birth of new enterprises. *Small Business Economics*, 215–223.
Wong, B. (2020). *How digital entrepreneurs will help shape the world after the COVID-19 pandemic*. Article for the World Economic Forum Website.
World Bank Group. (2019). *Ecuador: Trade and investment competitiveness report*. World Bank. Retrieved from https://openknowledge.worldbank.org/handle/10986/32430
World Bank Group. (2018). *Ecuador: Systematic country diagnostic*. World Bank. Retrieved from https://openknowledge.worldbank.org/handle/10986/30052
World Bank (2020). *Ease of Doing Business, World Bank Report.*
World Bank (2017). *Ease of Doing Business, World Bank Report.*
World Bank (2016). *Ease of Doing Business, World Bank Report.*
World Bank. (2012). *Ecuador: Las caras de la informalidad*. World Bank.
World Economic Forum. (n.d.-a). Global Competitiveness Report, various editions.
World Economic Forum. (n.d.-b). Global Entrepreneurship Monitor database, *Entrepreneurial Behavior and Attitudes*. Retrieved from https://www.gemconsortium.org/data/key-aps

Sara A. Wong, PhD in Economics from the University of California Los Angeles (UCLA), is a Professor with the ESPAE-Business School (https://www.espae.edu.ec/sara-wong/) and Director of the Center for Asia-Pacific Studies at the ESPOL Polytechnic University (www.ceap.espol.edu.ec) in Guayaquil, Ecuador. Her research interests include the analysis of impacts on productivity and poverty of changes in trade and labor policy. She has developed studies on family agriculture, trade openness, multidimensional poverty, and minimum wages. Her research has been published in *World Development*, *The Developing Economies*, *Journal of Business Research*, among others. She has been a consultant to the World Bank, FAO, ECLAC, RIMISP, IDB, etc. whose work has resulted in several publications.

Entrepreneurship in French Guiana

Nolywé Delannon, Djamila Delannon, and Mariana Royer

Abstract

This chapter proposes to delve into the history and current practice of entrepreneurship in French Guiana. It sheds light on the unique characteristics of entrepreneurship in this context, which is generally overlooked in the management literature. One of the insights gained from such a context is that collective entrepreneurship has historically served as a rehumanizing process in a post-slavery society. The chapter also illuminates how an unusually young and highly multicultural society experiences the emergence of an entrepreneurial ecosystem despite massive structural barriers, by leveraging its human potential and its uniquely rich biodiversity.

1 Introduction

French Guiana is a French overseas territory located in the northeast of South America. It shares lengthy borders with its two immediate neighbors, Brazil and Suriname. A post-slavery society and a former colony, Guiana was formally integrated to the French polity in 1946, its inhabitants then becoming French

N. Delannon (✉)
Département de Management, Faculté des sciences de l'administration, Université Laval, Quebec, Canada
e-mail: Nolywe.Delannon@fsa.ulaval.ca

D. Delannon
Département de sciences juridiques et économiques, Université de Guyane, Campus Troubiran, BP, Cayenne, Guyane
e-mail: djamila.delannon@alumni.lse.ac.uk

M. Royer
Bio Stratège Guyane, Matoury, Guyane
e-mail: mariana.royer@biostratege.com

L.-P. Dana et al. (eds.), *Entrepreneurship in South America*, Springer Texts in Business and Economics, https://doi.org/10.1007/978-3-030-97060-4_8

citizens. Guiana has later become one of the nine (9) ultra-peripheral regions of the European Union, a status that recognizes the significant challenges that result from it being attached to Europe while located so far away, and makes it eligible for targeted development programs and funding. With 83,534 km^2, Guiana has the smallest territory in South America but one of the largest when compared to the Caribbean region to which it also belongs. Ninety-five percent of its territory is made of primary Amazonian forest, a substantial natural wealth that has been well preserved over the centuries and has the potential to support local sustainable development. According to the latest census, Guiana has a population of 268,700 (INSEE, 2019), making it the territory with the smallest population of all South America, a characteristic that has certainly contributed to its economic, political and cultural invisibilization throughout history.

As of today, French Guiana remains an overlooked territory. Statistics about it are scarce and limited, and its uniqueness is often a reason for exclusion from comparative studies on South America, the Caribbean, or Europe, as if it were always too different from the rest. The fact is, by being South American/Caribbean on the one hand and European on the other, French Guiana is a hybrid context that is difficult to apprehend owing to a complex history and intertwined features of developed and developing countries. In that, it shares interesting commonalities with an island like Saint-Martin, a French overseas territory—distinct from the island of Guadeloupe since 2007—which has been shown to have followed a much different path of economic development compared to the other half of the island Sint Maarten (the Netherlands) in part because of the constraints resulting from the French regulatory framework (Dana, 1990). Going back to Guiana, among its developing country characteristics worthy of mention for our discussion on entrepreneurship, there is its demographic vitality. Over the 2010 decade, Guiana has had a spectacular population increase of 30% (INSEE, 2020a). It also has had a significant birth rate for years, and the latest data show an impressive level of 26.4 births per thousand in 2018 compared to 11.1 per thousand for France—which is itself above the European average.

With half of its population aged 25 years or under, Guiana is an exceptionally young society. It is also an extremely multicultural society which, building on the Indigenous, Creole, and Maroon populations that make the original matrix of the Guianese identity, continues to be shaped by successive waves of immigration coming mainly from South America and the whole Caribbean basin. An unusual fact resulting from both French settlement policies and geopolitical dynamics, the population of Guiana is made of an extremely high proportion of foreigners who are projected to outweigh the population holding the French citizenship during the 2020–2030 decade (Cambrézy, 2015). In any case, the territory's multicultural youth is both a tremendous opportunity in terms of development prospects and a formidable challenge because of worrisome social and economic indicators, poor infrastructure, and an education system under constant pressure. Before turning to the current socioeconomic and entrepreneurial context, it is insightful to delve into the history of the country to shed light on the colonial legacy that continues to shape its relationship with France and explain its lack of embeddedness in its geopolitical environment. This historical overview also helps understand the idiosyncrasies of entrepreneurship as it unfolds in Guiana.

1.1 Historical Context

1.1.1 Colonial Legacy

Guiana is one of the first territories acquired by the French colonial empire in the early seventeenth century, leading to a European imperial presence with a similar destructive impact on indigenous people as in the rest of the American continent. Like most territories in South America and the Caribbean, French Guiana has been used for the slave trade, an era during which European empires have wrenched millions of people from the African continent to enslave them on plantations in the Americas. During the centuries of slavery, institutionalized violence reigned in a constant effort to subjugate and dehumanize the enslaved (Dorlin, 2019). Such institutionalized violence culminated in 1685 with the adoption of the *Code noir* which codified the policing of slaves under French ruling and standardized the violent repression of slaves' resistance. The abolition of slavery was declared by France in 1848 and as a result Guiana became a French colony, like the islands of Martinique and Guadeloupe. Almost a century later, in 1946, another change of status occurred when Guiana was turned into a French overseas department, with the consequence that its inhabitants gained access to full citizenship—at least in theory.

The colonial legacy of France and its "legal, ethical, material and symbolic [obligations] towards those it once enslaved" were never discussed (Garraway, 2008, p. 366), neither through official addresses nor through history textbooks. It is as if forgetting had been a condition for moving forward with the post-colonial—and never achieved—project of creating a single French entity where all subjects would be equal. It is interesting to note that, when in 2001 France finally recognized that slavery was a crime against humanity, it was under the leadership of a Guianese member of the parliament who authored the law proposal. Commonly referred to as the Taubira bill owing to the name of its author, the law was unanimously adopted by the French parliament and one of its flagship articles demanded that the history of slavery be integrated into the national school curriculum.

1.2 Collective Entrepreneurship as Rehumanization in a Post-Slavery Society

The slave trade is a well-documented historical era that has led to the dehumanizing of millions of people. It has left profound scars in societies which, like French Guiana, have emerged from it. Such scars are not only physical, psychological, and cultural, they also have long-lasting socioeconomic implications (Fanon, 1963; Mbembe, 2011). Post-slavery societies have been shown to sustain extreme inequalities over the long term, a structural problem that can only be tackled by implementing significant public policies of reparation and redistribution (Piketty,

2019). Following the abolition of slavery, it is the former slaves' owners who were financially compensated for their alleged loss while the newly freed had to earn a living and start from nothing, struggling to secure a place in a social, economic, and political system that was racist by design. In such a context, deciding to live and to create anything new was in itself an act of resistance (Glissant, 1997). There is even evidence, drawn from the American antebellum context, of Black slaves' involvement in enterprise creation (see Walker, 1986).

In the Guianese context, the roots of entrepreneurship can also be traced back to slavery and to the immediate post-slavery period. By contrast with US slaves' individual entrepreneurship which seems to have been infused with the spirit of capitalism (see Walker, 1986), Guianese entrepreneurship during slavery and post-slavery was a fundamentally collective endeavor. Rooted in practices of solidarity and a sense of community belonging, such entrepreneurship took the main following forms:

- During slavery, entrepreneurial spirit guided not only the Maroons who successfully escaped the plantation to create free and self-sufficient communities in the forest, but also the slaves who remained trapped on the plantation but invented a common language—Guianese Creole—new cultural practices and a practical philosophy that were passed onto subsequent generations.
- Immediately after slavery, groups of Guianese men and women explored the entire country, including the inner land, in search of natural resources to sustain their livelihood (see Parépou, 1885). This is, for example, how gold was initially discovered in French Guiana, later giving birth to unique jewelry craftsmanship (see Fig. 1).

The entrepreneurship practices depicted above emerged out of absolute necessity (see O'Donnell et al., 2020's critical discussion of necessity entrepreneurship), namely the need to survive and to reaffirm one's human dignity. In that, entrepreneurship in French Guiana initially served as a rehumanizing means. Later on, entrepreneurship developed at a slow pace, especially following the country's change of status in 1946, when Guiana moved from being a colony to becoming an overseas department. Under departmentalization, the dominant logic of assimilation rewarded—both socially and economically—the mastery of the French language and culture (Fanon, 1952). Climbing the social and economic ladder required staying away from the land and manual work to embrace office work and life in the city. One of the visible manifestations of this was the creation of a Guianese class of civil servants appointed to low and intermediate positions within the local public administration. The apparent paralysis of entrepreneurial initiative during this era was reinforced by the complete absence of a supportive (financial) system. But as explained in the next sections of this chapter, a new generation of local entrepreneurs has emerged over the years 2010, launching a variety of ventures which are giving rise to a unique and promising ecosystem.

Fig. 1 Guianese jewelry craftsmanship. Photo © 2021 Efa K. Yana

2 The Environment for Entrepreneurship

2.1 Entrepreneurship at a Glance

This section starts with the presentation of the most relevant statistics among those that are available about the environment for entrepreneurship in French Guiana. As stressed earlier, data on this territory is scarce, incomplete, and fuzzy, all of this being a reflection of two main issues. First, there is a long tradition of limited investment of French statistics institutions in documenting the socioeconomic situation in Guiana. Second, because Guiana is not a sovereign country, it is systematically excluded from the production of data by international institutions such as the World Bank or the United Nations agencies. Despite these limitations, it is possible to give an overview of the recent evolution of entrepreneurship in French Guiana and to show that a promising dynamic has been emerging over the last few years.

First, there has been a steady increase in business creations over the last 20 years (Fig. 2), a clear sign of entrepreneurial vitality. There has also been a slight but

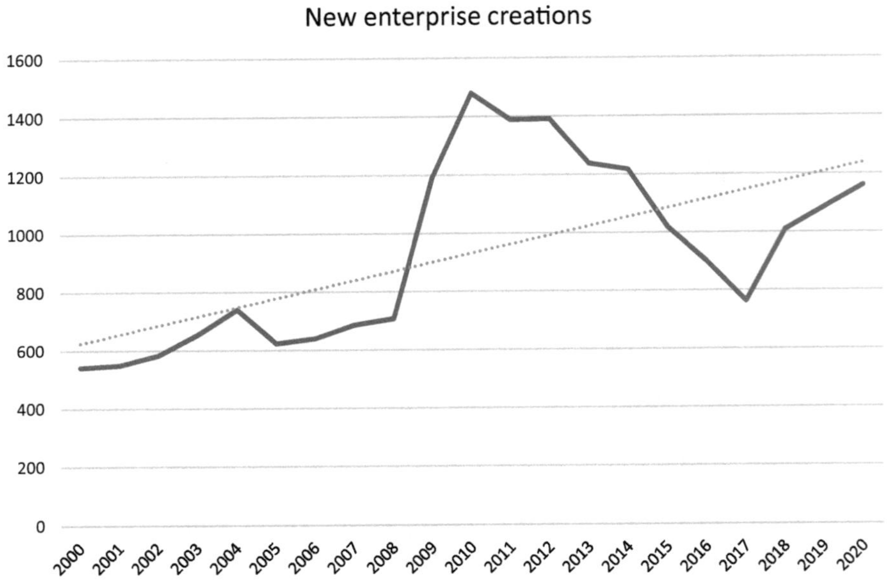

Fig. 2 Creation of new enterprises. Data: INSEE, 2021a

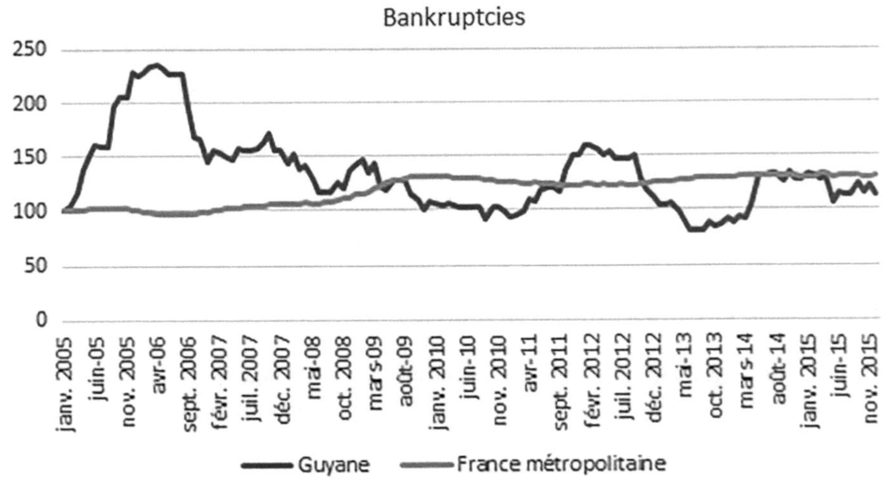

Fig. 3 Evolution of bankruptcies in French Guiana and in France. Source: INSEE, 2016

consistent drop in bankruptcies from 2005 to 2015, despite a peak in 2006 (Fig. 3). The Guianese economy is largely dominated by the tertiary sector, with market and nonmarket services, respectively, accounting for 44% and 36% of the added value (Fig. 4). Employment is primarily driven by small and medium-sized enterprises

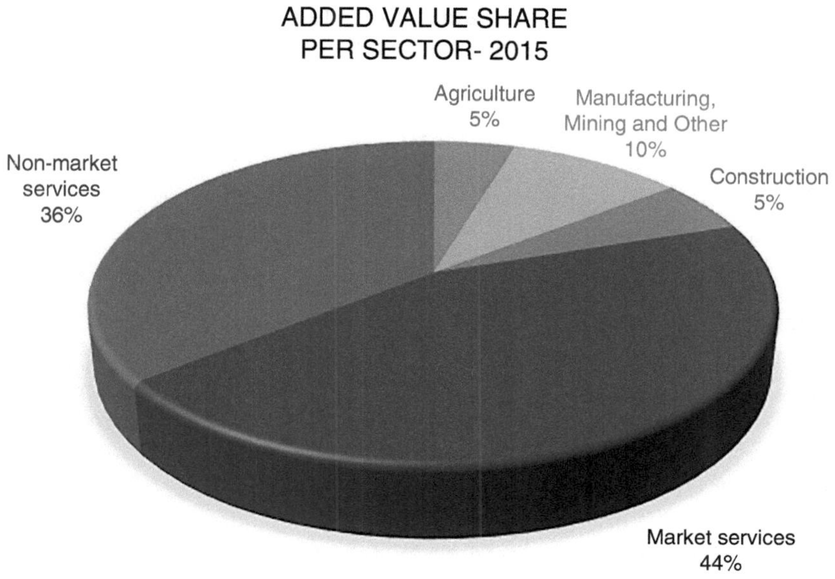

Fig. 4 Profile of the Guianese economy by sector. Source: INSEE, 2018a

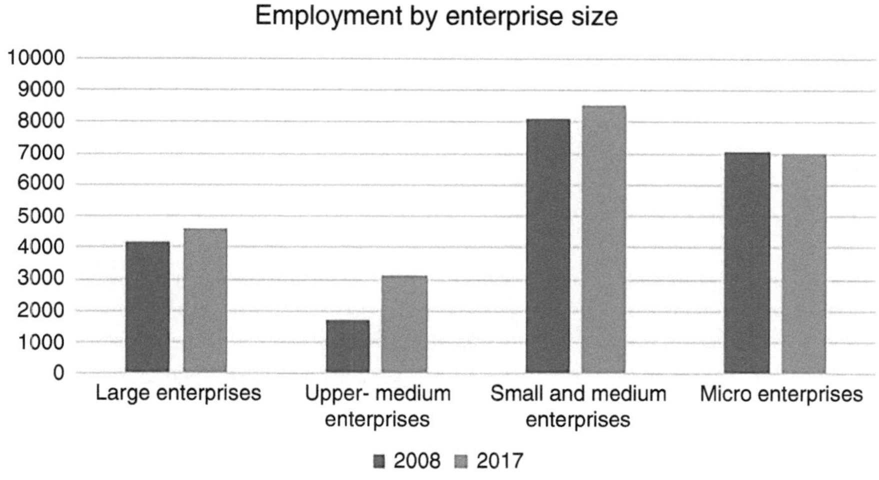

Fig. 5 Employment by enterprise size. Source: INSEE, 2021b

(SMEs), then by microenterprises (Fig. 5). Among SMEs, the biggest enterprises are the ones that account for the largest proportion of added value (Fig. 6). Likewise, these SMEs are the ones that invest the most (Fig. 7).

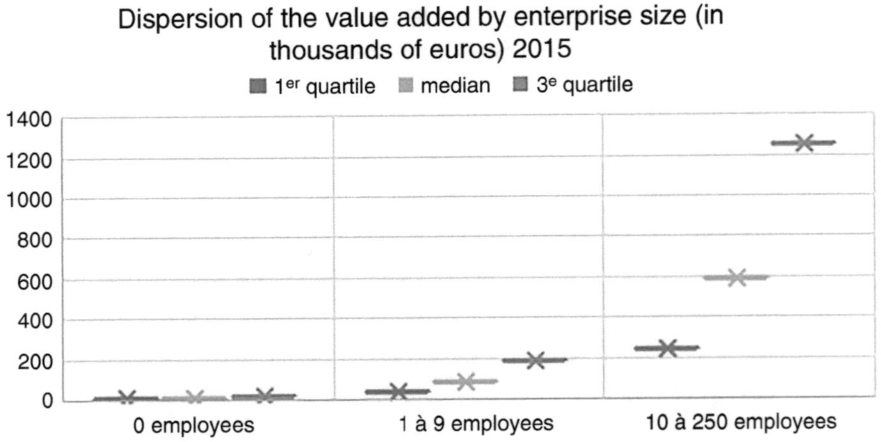

Fig. 6 Value added by enterprise size. Source: INSEE, 2018b

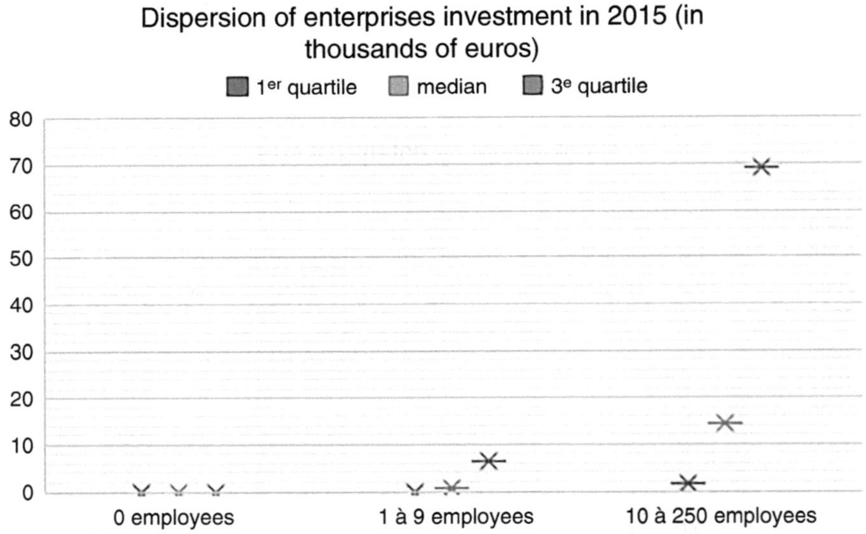

Fig. 7 Investment by enterprise size. Source: INSEE, 2018b

2.2 Current Challenges

From a business standpoint, French Guiana is primarily known for its space activity which has historically been portrayed as the main driver of the local economy (see INSEE, 1995). In fact, when France made the strategic decision to relocate its space activity in Guiana in 1964, the infrastructure needs of this economic sector dictated almost all the investments made in the territory over the following decades. This investment concentration has not been conducive to the emergence of an entrepreneurial ecosystem. Yet, as previously explained, collective entrepreneurship has a long history in Guiana. The local population and successive waves of immigration have struggled to thrive in a post-slavery and post-colonial country characterized by a rent economy with very low economic diversification and strong specialization in a few commodities sectors with little added value.

The current business environment is characterized by strong atomization and strong wealth concentration: while microenterprises represent 88% of the total number of businesses, only 10% of all companies account for 69% of the total added value (INSEE, 2020b). Although French Guiana is part of the European Union which offers a supportive macroeconomic framework for business development (e.g., through strong monetary policies and robust legal enforcement), the structural limitations of the local business environment explain the untapped potential of the country and the challenges faced by entrepreneurs to fully grasp market opportunities. In this section, we discuss the challenges and opportunities around three main aspects of the entrepreneurial environment, namely access to infrastructure, to natural resources, and finally to financing.

2.2.1 Access to Infrastructure

Access to transport and telecommunication networks is a key determinant of trade development, both at the domestic and at the international levels. Robust empirical studies show a causal link between access to such networks and trade expansion, and ultimately development, by increasing labor market efficiency, productivity, competition, and market opportunities between cities (Jensen, 2007; Straub, 2008; Donaldson, 2018). Transportation and telecommunication in French Guiana are poor both in breadth and in efficiency, with more than 90% of the country remaining inaccessible by any means of transport, and only 7% of the country covered by Internet and voice telecommunication (ARCEP, 2021). Concretely for entrepreneurs, this not only undermines the efficient flow of goods and information, it also reduces the array of business opportunities in specialized goods and services that would otherwise occur to respond to specific local needs. Moreover, the resulting spatial concentration of all activities on a small portion of the territory—80% of Guianese companies are located on less than 10% of the territory along the highway (INSEE, 2013)—comes at a high cost in terms of externalities.

When it comes to connectivity, French Guiana can be described as a commercial enclave, a legacy of its long colonial history of exclusive trade partnership with France. Such a situation is still being maintained through fiscal disincentives and lack of investment in transport facilities. Until today, commercial international airlines from and to Guiana only cover continental France and two French overseas territories in the West Indies on a regular basis. As a consequence, the aforementioned countries represent more than 50% share of Guiana's trade (INSEE, 2018a). In international trade where economies of scale matter, such narrow logistic routes preclude entrepreneurs from scaling up thanks to trading with South American partners. In the current context, trading with such partners would come at high costs, low speed, and high uncertainty. While it is difficult to assess the magnitude of these impediments for Guianese SMEs propensity to export, it is telling that exports are orchestrated by a few large companies mostly related to the space industry—73%, on average, of total exports between 2011 and 2016 (DIECCTE, 2017).

2.2.2 Access to Natural Resources

Until now, access to natural resources—which is instrumental for the development of entire supply chains—has remained restrictive, resulting in the underdevelopment of the industrial and agricultural sectors (respectively 10% and 5% of total added value, INSEE 2018a). Besides the inherent barriers due to the capital-intensive nature of extractive and natural resource-based industries, specific challenges that result from the Guianese context have hindered the development of businesses relying on natural resources. Indeed, there is high potential for a responsible exploitation of the Amazonian natural resources such as mining, biomass, or fisheries. While these resources have remained largely underexploited by legal businesses due to restrictive policies, they have been overexploited through illegal activities for decades. An eloquent illustration of this anomaly can be found in the field of gold mining where 204 illegal sites have been identified in 2015 (BRGM, 2016) compared to 27 legal concessions in activity for the same year (CPDP, 2018:15).

In the case of business projects that require access to natural resources, overlapping layers of regulatory constraints act as strong impediments. More specifically, the French Environmental Code coupled with land policy de facto deprives more than 60% of the territory from hosting an economic activity (see DEAL, 2014). In all, these regulations impose practices that weaken competitiveness—e.g., the constant strengthening of regulatory constraints on forest management and exploitation generates very high costs and millions of deficits for the national forestry organization. While it is hard to dispute the legitimacy of sustainability-oriented policies, the exceptional magnitude of their application in French Guiana causes two deleterious effects. Firstly, by creating artificial scarcity, it makes the exploitation and valorization of natural resources economically unappealing for entrepreneurs. Secondly, at a policy level, it reinforces the oligopolistic structure of the extractive and natural resources sectors. Ultimately, such a situation reduces the bargaining power of public institutions with private actors for the implementation of more sustainable and innovative practices.

2.2.3 Access to Finance

Financing is one of the few characteristics of the business environment that is robustly linked to firm growth (Ayyagari et al., 2006). Guianese SMEs evolve in a very small financial market. The narrowness of financial instruments leads entrepreneurs to rely heavily on traditional debt instruments characterized by a high cost of credit—4 points difference between France and Guiana, at the disadvantage of the latter (IEDOM, 2007, p. 7). The lack of both alternative sources of funding (e.g., asset-based and equity funding) and lenders willing to invest at the riskier stages of development of entrepreneurial ventures (i.e., capital risk), further erode their competitiveness, if not excluding them altogether from the financial market. Ultimately, this situation strengthens wealth concentration as illustrated by the fact that 10% of companies that operate in French Guiana account for 96% of total investment (INSEE, 2018b).

Over the last decade, public authorities have developed a number of mechanisms to support the financial inclusion of businesses such as microcredit which has increased at a steady rate of 17% per year on average since 2008 (IEDOM, 2020). However, these recent efforts can hardly produce significant change unless they become embedded in a holistic approach to entrepreneurial support. Indeed, there is growing evidence showing only mixed positive effects of microcredit on business creation (Banerjee et al., 2015) or on business expansion (Crépon et al., 2011).

3 Toward the Future

While the structural challenges to entrepreneurship discussed in the previous section are significant, the opportunities are tremendous. With the acknowledgment of the role of Guianese SMEs as the most promising drivers of local development, public authorities have implemented an increasing range of measures and stimulus policies over the recent years, among which:

- Fiscal and regulatory incentives for investments.
- Direct program of financial support.
- Indirect program of export support (tax credit).
- R&D programs.

Hence, along with the mobilization triggered by the 2017 social movement which called for a more inclusive and local growth (Breeden, 2017), an impressive number of supportive entrepreneurial organizations has emerged in the last few years. Among other things, a cluster for innovative start-ups has been created within the University of French Guiana; training in soft entrepreneurial skills has multiplied to support the emergence and growth of different types of organizations; specialized incubators for innovative women entrepreneurs or Fintech have emerged. For SMEs that depend on external sources of information, knowledge, know-how, and technologies in order to build their own innovative capability, such dynamics and networks offer the prospect of inclusive innovation. Notwithstanding that the process and its economic spillovers are nonlinear and are shaped by the interplay of market and nonmarket organizations (OECD, 2004, p.12), there are serious reasons to be optimistic about the future of entrepreneurship in French Guiana.

A telling illustration of this promising context can be found in the unprecedented proportion of Guianese ventures considered to have significant development potential by the French public authorities. In the perspective of the post-pandemic recovery, the French government launched a call for projects named "France Relance" (Ministère de l'Économie, 2020). Among the 8 projects from overseas territories that were selected to be funded, 4 were Guianese. One of such projects is the AmazonActiv Valley which envisions the creation of an entire supply chain of natural and ecological products from the rich Amazonian forest. Another laureate is

Yana Wassaï, an agribusiness SME engaged in the transformation of a selection of premium palm trees for the food and cosmetics industries.

4 Case Study. "Guiana Immunity": Leveraging Green Innovation and Local Knowledge during a Pandemic

Guiana Immunity is an innovative project developed in 2020 by the Guianese startup Bio Stratège Guyane. In the midst of the COVID-19 pandemic, while the global economy was experiencing a major slowdown which exposed the fragility of global value chains (see UNCTAD, 2020), remote territories like French Guiana appeared to be highly exposed to shortages in a variety of domains, including health. At the same time, a growing number of people were searching for more sustainable ways to live and consume, and for avenues to support a greener economy. Bio Stratège Guyane came up with the idea of leveraging local knowledge of medicinal plants to create a green product based on an entirely local value chain. Bringing together chemists, pharmacists, botanists, ethno-pharmacologists, farmers, cooperatives, retailers, and distributors, this project created a new ecosystem based on the pre-industrial implementation of plant processing and their standardization for the design of natural products (see Fig. 8). The project has bridged local traditional knowledge with codified scientific knowledge to create a viable business model which has already yielded impressive results.

More concretely, the project started with the selection of 15 local plant species with properties of interest. Among them, 5 plants were the subject of a 6-months pilot study, the objective of which was to generate technical and economic specifications for the implementation of the processing chain, from the collection of the various selected plants to the market. Bio Stratège has been able to create a support community around its project, by directly involving the consumer through the crowdfunding of the pilot study and then through the commercial launch on the local market. By regularly informing the public of the project's continuous progress (through a newsletter and videos posted on social networks), the company has stimulated a real appropriation of the project by the consumer who becomes a key actor to promote the development of this sector, by expressing their expectations or providing feedback.

During the pilot study, the proof of concept has been made with 200 local contributors/consumers who received the first "Guiana Immunity" boxes with the carefully selected and normalized herbal teas by the end of the year 2020 (see Figs. 9 and 10). The box includes a digital book bridging scientific data and traditional knowledge on medicinal plants, by providing key information to increase the consumer's awareness and knowledge about local bio-resources. The demand increased rapidly and, 3 months only after the pilot study, the company had already tripled its pool of customers. This promising growth has so far allowed the startup to consolidate its business model and to increase its own product demand to local farmers and suppliers. The startup projects to industrialize the transformation

Fig. 8 Pre-industrial plant processing and standardization. Photo © 2020 Bio Stratège Guyane

process in order to upscale its business model, thereby contributing to the industrialization of French Guiana which is still very limited.

5 Conclusion

The successful experience of Bio Stratège, in the midst of the COVID-19 crisis, is an eloquent demonstration of the potential to develop sustainable business models based on local natural resources—in this case, the processing and transformation of traditional plants known to be effective against microbiological infections. The challenge is now to achieve replication and upscaling. In this spirit, cross-sectoral

Fig. 9 Guiana Immunity box. Photo © 2020 Bio Stratège Guyane

Fig. 10 Raw medicinal plant to be transformed for the Guiana Immunity box. Photo © 2020 Bio Stratège Guyane

partnerships between rural municipalities and innovative start-ups could allow for an endogenous industrialization based on the transformation of local plants into natural products likely to generate high added value. Amazonian palm trees like comou (*Astrocaryum vulgare*), awara (*Oenocarpus bacaba*), or parépou (*Bactris gasipaes*) contain active molecules that innovative startups like BioStatège or Yana Wassaï could transform and enhance into finished products designed for a niche market at the international level. While bridging tradition and modernity, the emergence of such an ecosystem could pave the way for a sustainable local development that generates employment and fosters growing economic dynamism.

References

ARCEP. (2021). *Mon réseau mobile–Service public certifié* [My mobile network–Certified public service]. Retrieved from https://www.monreseaumobile.fr

Ayyagari, M., Kunt, A. D., & Maksimovic, V. (2006). *How important are financing constraints?: The role of finance in the business environment* (Vol. 3820). World Bank Publications.

Banerjee, A., Duflo, E., Glennerster, R., & Kinnan, C. (2015). The miracle of microfinance? Evidence from a randomized evaluation. *American Economic Journal: Applied Economics, 7*(1), 22–53.

BRGM. (2016). *En Guyane, des recherches qui valent de l'or. [In French Guiana, researches that are worth their weight in gold].*[Online]. Retrieved April, 2021, from https://www.brgm.fr/fr/reference-projet-acheve/guyane-recherches-valent-or

Breeden, A. (2017). *Strikes shut down French Guiana, with effects resonating in Paris.* The New York Times.

Cambrézy, L. (2015). Immigration et statistiques en Guyane [Immigration and statistics in Guiana]. *Autrepart, 2*, 193–214.

CPDP. (2018). *Projet de mine d'or en Guyane.* [Gold mine project in Guiana]. Retrieved from: https://cpdp.debatpublic.fr/cpdp-montagnedor/images/Documents-Mo-montagnedor/Montagnedor-dossier-maitre-ouvrage-vweb.pdf

Crépon, B., Devoto, F., Duflo, E., & Pariente, W. (2011). Impact of microcredit in rural areas of Morocco: Evidence from a randomized evaluation.

Dana, L. P. (1990). Saint Martin/Sint Maarten: A case study of the effects of culture on economic development. *Journal of Small Business Management, 28*(4), 91.

DEAL, (2014). *Atlas des sites et espaces protégés de Guyane. [Atlas of protected sites and spaces in Guiana].* Retrieved from: http://www.guyane.developpement-durable.gouv.fr/IMG/pdf/Atlas_des_Sites_proteges_Chapitre1.pdf

DIECCTE. (2017). *Les échanges commerciaux de la Guyane avec les pays tiers en 2016 [Guiana's trade with third countries in 2016].* Retrieved from https://guyane.dieccte.gouv.fr/sites/guyane.dieccte.gouv.fr/IMG/pdf/le_commerce_exterieur_de_la_guyane_en_2016.pdf

Donaldson, D. (2018). Railroads of the raj: Estimating the impact of transportation infrastructure. *American Economic Review, 108*(4–5), 899–934.

Dorlin, E. (2019). *Se défendre: Une philosophie de la violence [defending oneself: A philosophy of violence].* La Découverte.

Fanon, F. (1963/1961). The wretched of the earth. : Présence africaine.

Fanon, F. (1952). *Peau noire, Masques blancs [Black skin, White masks].* Éditions du Seuil.

Fortunato, P. (2020). *How COVID-19 is changing global value chains.* UNCTAD. Retrieved from https://unctad.org/news/how-covid-19-changing-global-value-chains

Garraway, D. L. (2008). Memory as reparation? The politics of remembering slavery in France from abolition to the Loi Taubira (2001). *International Journal of Francophone Studies, 11*(3), 365–386.

Glissant, E. (1997). *Le Discours antillais* [The Caribbean discourse]. Gallimard.

IEDOM. (2007). *Quel impact de la politique monétaire sur le coût du crédit aux entreprises en outre-mer?* [What impact does monetary policy have on credit costs for businesses in overseas France?] Retrieved from: https://www.ieom.fr/IMG/pdf/note_ie_politique_monetaire_sur_cout_credit.pdf

IEDOM. (2020). *Le microcrédit en Guyane.* [Microcredit in Guiana] Retrieved from: https://www.insee.fr/fr/statistiques/3596346

INSEE. (1995). Dans l'orbite du spatial (in the space industry's orbit). *Antiane, 29.*
INSEE. (2013). *Le tissu productif guyanais: des petites aux grandes entreprises.* [The Guianese productive structure: from small to large companies].
INSEE. (2016). *Évolution des défaillances d'entreprises dans la région Guyane* [Business bankruptcies in French Guiana]. Retrieved from https://www.insee.fr/fr/statistiques/2018783?sommaire=2018790#graphique-Figure_6
INSEE. (2018a). *Produits intérieurs bruts régionaux et valeurs ajoutées régionales de 1990 à 2015* [Regional gross domestic product and regional value added from 1990 to 2015]. Retrieved from https://www.insee.fr/fr/statistiques/1893220
INSEE. (2018b). *En 2015, le secteur de la construction demeure fragile* [In 2015, the construction industry remains fragile]. Retrieved from https://www.insee.fr/fr/statistiques/3596346
INSEE. (2019). *Recensement de la population–973 Guyane [Population Census–973 Guiana].* Retrieved from https://www.insee.fr/fr/statistiques/fichier/4265439/dep973.pdf
INSEE. (2020a). *Bilan démographique de Guyane 2018. Une croissance démographique toujours soutenue [Guiana demographic report 2018. Demographic growth is still sustained].* Retrieved from https://www.insee.fr/fr/statistiques/4285434
INSEE. (2020b). *Les entreprises guyanaises génèrent 1,2 milliard d'euros de richesse en 2017 [Guianese companies generate 1.2 billion euros in wealth in 2017].*
INSEE. (2021a). *Nombre de créations d'entreprises - Entreprises individuelles y compris micro-entrepreneurs – Guyane* [Number of business creations - Sole proprietorships including micro-entrepreneurs – French Guiana]. Retrieved from https://www.insee.fr/fr/statistiques/serie/001577506#Tableau
INSEE. (2021b). *Guyane : les entreprises de taille intermédiaire en fort développement* [French Guiana: mid-sized companies in strong development]. Retrieved from: Guyane: https://www.insee.fr/fr/statistiques/5056368
Jensen, R. (2007). The digital provide: Information (technology), market performance, and welfare in the south Indian fisheries sector. *The Quarterly Journal of Economics, 122*(3), 879–924.
Mbembe, A. (2011). Préface. L'universalité de Frantz Fanon [preface. The universality of Frantz Fanon]. In F. Fanon (Ed.), *Frantz Fanon–Oeuvres* (pp. 9–21). La Découverte.
Ministère de l'économie, des finances et de la relance. (2020). *Appels à projets France Relance.* Retrieved from https://www.economie.gouv.fr/plan-de-relance/appels-projets
O'Donnell, P., O'Gorman, C., & Clinton, E. (2020). Rethinking the "necessity" in necessity entrepreneurship. *Academy of Management Review.*
OECD. (2004). *Promoting entrepreneurship and innovative SMEs in a global economy: towards a more responsible and inclusive globalisation.* Paper presented at the Second OECD Conference of Ministers responsible for Small and Medium-sized Enterprises (SMEs), Istanbul.
Parépou, A. (1885). *Atipa. Roman guyanais [Atipa. Guianese novel]. Reprint (2016).* L'Harmattan.
Piketty, T. (2019). *Capital et idéologie [Capital and ideology].* Le Seuil.
Straub, S. (2008). Infrastructure and growth in developing countries: Recent advances and research challenges. *World Bank Policy Research Working Paper Series, Vol.*
Walker, J. E. (1986). Racism, slavery, and free enterprise: Black entrepreneurship in the United States before the civil war. *The Business History Review*, 343–382.

Nolywé Delannon is an Associate Professor at the Faculty of Business Administration at Université Laval in Canada. She holds a Ph.D. from HEC Montréal. Born and raised in French Guiana, she has conducted in-depth fieldwork in her home country as well as in Brazil, Chile and France. Drawing from her expertise in corporate social responsibility (CSR), her work delves into power dynamics between business, government and marginalized civil society. She has published book chapters and articles in both French and English, some of which appear in *Human Relations*, the *Journal of Cleaner Production* and *Business Ethics, the Environment & Responsibility.*

Djamila Delannon is a consultant and lecturer at Université de Guyane. She holds a M.Sc. in public administration from the London School of Economics. She has worked at UNESCO where she developed an expertise in public financial management for development, with an emphasis on accountability, the transparency of financial funds and the financing for Sustainable Development Goals. Her concern for upscaling development programs has led her to explore the effectiveness determinants of said programs. One of her latest mandates as a consultant resulted in her co-designing of the protocol for the impact evaluation of a Colombian cultural center program on violence.

Dr. Mariana Royer is the founder and CEO of the startup Bio Stratège Guyane, multiple winner of French and European innovation prizes. A chemist specialized in natural products, in 2013 she founded Bio ForeXtra Laboratories, a startup based in Québec City, Canada. The company's promising growth on the international cosmetics market led to its acquisition by a multinational group in 2018. Dr. Royer took this opportunity to invest in her home country, French Guiana, by starting Bio Stratège Guyane which mission is to develop eco-value chains from natural resources to markets, by valorizing Amazonian bio-resources and biomolecules.

Entrepreneurship in Guyana

George K. Danns and Donna E. Danns

Abstract

Guyana, formerly British Guiana, is located in the northern region of South America, bordered by Venezuela, Suriname, Brazil, and the Atlantic Ocean. It has an area of 214,969 square kilometers, a population of 782,766, and is the third smallest country on the continent. The country is sparsely populated and underdeveloped but has an abundance of untapped natural resources. Historically, the local private sector has been marginalized and dominated, first by the colonial government and the foreign private sector, then by successive postcolonial socialist-oriented governments that privileged state entrepreneurship and state economic control. In the latter half of the 1980s, a collapsing economy led to austerity measures by way of an IMF-enforced structural adjustment program, the abandonment of the atrophied socialist pathway, divestment and privatization of state-owned enterprises, and wooing of foreign investment through a policy of industrialization by invitation. Guyana's entrepreneurial ecosystem is burdened by poor infrastructure, high taxes, excessive regulations, and inadequate financing for borrowing and investment. Much of Guyana's local entrepreneurship is conducted in the informal sector and underground economy which have been spawning a revenant capitalist culture opposed to state control and paying taxes. Over the past five years, successive governments have been making positive policy pronouncements, privileging entrepreneurs, and primacy for the private sector. The discovery of large deposits of oil and natural gas in 2015 and subsequent production by a plethora of prominent transnational enterprises in 2020 have catapulted the country's fortunes, making Guyana the fastest growing

G. K. Danns
Department of Sociology and Human Services, University of North Georgia, Gainesville, GA, USA

D. E. Danns (✉)
Department of Economics and Finance, University of North Georgia, Gainesville, GA, USA
e-mail: donna.danns@ung.edu

L.-P. Dana et al. (eds.), *Entrepreneurship in South America*, Springer Texts in Business and Economics, https://doi.org/10.1007/978-3-030-97060-4_9

economy in the world and opening previously unimagined vistas for foreign and local entrepreneurs.

1 Introduction

Guyana, formerly known as British Guiana, was a colony of Britain, obtained its political independence on May 26, 1966, and later became the Cooperative Republic of Guyana on February 23, 1970. Figure 1 shows the flag of Guyana adopted after nationhood. Guyana is situated on the northern coast of South America and is bordered by Venezuela to the west, Suriname to the east, Brazil to the south, and the Atlantic Ocean to the north (See Fig. 2). It is the only English-speaking country in South America. As a British colony, Guyana was culturally oriented to the Anglo-Caribbean islands and not allowed to embrace its continental neighbors who spoke Spanish, Dutch, and Portuguese, respectively. As the third smallest country on the continent of South America, Guyana occupies a landmass of 214, 969 square kilometers or about 83,000 square miles (Bureau of Statistics, Government of Guyana, 2020). Based on the 2012 Census, Guyana's population was 747,884, reflecting a negative growth of 0.04% per annum during the inter-census period 2002 to 2012 (Bureau of Statistics, Government of Guyana, 2020). Recent estimates, however, show a population of 782,766 in 2019 (The World Bank, 2020a). Migration from Guyana is among the highest in the world with 60.8% of its citizens estimated to be living abroad. Further, Guyana leads the world with 93% of its tertiary educated population having migrated (The World Bank, 2016).

The race distribution of Guyana's population is East Indian 39.8%, African/Black 29.3%, mixed race 19.9%, Amerindian 10.5%, others 0.5% (includes Portuguese, Chinese, White) (Bureau of Statistics, Guyana, 2012). The population density is 3.5 persons per square kilometer. Almost 90% of Guyana's population resides on

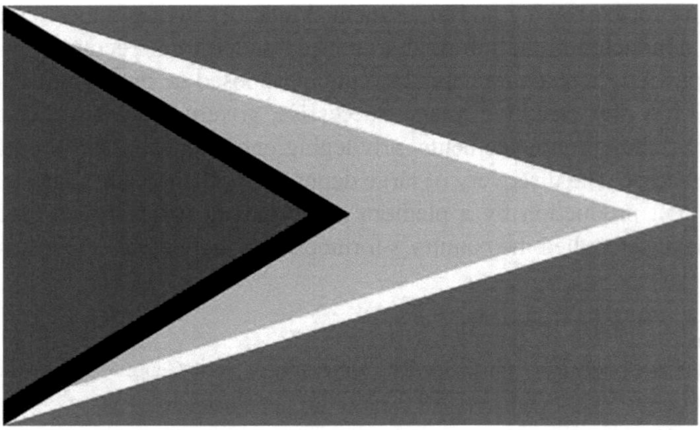

Fig. 1 Flag of Guyana. Source: Nations Online Project

Fig. 2 Map of Guyana. Source: Nations Online Project

approximately 5% of Guyana's land space, along its low coastlands. Just 26.4% of the total population live in urban areas and 62% of those urban dwellers reside in the capital city of Georgetown. (Bureau of Statistics, Guyana, 2012).

Guyana's gross domestic product (GDP) in 2019 was US$5.2 billion reflecting a 4.7% growth from the previous year. Per capita income (current US$) was $6609.6 in 2019 compared to the world average of US$11,441.7 and an average of US$8,869 for the Latin America and the Caribbean region (The World Bank, 2020b). Guyana,

Fig. 3 Aerial view of the Skeldon Sugar estate in Guyana. Picture Source: https://www.kaieteurnewsonline.com/images/2017/05/skeldon-copy-1.jpg

therefore, is one of the poorer countries in the Western Hemisphere. The Inter-American Development Bank (IDB) (2020) reported that one estimate, using a US $5.50 per day threshold, placed Guyana's poverty rate at 41.2% in 2017. The country's major economic activities have been agriculture (sugar, rice, and other crops), mining and quarrying (bauxite, gold, diamond, and stone), fishing and forestry, services, and limited manufacturing, mainly tied to the agriculture and mining sectors. For decades, the performance of the overall economy was inextricably tied to the performance of the sugar and bauxite industries, both of which experienced major declines over the last two decades. Figure 3 provides an aerial view of the sugar estate and factory where production has declined over the last decade.

The production of gold, diamonds, forestry, fishing, and other agriculture filled this void for some years allowing the country to experience real growth rates of between 2.1% and 5.4% in the decade between 2010 and 2019 (Bank of Guyana, 2020). The Inter-American Development Bank (2014) noted that although Guyana is small and sparsely populated, its largest asset was its natural-resource endowment much of which remained underexploited. However, with the recent discovery of large reserves of oil and gas, the associated capital investment and production by major transnational companies will have transformative and developmental impacts on Guyana in the medium and long terms. The Guyana economy has become the fastest-growing economy in the world with an estimated growth rate of 26.2% in 2020 (International Monetary Fund, 2019).

Bureau of Statistics, Guyana (2020) reported a 12.8% unemployment rate and a youth unemployment rate of 30.2% for the first quarter of 2020. The rural unemployed population represents the vast majority of the total unemployed and the

Fig. 4 Demerara Distilleries Ltd. Factory—A Medium-sized Guyanese business. Source: https://www.kaieteurnewsonline.com/

unemployment rate for women is higher than that for men. Most of the Guyanese labor force is employed in agriculture, forestry and fishing, wholesale and retail trade, in public administration and defense, mining, manufacturing, and construction (Bureau of Statistics, Guyana, 2020). A majority of the working population is employed in the private sector. The labor force is composed of 303,834 persons with 264,862 being employed. Of the employed, 5.5% are employers while 27.7% are own account workers/self-employed (Bureau of Statistics, Guyana, 2020). The labor force in general is lowly paid with a public sector minimum monthly salary of G$70,000 (approx. US$333) and a private sector minimum monthly salary of $44,200 (approx. US$210).

The local private sector and the culture of entrepreneurship: The local private sector comprises homegrown foundational business enterprises defined by the liberty and imperative of their economic actions, making invaluable contributions to gross domestic product, government revenue, employment, and the very lives and sustenance of the Guyanese people. Historically, the private sector has been dominated and marginalized by the state sector, the foreign private sector, and the government. Yet, it has been very resilient and survived. Some local private sector enterprises have thrived in areas such as beverage manufacturing, forestry and sawmilling, banking and financial services, rice farming, and ecotourism. Some Guyanese business leaders of companies such as Banks DIH Ltd., Demerara Distilleries Ltd. (See Fig. 4), and Edward B. Beharry & Co. Ltd. have used their entrepreneurial drive, sustained and expanded their companies over decades of ebbs and flows of the Guyana economy. These companies have thrived by evolving and expanding beyond their initial manufacturing operations to include, in some instances, banking and financial services, automotive sales, restaurant businesses, marketing operations, and much more (Georgetown Chamber of Commerce, 2019).

Fig. 5 Coconut farmers (small entrepreneurs) using labor-intensive methods. Picture source: https://www.kaieteurnewsonline.com

As currently constituted, the broader local private sector in Guyana is transactional rather than transformational and is limited in its capabilities to engender sustainable development of the country. A sizeable proportion of the private sector operates in the informal economy as opposed to the formal economic sector. Many private sector operatives are "necessity entrepreneurs" as opposed to "opportunity entrepreneurs" (Global Entrepreneurship Monitor, 2020).

Local entrepreneurs in Guyana, with some exceptions, are by no means wealthy and are not enamored of a dynamic entrepreneurial disposition. They are seemingly contented to make a surplus on their investments and earn a living rather than to generate serious profit. They stick with what works (See Fig. 5) and eschew the creative risk taking that may result in major entrepreneurial successes. These local private sector operatives are mainly entrepreneurs who buy and sell products from abroad or locally, engage in farming, small-scale mining, and the provision of limited services. They operate mainly small businesses with fewer than twenty employees. Many have four or less employees. Some are involved in manufacturing and other value-added production. The majority do not readily embrace technology. Rather, technology embraces them.

In general, the organizational mode of the Guyana private sector is that of sole proprietorships or family businesses. They invariably eschew the creation of corporations where ownership resides with shareholders. They are largely insular and uncurious and are more contented with survival rather than growth (Danns, 1994). There is a paucity of cross border trade with contiguous South American countries. Local entrepreneurs generally present little rivalry to the foreign private sector and have few partnerships with these. They seek favors from the government when necessary, circumvent regulations where possible and otherwise avoid engagement with public officialdom. Figure 6 shows a network of fruit and vegetable vendors, mini-bus and taxi drivers, traditional small businesses, and other small

Fig. 6 A network of fruit and vegetable vendors, mini-bus and taxi drivers, traditional small businesses in background and hundreds of other small entrepreneurs in and around Stabroek Market, Georgetown (the capital city of Guyana). Picture source: https://guyanachronicle.com/2020/01/20/the-transportation-network-in-guyana/

entrepreneurs around the Stabroek Market, in Georgetown, the capital city of Guyana.

2 Historical Context

But, how did the local private sector get to be this way? Why is it that they are seemingly characterized by a poverty of purpose and of growth? For most of the known history of Guyana, the leading entrepreneurs have been expatriates. The early planters established sugar and cotton plantations. These entrepreneurs were absentee proprietors, expatriates to the country. Their attorneys and other personnel from Britain managed their plantations. Foreign multinational companies produced sugar, bauxite, and manganese further heightening the remoteness of the expatriate entrepreneur from Guyana. The leading businesses in Guyana, then, lacked the visible presence of the entrepreneurs who created them. Because of this tradition of absentee ownership of the commanding heights of the Guyana economy, a culture of viable entrepreneurship failed to develop (Danns, 1994). The colonized peoples were imported either as slaves, from Africa or as indentured laborers, from India, China, and Portugal, strictly as a workforce. The colonized were hardly permitted the kind of freedom space and access to capital required for the emergence of anything other than small-scale entrepreneurship.

The colonial government in British Guiana played a key role in inhibiting the development of the local private sector. Preference was given to the expatriate multinational companies such as Bookers McConnell and Aluminum Company of Canada (ALCAN), which were involved in sugar cane farming and manufacture, bauxite mining, and other exploits. Local entrepreneurship emerged after liberation from plantation labor but was confined largely to retail trade, services, and small-scale farming. Portuguese and Chinese businesses were privileged in the commercial sector over those of the majority East Indian and African Guyanese populations. The colonial economy relied almost exclusively on exports of primary commodities, and imports of everything else, which economists have argued has been the basis for sustained underdevelopment (Beckford, 1972; Thomas, 1974). The colonial government, however, strongly encouraged and incentivized the local private sector to produce during World War II because British merchant ships could not have travelled safely to bring imported commodities to the colony. This "Grow More Food" campaign was highly successful. The then British Guiana ably survived without accustomed imports. As soon as the war ended, the colonial government reversed this beneficial trend by ending the "Grow More Food" campaign and withdrawing its support and incentives so that imported commodities primarily from Great Britain, would once again dominate (Danns & Matthews, 1989). The lesson here is that the powers and policies of government can go a far way toward enabling or restricting the growth of the private sector and a viable entrepreneurship culture.

The biggest challenge that faced the development of entrepreneurship in post-colonial Guyana was that the two major political parties were both socialist and viewed the private sector as promoting capitalism and imperialism and sought to limit its role. An independent Guyana soon embraced "cooperative socialism" (Hope, 1973). The cooperative experiment as a mode for economic development failed. The state sector, through nationalization of an estimated 80% of the economy, replaced the foreign private sector as the dominant economic sector. Socialism proved an anathema to the viability of entrepreneurship. Deliberate socialist policies by the Forbes Burnham Government from 1968 to 1985, then, resulted in the marginalization of the local private sector (Danns, 2017). These policies, combined with declining world prices for primary exports on the world market, high oil prices, internal and external imbalances, escalating external debt and foreign exchange crises, high inflation, and other economic pathologies swung the economy into a vortex of underdevelopment creating severe shortages and hardships for the population (Danns, 1990).

The Guyana economy was on the verge of collapse. Guerilla entrepreneurs, traders, and vendors using unconventional means emerged during this crisis period as part of a thriving underground economic movement in marked resistance to the state dominated economy. Private enterprises became an expression of freedom (Danns, 1994). Entrepreneurs flourished in the informal sector, the underground economy and black market for currency, as businesses sought to avoid taxation, the formal foreign exchange market, and other government regulations. Reportedly, even public sector workers, unable to survive on their low salaries during a period of extraordinarily high inflation, embraced their innate entrepreneurial abilities.

The Desmond Hoyte led PNC Reform Government succeeded the socialist Burnham Government after the death of Forbes Burnham in 1985 and abandoned the failed socialist development path. Through adoption of an Economic Recovery Program informed by an IMF structural adjustment regime in 1989, it ideologically embraced free-market principles restoring the primacy of the private sector as the engine for economic growth. The local private sector, whose operatives were politically opposed to socialism, was no longer discouraged. Nationalized industries were subjected to divestment and privatization with the President declaring that there are "no sacred cows" (Danns, D., 1990 p. 143). Once again, the foreign private sector was privileged over the local private sector by the Hoyte Government, which pursued an "industrialization by invitation" policy. President Hoyte had declared that Guyana was open for business and granted generous tax and other concessions to foreign mining, forestry, and other foreign direct investors.

The socialist Cheddi Jagan-led PPP Civic Government replaced Hoyte's PNC Reform in 1992. Once again, the local private sector was confronted with a paramount socialist party that sustained an ambivalent disposition toward it. However, Hoyte's policies toward the private sector and foreign investment were found to be politically expedient and were retained by the PPP government in a country constrained to adhere to the structural adjustment program and debt restructuring conditionalities. The Guyana populace had also grown tired of failed socialist ideologies. Still, not enough was done to create a positive environment for business and to empower local entrepreneurs. Instead, it was widely reported that corruption and the payment of bribes to government officials and politicians became the mechanism for selected elements of the local private sector's engagement with the government. Guyanese investors from the diaspora played leading roles in government/private sector partnerships. The sale of government property, the awarding of government contracts, and government/private sector partnerships were widely reported as tainted with venality (Danns, 2014). In 2013, Guyana was perceived as a very corrupt country and was ranked 136 out of 177 countries in the Corruption Perception Index. In 2015, the David Granger, APNU/AFC government replaced the PPP government, which had ruled for 23 years, and Guyana's ranking improved steadily to 85 out of 170 countries in the 2019 Corruption Perception Index (Transparency International, 2014, 2019). In 2020, the PPP government returned to power.

3 The Environment for Entrepreneurship

Obrecht (2021) pointed to the importance of recognizing contextual, cultural, and other environmental factors influencing entrepreneurial action in any analysis of the entrepreneur and entrepreneurship. Dana (1993) pinpointed some of the environmental factors, which conditioned the range and scope of entrepreneurial activity of countries in the Caribbean. Among these were government, laws, regulations, and procedures. He advanced that the attitude of the government springs from the culture of the people it governs and this was confirmed in the case of Guyana. Further, Dana explained that a "government may perceive entrepreneurship as (i) having a high social value worth being encouraged, (ii) being a socially acceptable activity but not worth promoting actively; or (iii) undesirable behaviour." (1993, p. 2–3). Governments in a post-colonial Guyana have traversed all three dispositions, currently embracing the first as Guyanese, faced by high unemployment and low wages, have resorted either to survival entrepreneurship or migration mainly to the United States and Canada seeking improved life chances. However, the Government's embrace and encouragement of entrepreneurship and, viewing it as having high social value will not readily bring about the desired developmental economic transformation.

The Inter-American Development Bank (IDB) (2014) reported that "Guyana's private sector is fragile, and the incentive framework is such that companies tend not to invest adequately. Because of this underinvestment, companies do not modernize, and practices in mining and agriculture have not changed significantly for many years. Miners use obsolete extractive technologies, and they are frequently responsible for significant environmental damage, including water pollution." (Private Sector Report Guyana IDB, p.3). Guyana's largest asset is its natural-resource endowment.

The World Bank Group (2020c) *Doing Business Project* ranks Guyana 134 out of 190 countries for the ease of doing business. The Project measured ten important dimensions of the regulatory environment as it applies to local firms. Ranking Guyana in relation to other nations, the *Doing Business Project* provided quantitative indicators on regulation for starting a business (111), dealing with construction permits (167), getting electricity (170), registering property (128), getting credit (94), protecting minority investors (88), paying taxes (122), trading across borders (151), enforcing contracts (92), and resolving insolvency (163). Guyana invariably fared less well on all indices for doing business compared to OECD countries and countries in Latin America and the Caribbean as a whole.

The main problem with developing entrepreneurship in Guyana is that it existed and survived in an environment where the state, both colonial and post-colonial, adumbrated policies and regulations that limited the growth of local private enterprises. Educational institutions in Guyana, trained persons for the public sector, for the teaching profession, and other professional roles, paying inadequate attention to the development of entrepreneurship and innovation. Danns (1994) noted that it is quite possible that the content of the Caribbean region's education curricula has induced a trained incapacity in people to adopt values essential to the generation of wealth. He concluded: "The region's peoples are job seekers rather than job creators. The brightest and most creative workers seek good jobs and often with the state" (p. 45). Guyana's limitations on local entrepreneurship development fit a pattern experienced elsewhere in the English-speaking Caribbean. Lashley (2016) partially blames this on a general public policy framework that embraced "entrepreneurship as a panacea for social and economic ills" (p. 83), leading to a diluted policy approach to entrepreneurship. Further, he posited that a poor quality of entrepreneurship in the Caribbean (including Guyana) rendered entrepreneurs unable to leverage fully the resources provided through any governmental programs.

Currently, however, local entrepreneurship is being strongly encouraged although the environment for business development continues to be less than enabling. National policies geared towards the private sector are targeted primarily at attracting foreign direct investment rather than empowering local entrepreneurs. The last and current governmental administrations have unequivocally targeted the private sector as the focal point for generating the country's development. Strong initiatives were and are being adumbrated to actively promote and incentivize entrepreneurial activities in the various regions of the country, particularly among the nation's women and youth (Danns & Danns, 2019). The aim is to generate employment and in the process, expand, and diversify the local private sector beyond its traditional existence. The past APNU/AFC government affirmed that it was promulgating "local content" legislation to ensure that local businesses and workers have a fair share and opportunity within the developing oil industry. Additionally, the APNU/ANC Government accessed US$86.1 million in concessional financing from the IDB to enable Guyana's pursuit of inclusive growth by focusing on institutions to deliver services, critical infrastructure, and improve the basic conditions that enhance the private sector's role in the economy (Kaieteur News, 2017).

For the first time a Government of Guyana was unequivocally supporting the expansion and development of the local private sector while simultaneously courting foreign direct investment. Still, much more needs to be done to empower and incentivize the growth of entrepreneurship and transformation of the traditional private sector, which has survived centuries of discouragement and subordination.

4 Toward the Future

In recent times, scholars of entrepreneurship have touted the notion of an entrepreneurship ecosystem (Malecki, 2018). Daniel Isenberg, a proponent of a comprehensive entrepreneurship ecosystem perspective for analyzing and supporting entrepreneurship within nations, pointed to a combination of elements and sub-elements or factors operating within the realm of this ecosystem. Broad elements or domains include policy, markets, finance, human capital, support systems, and culture, while sub-elements include a confluence of customers, entrepreneurial networks, labor, educational institutions, infrastructure, support professions, non-governmental institutions, societal norms and stories, financial capital, leadership, and government (institutions, research institutes, legislation, tax systems, etc.). Isenberg recognized that one policy implication of the entrepreneurship ecosystem perspective is that there is a need for a coordinating organization that has "the mandate, competence and motivation to enhance the entrepreneurship ecosystem in order to achieve a self-sustaining amount of entrepreneurship" (p.12) and that, public leaders should explicitly communicate entrepreneurship as a high social priority (Isenberg, 2011). From the Guyana perspective, while there may not be a distinctly evidential confluence of all elements and factors mapping the entrepreneurship ecosystem, some elements may be converging at this time.

The future of entrepreneurship in Guyana is bright. The motivation that the local private sector needs to unleash its entrepreneurial potential is the knowledge that their government supports them. Guyana's entrepreneurs need to adopt a disposition towards twenty-first-century innovation; change the entrepreneurial culture of instinctual aversion to governance and the formal economic sector; become more corporate and inclusive in their business ownership; be willing to engage aggressively with similar or related enterprises both local and foreign and possibly form alliances to hone skills and capital of the diaspora.

The newly elected PPP/C government, which took office in August 2020, buoyed by the advent and ebullience of the oil and gas sector, pledged to transform the culture of entrepreneurship in Guyana. The government announced that it would be establishing a National Entrepreneurship Council to create an enabling environment for business development and to ensure that entrepreneurs are able to "keep up" (Seoraj, 2020). Guyana's President, Irfaan Ali, in an address to the American Chamber of Commerce's (AMCHAM's) virtual Annual General Meeting stated that: "This body will radically reform the culture of entrepreneurship and encourage the emergence of new entrepreneurs while supporting existing ones" (Seoraj, 2020). The Minister of Tourism, Industry, and Commerce, Oneidge Waldron, added that: "The national entrepreneurship body will act in concert with business incubators to form a breeding ground for new entrepreneurs, supporting them institutionally, financially and technically" (Seoraj, 2020). (Figs. 7 and 8 show the environment for the development of ecotourism businesses in Guyana's vast interior.)

The National Entrepreneurship Council is being developed against the background of a previously announced seven-point plan which included preserving the rule of law and democracy; improving the ease of doing business; enhancing national competitiveness; facilitating trade and investment; and supporting small businesses. The new government views business as the lifeblood of the economy and as enabling entrepreneurs to generate jobs and foster their local economies. It is committed to fostering the development and competitiveness of micro and small businesses as a strategy for job creation, income distribution, social inclusion, reducing informality, and strengthening the economy. In 2020, the government's Small Business Bureau increased the grant size for small businesses by 100 percent and promised to expand the range of procurement opportunities for small businesses from the government (Seoraj, 2020).

The challenge to the local entrepreneurs is that while government now seeks to engender private sector development, local entrepreneurs will face stiff competition from the foreign investors who are better funded and provided with significant government concessions, such as tax breaks and duty-free imports, as a condition for their investing. Local entrepreneurs are also more dependent on access to the limited pool of government-supported loans and grants and challenged by barriers to borrowing from the financial sector (Danns & Danns, in press). The influx of foreign business enterprises may, however, provide models of successful entrepreneurship and partnerships for local entrepreneurs.

Fig. 7 Kaieteur Falls, Guyana. Picture source: http://exploreguyana.org/

Fig. 8 The Iwokrama Lodge, Iwokrama, Guyana https://www.livingdreams.tv/environment/ecotourism-in-guyana

Guyana is steadily being incorporated into the expansive global transnational capitalist system and its political economy seems destined to be overrun by entrepreneurs both foreign and local. Local entrepreneurs are concerned about being marginalized from meaningful involvement in the oil and gas industry. They have urged the Guyana government to put in place the framework and enabling environment so that local businesses can be availed salient opportunities to participate in the oil and gas value chain which sector is poised for significant growth in the coming years. The Private Sector Commission (PSC) and the Guyana Manufacturing and Services Association (GMSA), in a joint statement, indicated that they are looking forward to "meaningful local content and greater transparency in procurement opportunities through unbundling and moving away from sole sourcing so that local businesses can be part of the value chain either directly or through partnerships and joint ventures." (Stabroek News, December 17, 2020).

5 Case Study: Banks DIH Ltd.

Banks DIH Limited is an iconic local private sector company and one of several companies in Guyana that have broken with the genre of ownership that the traditional private sector has embraced. What distinguishes the Banks DIH company and its myriad successes is that it is neither a sole proprietorship nor a family business but is instead a publicly traded limited liability company whose corporate growth and successes are reflective of this changed organizational mode. Banks DIH is the longest established and leading local manufacturer of food and beverages in Guyana. The company produces soft drinks, alcoholic beverages, and food products, and owns and operates restaurants and bars across the country. It has agents and distributors throughout the country and owns a large fleet of delivery vehicles. It is also the local distributor for some brands of foreign whiskey, vodka, and a variety of other products (Things Guyana, 2019). Banks DIH's leadership are opportunity entrepreneurs and over time expanded into other areas. The company is a major player in the local financial sector having a controlling interest in Citizens Bank Inc. and has recently entered the automobile sales industry. Further, Banks DIH exports its products to the Caribbean and other countries and currently holds franchising rights for Coca-Cola and other alcoholic beverages.

As at the end of September 2019, Banks DIH had assets totaling G$87.5 billion (approx. US$420 million). The company reported revenue of G$16.7 billion (approx. US$80 million) and before tax profits of G$3.48 billion (US$ 16.2 million) for the six-month period ending March 2020. Eighty percent of company revenue derived from sales of beverages.

Banks DIH traces its origins as a single proprietorship over 170 years ago in the 1840s when its founder a Portuguese businessman, Jose Gomes D'Aguiar, started a rum business which by 1885 had expanded to include a Cocoa and Chocolate Factory and Schooner Shipping Agency. Jose Gomes D'Aguiar died in 1893 and his four sons inherited and formed a partnership, which later became the D'Aguiar Brothers family business. D'Aguiar Brothers purchased the Demerara Ice House

Fig. 9 Inside the Banks DIH Factory: Producing Banks Beer: Picture source: Mr. Troy Peters, Public Relations Officer, Banks DIH Ltd. https://exploreguyana.org/

(DIH), which had owned a hotel, liquor bar, and an aerated soft drink plant. "The name 'Ice House' was derived from the fact that ice was imported in schooners from Canada, hence the initials DIH" (Banks DIH, 2020a). By 1934, the brothers had all died and Peter D'Aguiar, a grandson of the founder, at the young age of 22 years, took over the business, which was on the verge of bankruptcy. The company had earlier shed the Cocoa and Chocolate factory and Schooner Shipping business. By borrowing heavily and paying off debts, Peter D'Aguiar not only restored the viability of the business but he also expanded it. Of note was the acquisition of the franchise for Pepsi-Cola in 1942 making the then British Guiana the first South American country to bottle Pepsi. The award-winning XM Rum the company patented and manufactured became the number one rum in 1959. Peter D'Aguiar proved to be an outstanding entrepreneur by any international metric. In 1955, he introduced the very successful Banks Breweries Limited, which produced the locally brewed Banks beer (See Fig. 9). Banks Breweries Limited was the first public company in Guyana with a widespread ownership. In 1966, Peter D'Aguiar converted D'Aguiar Brothers into a public company D'Aguiar Brothers (DIH Limited) with a share capital of G$one million (Banks DIH, 2020a).

In 1969, D'Aguiar Bros. (DIH) Ltd. was merged with Banks Breweries Ltd. into a new company called Banks DIH Ltd. with a share capital of G$4,140,000.00. Banks DIH Ltd. built its headquarters, the Rotunda (See Fig. 10) on 13.2 acres of land, popularly known as Thirst Park. Shareholders from this company grew from 5000 to 14,000 and over 500 employees are shareholders (Banks DIH, 2020a). Peter D'Aguiar died in 1989 but by then had built the most famous Guyanese private sector business. "During his tenure of service (1934–1989) the company showed a record of rapid development and continued progress and has emerged as one of the most dynamic, efficient and profitable businesses in the Caribbean" (Things Guyana, 2019).

Fig. 10 The Rotunda Banks DIH Ltd. Source: https://banksdih.com/?q=content/banks-tour

Banks DIH Limited matured over the years from a private proprietorship to a family business and then a publicly traded limited liability company that had welcomed the Guyanese people including its employees as shareholders. D'Aguiar was succeeded by Clifford Reis, under whose leadership Banks DIH continued to grow, produce and promote globally competitive products, which have gained international reputation and won many awards. Banks DIH's XM Supreme 15-year old and XM Special 12-year old received Grand Gold awards; XM Royal 10-year old and 5-year old were bestowed gold awards by Monde Selection, an International Institute for Quality Selection based in Brussels. XM 15, 12, and 10-year rum won gold medals at the Rum Masters tasting competition in England in 2013 while XM 10-year old was a gold medalist at the Caribbean Rum Festival in 2014. The flagship Banks Beer and GT Beer, both won gold medals at 2018 Monde Selection for quality and the company won the prestigious Coca Cola Excellence Cup for performance excellence (Small Markets) at the Coca Cola Latin Centre Business Unit Regional Conference in 2016 (Banks DIH, 2020a, b). Figure 11 shows one of the Banks DIH award winning products.

5.1 Challenges for the Company

Banks DIH invariably brands itself as the "Pacesetter" and insofar as local private sector companies in Guyana are concerned, it meets that moniker. The company is seen as having the "Midas Touch" in making a great success of almost every product or line of business it embraces. The company earns high marks for the inclusive way in which it treats its diverse groups of employees, its workers' participation, and the profit sharing and bonuses they are normally paid. Employees also benefit from houses built by the company and sold to them at cost. There is no record of workers ever calling a strike against or engaging in industrial action. Banks DIH has an upstanding record as a good corporate citizen, contributes to the community and is not known to court government support for its business initiatives. Demerara

Fig. 11 An Award winning rum produced by Bank DIH

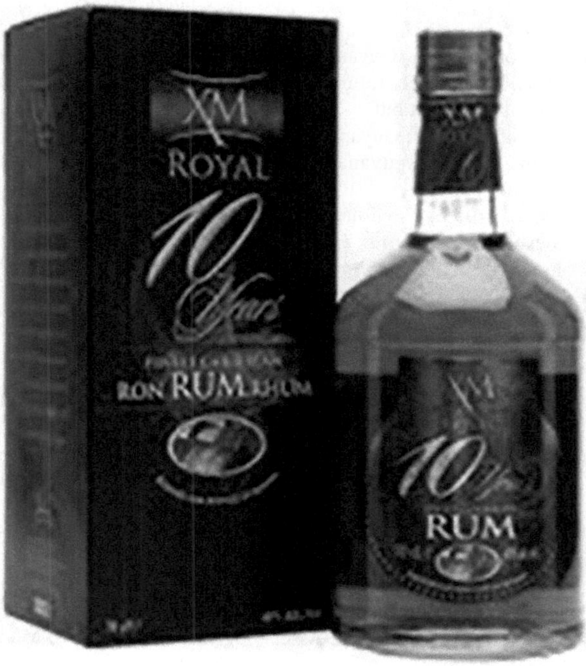

Distilleries Ltd. (DDL) is Banks DIH strongest competitor in the food and beverage industry. DDL produces the award winning El Dorado Rum, soft drinks and is the local manufacturer for a variety of imported beers and liquors. DDL has majority shares in Demerara Bank in Guyana.

Banks DIH has a much-diversified manufacturing and service portfolio, which evolved because of discerned business opportunities and the inadequacy of other business enterprises to meet these. As the Guyana economy expands because of the oil boom, Banks DIH will be faced with the dilemma of further diversifying its business portfolio in other areas and consolidating its brand in the face of inevitable competition from the surge of companies likely to be established by foreign investors and the Guyanese and Caribbean Diasporas.

References

Bank of Guyana. (2020). *Bank of Guyana annual report 2019*. Retrieved from https://www.bankofguyana.org.gy/bog/images/research/Reports/ANNREP2019.pdf

Banks DIH Ltd. (2020a). *About us: History*. Retrieved from https://www.banksdih.com/?q=about-us/history

Banks DIH Ltd. (2020b). *Banks DIH and its subsidiaries: Interim financial report for the half year ended March 30, 2020*. Retrieved from https://www.banksdih.com/files/Interim%20Financial%20Report%20May%202020_0.pdf

Beckford, G. (1972). *Persistent poverty: Underdevelopment in plantation economies of the third world*. Oxford University Press.

Bureau of Statistics, Guyana. (2012). *Guyana population and housing census, 2012 preliminary report*. Retrieved from https://statisticsguyana.gov.gy/wp-content/uploads/2019/10/2012_Preliminary_Report.pdf

Bureau of Statistics, Guyana. (2020). *Guyana labour force survey: October 2020*. Retrieved from https://statisticsguyana.gov.gy/wp-content/uploads/2020/10/GLFS_Bulletin_2020_First_Quarter.pdf

Dana, L. (1993). Environment for entrepreneurship: A model of public policy and economic development. *Journal of Entrepreneurship, 1993*(2).

Danns, D. (1990). *The history of the Bank of Guyana: 1965–1990*. Bank of Guyana.

Danns, D. & Danns, G. (in press). Institutional support and the challenges facing youth entrepreneurs in developing countries: A Guyana case study. *Journal of Entrepreneurship and Small Business*. https://www.inderscience.com/info/ingeneral/forthcoming.php?jcode=ijesb

Danns, D., & Danns, G. (2019). Financing youth entrepreneurship in a developing country. *Quarterly Review of Business Disciplines, 6*(3).

Danns, G. (1994). The role of the entrepreneur in the development strategy of the Caribbean. In S. Ryan & T. Stewart (Eds.), *Entrepreneurship in the Caribbean*. Institute of Social and Economic Research (ISER), University of the West Indies.

Danns, G. (2014). The impact of identity, ethnicity and class on Guyana's strategic culture. *American Journal of Contemporary Research, 4*, 11.

Danns, G. (2017). *Domination and power in Guyana*. Routledge Press.

Danns, G., & Matthews, L. (1989). Perspectives of the development and underdevelopment of communities in Guyana: A sociological analysis. In M. Martin & T. Kandal (Eds.), *Development and change in the modern world*. Oxford University Press.

Georgetown Chamber of Commerce. (2019). Guyana: Potential unleashed. *Business Guyana*. Guyana: Georgetown Chamber of Commerce. Retrieved from https://gcci.gy/business-guyana-2018-guyana-on-the-rise-2/

Global Entrepreneurship Monitor. (2020). GEM Project 2019/2020 Global Report. Retrieved from https://www.gemconsortium.org/report/gem-2019-2020-global-report

Hope, K. (1973). A note on co-operative socialism in Guyana. *Annals of Public and Cooperative Economics, 44*(3), 233–240.

Inter-American Development Bank (IDB). (2014). *Private sector assessment of Guyana*. Inter-American Development Bank.

Inter-American Development Bank (IDB). (2020). *LAC post COVID-19: Challenges and opportunities*. Inter-American Development Bank, Country Department Caribbean. Retrieved from https://publications.iadb.org/publications/english/document/LAC-Post-COVID-19-Challenges-and-Opportunities-for-CCB.pdf

International Monetary Fund. (2019). *2019 Article IV Consultation press release: staff report and statement by the executive director for Guyana*. Retrieved from https://www.imf.org/en/Publications/CR/Issues/2019/09/16/Guyana-2019-Article-IV-Consultation-Press-Release-Staff-Report-and-Statement-by-the-48678

Isenberg, D. (2011). *The entrepreneurship ecosystem strategy as a new paradigm for economic policy: Principles for cultivating entrepreneurship* (p. 12). Invited presentation at the Institute of International and European Affairs.

Kaieteur News. (2017, December 21). IDB predicts: Oil production will see reduction in concessional loans. *Kaieteur News*. Retrieved from https://www.kaieteurnewsonline.com/2017/12/21/idb-predicts-oil-production-will-see-reduction-in-concessional-loans/

Lashley, J. G. (2016). SME and entrepreneurship in the Caribbean. In R. Blackburn & M. Schaper (Eds.), *Government, SMEs and entrepreneurship development: Policy, practice and challenge*. Routledge, Taylor and Francis Group.

Malecki, E. J. (2018). Entrepreneurship and entrepreneurial ecosystems. *Geography Compass.* https://doi.org/10.1111/gec3.12359. Retrieved from https://onlinelibrary.wiley.com/doi/epdf/10.1111/gec3.12359

Obrecht, J. J. (2021). Environment of entrepreneurship. In L.-P. Dana (Ed.), *World encyclopedia of entrepreneurship* (2nd ed.). Edward Elgar Publishing.

Seoraj, N. (2020, November 16). Culture of entrepreneurship to be radically transformed. *The Guyana Chronicle* https://guyanachronicle.com/2020/11/16/culture-of-entrepreneurship-to-be-radically-transformed/

Stabroek News. (2020, December 17). Private sector seeking "meaningful" opportunities in oil and gas value chain. *Stabroek News.* https://www.stabroeknews.com/2020/12/17/news/guyana/private-sector-says-seeking-meaningful-opportunities-in-oil-and-gas-value-chain/

Things Guyana. (2019). *Banks, DIH-Guyana's leading beverage company.* Retrieved from https://www.thingsguyana.com/banks-dih-guyanas-leading-beverage-company/

Thomas, C. Y. (1974). *Dependence and transformation: The economics of the transition to socialism.* Monthly Review Press.

Transparency International. (2019). *Corruption Perception Index.* https://www.transparency.org/en/cpi/2019/results

The World Bank. (2020a). *Population, total–Guyana*: Retrieved from https://data.worldbank.org/indicator/SP.POP.TOTL?locations=GY

The World Bank. (2020b). *GDP per capita (current US$).* https://data.worldbank.org/indicator/NY.GDP.PCAP.CD

The World Bank. (2020c). *Doing business 2020: Comparing business regulation in 190 economies.* World Bank Group. Retrieved from http://documents1.worldbank.org/curated/en/688761571934946384/pdf/Doing-Business-2020-Comparing-Business-Regulation-in-190-Economies.pdf

The World Bank. (2016). *Migration and remittances factbook, 2016* (3rd ed). Retrieved from https://openknowledge.worldbank.org/bitstream/handle/10986/23743/9781464803192.pdf

George K. Danns is a Professor of Sociology, University of North Georgia. He has a PhD in Sociology from the State University of New York at Stony Brook and was awarded a Ford Foundation Fellowship for Doctoral Research in Latin America and the Caribbean. He was a Visiting Fulbright Professor in the Department of Sociology, University of Michigan, Ann Arbor; and Dean, Faculty of Social Sciences, University of Guyana. Dr. Danns has conducted extensive research in Guyana and the LAC region and has published in areas such as entrepreneurship, diaspora engagement, and development issues. Among his publications are *Dynamics of Caribbean Diaspora Engagement: People, Policy, Practice*, University of Guyana Press, 2018; *Domination and Power in Guyana,* Routledge 2017; He has published in a variety of journals including *Quarterly Review of Business Disciplines; Journal of Business and Economic Policy;* and *International Journal of Entrepreneurship and Small Business.*

Donna E. Danns is a Professor of Economics, University of North Georgia and earned her PhD from the University of Georgia. She previously served as an Assistant Chief Economist, Central Bank of Guyana and as a consultant to the Caribbean Center for Monetary Studies. She was a Hubert Humphrey Fellow, American University, Washington, DC. She is the author of three books *Financial Education in US State Colleges and Universities; A History of the Bank of Guyana;* and *The Financial Evolution of the Caribbean Community.* She has researched and published in the areas of banking, debt, monetary policy, financial literacy, economic crises in LAC countries, entrepreneurship in the Caribbean, and the economic role of China in Latin America and the Caribbean. She has published in a variety of journals including *Quarterly Review of Business Disciplines; Journal of Business and Economic Policy; International Journal of Entrepreneurship and Small Business; Family & Consumer Sciences Research Journal; and Social and Economic Studies.*

Entrepreneurship in Paraguay

Aidin Salamzadeh and Léo-Paul Dana

Abstract

With a remarkable history, Paraguay has evolved throughout the centuries. During those eras, the country has turned into the Republic of Paraguay, and its economy has changed dramatically. Like most South American countries, the entrepreneurial ecosystem is changing gradually. In this chapter, the authors review the historical context and then discuss the environment for entrepreneurship. Some future directions are explored, and collective entrepreneurship is elaborated upon by exploring the Mennonite community in Paraguay. Finally, the chapter concludes with some remarks for policymakers, practitioners, and scholars.

1 Introduction

The Republic of Paraguay is a South American country that is neighbouring Argentina (south and southwest), Brazil (east and northeast), and Bolivia (northwest). Figure 1 shows a typical scene in eastern Paraguay. With an estimated population of 7,253,000 in 2020, it has one of the most homogenous populations in South America, mainly of European (especially Germany, Italy, Spain) and Guaraní ancestry (Simão et al., 2017). One of our Guarani informants is featured in Fig. 2.

A. Salamzadeh (✉)
Faculty of Management, University of Tehran, Tehran, Iran
e-mail: Salamzadeh@ut.ac.ir

L.-P. Dana
Dalhousie University, Halifax, NS, Canada
e-mail: lp762359@dal.ca

L.-P. Dana et al. (eds.), *Entrepreneurship in South America*, Springer Texts in Business and Economics, https://doi.org/10.1007/978-3-030-97060-4_10

Fig. 1 Oxcart near Piribebuy; photo © 2021 by Léo-Paul Dana

Thousands of Brazilians also immigrated to Paraguay in the 1970s (Blanc, 2015). Its population follows the culture and customs of Guaraní, which is extensively evident in various aspects of their lives, including arts, festivals, carnivals, and even their daily habits. Most people feel proud of speaking the Guaraní language, which in 1992, became an official language in its constitution (Nickson, 2009). The official institutions and the public predominantly use Spanish; an important Mennonite minority uses German (Fig. 3), and Paraguayans prefer to speak in the Guaraní language in their daily communications (Garvin & Mathiot, 2017). Paraguay's name was derived from a Guaraní word which means "river that gives birth to the sea". Figure 4 shows a boat docking at Asuncion.

Indeed, rivers have long been an integral part of life in Paraguay, and the economy (Barclay, 1909). They could access the Atlantic Ocean, produce electricity, export and import goods, and enjoy the riverside lifestyle. Besides, due to the country's geographic location, they have become experts in producing hydropower, agricultural products such as soybeans, and many other related products (Blanco et al., 2017). Paraguayans enjoy the subtropical climate, and the Chaco (Fig. 5) is considered to be semi-arid, but, farmers also experience periodic floods (Fig. 6) and droughts (Fig. 7) harmful to their agricultural sector.

Paraguay is the home of numerous entrepreneurs. Its GNI per capita is 5680, which puts it in the upper-middle-income countries (Salas-Pilco & Yang, 2020). The government also supports entrepreneurial activities through initiatives such as pushing a free trade agenda to improve the business environment. Free trade agreements signed with countries like Colombia, Chile, and Peru are examples of such initiatives (Beck et al., 2019). Besides, the government has negotiations with other regional powers such as the European Union to expand its business and entrepreneurial activities (Cano et al., 2017). Decreased taxes, considering the diverse economy,

Fig. 2 Guarani informant; photo © 2021 by Léo-Paul Dana

and improved fiscal responsibility are among the other issues to be considered while studying entrepreneurship in Paraguay. Therefore, this chapter aims to review the country's historical context, which is of paramount importance to learn more about entrepreneurship in Paraguay. Then, the environment for entrepreneurship is elaborated accordingly. Next, based on the aforementioned issues, the authors propose some directions for the future. Finally, a case is discussed to highlight how entrepreneurs act in this context.

2 Historical Context

The country has gone through several historical periods. For more than a millennium, the indigenous Guaraní used to live in that area, until the Spanish arrived (Sarreal, 2014). Guarani people were primarily involved in agricultural activities, especially near the Paraguay River. Besides, they were known for their warrior

Fig. 3 Bilingual signage; photo © 2021 by Léo-Paul Dana

traditions (The Pre-Columbian era) (McRostie et al., 2017). In the next period (the Colonisation era), the Spanish entered the country and shaped the Spanish colonisation of the Americas (Nickson, 1989). As a result, they tried to expand their traditions and religion. Then, people started to convert to Christianity, and slavery was fading away. The Jesuit Missions of La Santísima Trinidad de Paraná and Jesús de Tavarangue, listed as the World Heritage Sites by UNESCO, are among the main testimonies of the country's history (Santiago-Vendrell, 2018). Nevertheless, the nomadic Guaycuru and other nomads resisted this religious movement, especially after the sixteenth century.

In 1811, the new era began (Independence and rule of José Gaspar Rodríguez de Francia), and the Spanish were overthrown from Paraguay by José Gaspar Rodríguez de Francia (*El Supremo*), who ruled over the country until his death in 1840 (Cooney, 1983). He attempted to create a Utopian society according to the French theorist's views of Jean-Jacques Rousseau (García, 2008). He put many limitations at national and international levels, restricting freedom and international

Fig. 4 Docking at Asuncion; photo © 2021 by Léo-Paul Dana

Fig. 5 The Chaco; photo © 2021 by Léo-Paul Dana

collaborations with other countries. After his death, various military officers ruled over the country until 1841, when Carlos Antonio López became the ruler (Rule of the López family) (Krauer, 1982). Unlike Francia, López opened the economy and started collaborating with various countries. Paraguay declared its independence in 1842 and commissioned the construction of the Legislative Palace (Fig. 8) at Independence Square in Asuncion.

López's son Francisco Solano López became the ruler after his death in 1862 (Saeger, 2007). Although he seemed to be a more diminutive dictator than his father,

Fig. 6 After a flood; photo © 2021 by Léo-Paul Dana

Fig. 7 Drought; photo © 2021 by Léo-Paul Dana

still liked to control most of the economy. Both modernised the economy and socioeconomically developed the country. In 1864 Asuncion's new train station (Fig. 9) contributed to the economy.

The Paraguayan War lasted from 1864 to 1870 (Williams, 1977). In 1864, Brazil initiated a war with the Republic of Uruguay and the Paraguayan War was started, as

Fig. 8 Legislative Palace in Asuncion; photo © 2021 by Léo-Paul Dana

Fig. 9 Train station, Asuncion; photo © 2021 by Léo-Paul Dana

Fig. 10 Forces keeping control; photo © 2021 by Léo-Paul Dana

they had already warned Brazil not to do so. Argentina also became a part of this war. In 1865, the three countries signed a secret treaty against the Paraguayan government. The war ended in 1870 by killing Marshal Solano López, who refused to surrender (Whigham, 2018). According to estimations, the country lost more than half of its population and many resources due to this war. Thus, the war became a catastrophe that will not be removed from its history. Furthermore, the Brazilian army took the national archives to Rio de Janerio; therefore, some parts of Paraguayan history are missing (Blinn Reber, 1999).

The first half of the twentieth century witnessed much socio-political instability. As a notion of such instability, one could mention the 31 presidents who governed the country between 1904 and 1954 (Chesterton, 2013). In addition to this, the civil wars of 1922 and 1947 (Lambert, 2008) and the Chaco War in the 1930s (Fogelquist, 1949) worsened the situation. Finally, Alfredo Stroessner overthrew the previous ruler in his military coup in 1954, and the new era began (Alfredo Stroessner era) (Lewis, 1980). They ruled over the country until 1989. As a dictator, his office dealt with the modernisation of the economy, but he overlooked the human rights and internationalisation related issues (Birch, 1996). In 1989, history repeated itself, and General Andrés Rodríguez overthrew Stroessner in a military coup (Stroessner's overthrow era) (Abente-Brun, 1999). Although police and military are very visible (Fig. 10), this new era brought socio-economic development for the country, and a democratic system of governance established in 1992 (Duarte Recalde, 2017). Today, the Republic of Paraguay is experiencing further developed socio-economic development in light of its remarkable history that is full of lessons for its politicians and the general public.

3 The Environment for Entrepreneurship

The country represents less than 0.5% of the world economy in terms of its GDP. Nevertheless, Paraguay is a key producer of hydroelectricity and renewable energy, especially near the Paraná River. Its average growth rate between 1970 and 2013 was almost 7.2% annually, making it the leading country in South America. As one of the leading countries in the agriculture sector, it stands in second place as a producer of stevia and tung oil, and sixth place for producing soybeans and corn. Nevertheless, the country is poor as many of its population could not afford their basic needs (Grassi, 2014). Therefore, it makes the country an exciting place to establish social enterprises, agricultural firms, and other ventures.

Entrepreneurship is a critical concern and solution for those at the bottom of the pyramid (Hall et al., 2012). There are some factories (Fig. 11), making bricks (Fig. 12) or roof tiles (Fig. 13), for example, and some individuals own shops (Fig. 14) while other entrepreneurs own restaurants (Fig. 15), but poorer self-employed people manage much smaller-scale operations, such as a fruit stand (Fig. 16). Many sell from impromptu stalls (Fig. 17). Some business is even less formal (Fig. 18). The emergence of water entrepreneurs is another evidence of paying attention to the basic needs of society (Schaub-Jones, 2008, 2011).

Fig. 11 Factory in Tobatí; photo © 2021 by Léo-Paul Dana

Fig. 12 Making bricks; photo © 2021 by Léo-Paul Dana

Fig. 13 Making roof tiles; photo © 2021 by Léo-Paul Dana

Fig. 14 Butcher; photo © 2021 by Léo-Paul Dana

It is noteworthy that the context of business is very significant (Dana et al., 2022). Hopefully, as the ICT industry has developed significantly (Grazzi & Vergara, 2012), the cell phone penetration rate has increased during the past decade, and investors could enjoy the available entrepreneurial opportunities in this technological context. Nevertheless, according to the Ease of Doing Business reports, in 2021, starting a business is not an easy task, as the country is ranked 160th in the world. Moreover, the index is not well enough in terms of protecting minority investors (143rd), getting credit (132nd), trading across borders (128th), paying taxes (126th), getting electricity (109th), and resolving insolvency (105th). However, its situation is much better in terms of registering property (80th), dealing with construction permits (75th), and enforcing contracts (72nd) (Llamosas et al., 2021).

Besides, the government has marginally facilitated foreign direct investment and capital inflow/outflow, and therefore, interested investors could invest in various projects. Nevertheless, tax exemptions are not good enough to motivate foreign investors. For instance, foreign investors are obliged to pay a 5% additional tax, or nonresidents must pay 15% on any international remittances. Also, to establish and manage a company as a member of the board of directors, one must be a resident. Otherwise, one might find a local partner to face this restriction. Like many similar countries, Paraguay witnesses corruption and a lack of sufficient transparency. It makes it hard for one to compete in global markets, which oblige companies to be transparent and corruption-free. In addition, workforce rights and child labours are dark sides of the economy (Larrouqué, 2019). Women entrepreneurship is also a concern for them as women are marginalised to some extent (Ajjan et al., 2014).

Fig. 15 Restaurant owner; photo © 2021 by Léo-Paul Dana

The number of community-based entrepreneurship projects has increased during the last two decades. These projects are generally defined and established to alleviate poverty by helping poor people increase their capacity and making them capable of earning money by identifying, evaluating, and exploiting entrepreneurial opportunities. The PRODECO is a perfect example of such projects designed to improve community-based entrepreneurship (Gallardo & Raufflet, 2014). In

Fig. 16 Fruit stand; photo © 2021 by Léo-Paul Dana

Fig. 17 Impromptu stall; photo © 2021 by Léo-Paul Dana

Fig. 18 Informal deal; photo © 2021 by Léo-Paul Dana

addition, entrepreneurship education and promotion of startup creation are other critical aspects of entrepreneurship promotion in Paraguay (Gonzalez, 2019).

The country's entrepreneurship ecosystem is young, and a limited number of startups and new ventures are playing marginal roles in its economy (Villalba Benítez & Ortega Carrasco, 2021). Nevertheless, co-working spaces (such as Loffice and Welco), incubators (mostly university-based), accelerators (such as Startup Lab-FPUNA, and Bono Plus Creativo), and such mechanisms are finding their way of contributing to the knowledge-based economy of Paraguay. A positive point of the ecosystem is that the young generation of Paraguay includes around 70% of the whole population. For instance, the *"Jóvenes Empresarios del Paraguay"*[1] provides a fertile ground for helping young entrepreneurs contribute to the country's sustainable development. Besides, entities such as *"Fundación Paraguaya"* are active players in this entrepreneurial ecosystem that help startups and entrepreneurs (Maak & Stoetter, 2012). Also, some of the existing Paraguayan startups have targeted international markets to render their services or sell their products.

The Paraguayan government has proposed various initiatives to increase total entrepreneurial activities. These initiatives are quite new. For instance, in 2009, they initiated INCUPAR,[2] which after some years, offered a new startup programme called Innovandopy in 2015. In 2017, Karakú Emprendedor was created to connect public and private sector players to increase their synergy. In 2018, the DINAEM[3] was proposed by the Ministry of Industry and Commerce that improved entrepreneurial activities throughout the country (Esteche et al., 2020). Besides, the Law of

[1] Young Entrepreneurs of Paraguay.

[2] Asociación Paraguaya de Incubadoras de Empresas y Parques Tecnológicos.

[3] Paraguayan National Entrepreneurship Directorate.

Simplified Stock Companies, which Congress passed, facilitated easy, fast, digital, and free new venture creation. Finally, CEE[4] was another initiative to support entrepreneurs.

Hopefully, Paraguay became a partner country in GEM[5] and is then included in the 2019/2020 GEM Global Report. Several partners were involved in this new wave of improving entrepreneurship through GEM-based surveys. These partners include: Asociación de Emprendedores de Paraguay,[6] MIC,[7] GEN,[8] Koga Impact Lab, Karaku Emprendedor, and UPA.[9] According to the GEM 2019/2020 report, the country's NECI[10] score was among the last three studied ones among 54 economies. All the country scores were lower than the average GEM scores for various countries. It reveals that the entrepreneurial ecosystem is not perfectly developed.

Religion and culture are also critical factors to be considered in scrutinising the entrepreneurial ecosystem in Paraguay (Dana & Dana, 2008a, 2008b; Kraybill et al., 2010). Many Paraguayans follow the Guarani culture, which is respected by the general public and led to increased collective entrepreneurship (Aponte & Álvarez, 2017). Besides, as Masi (2013) argued, various stakeholders, including the general public, public and private sectors, international bodies, universities, and research centres, agree that these players do not have enough capability and readiness to efficiently use their expertise and resources. It should be noted that public universities and state agencies have limited access to financial support, and therefore, entrepreneurship research is limited.

Considering all the issues mentioned above, one could argue that the country's entrepreneurial ecosystem is not well-developed, and there would not be an easy entrepreneurial journey for those who want to establish their business, initiate their ventures, or start their startups in this context. However, on the other hand, there are many entrepreneurial opportunities in the country, especially in terms of clean energy, agricultural, and social issues. Nevertheless, one should take the formal and informal issues, such as bribery, embezzlement, and corruption, into account (Jurik, 2018; Wilhelm, 2002).

4 Toward the Future

Based on its fascinating history, potentials, and developments of the entrepreneurial ecosystem of Paraguay, the country needs to be more focused on various aspects of its ecosystem. On the one hand, policymakers might consider various actions to

[4] Entrepreneurs Training Centre.

[5] Global Entrepreneurship Monitor.

[6] ASEPY, the lead institution in the GEM Paraguay project.

[7] Ministerio de Industria y Comercio.

[8] Global Entrepreneurship Network.

[9] Universidad Paraguayo Alemana.

[10] National Entrepreneurship Context Index.

facilitate entrepreneurship development throughout the country. On the other hand, they need to take necessary actions to remove barriers in front of the potential and existing entrepreneurs. In this sense, the data published by GEM, ASEPY, or other surveys and studies could provide them with a more precise big picture of the country.

As the level of trust affects the propensity to act entrepreneurially and take risks, the Paraguayan society, which suffers from a low trust level, is less prone to act entrepreneurially (Sohn & Kwon, 2018). Therefore, policymakers and officials must pay more attention to solving this problem to facilitate entrepreneurial activities. Besides, as Pathak et al. (2009) and Ibrahim et al. (2020) mentioned, the internationalisation behaviours of Paraguayan SMEs and entrepreneurs must be strengthened to make them more capable of exporting their products and rendering services to customers from other countries. In addition, according to the potentials of social entrepreneurial activities, the country could be a perfect destination for globally well-known social entrepreneurs and social enterprises, such as *Yunus Social Business*. Therefore, by improving entrepreneurship at the bottom of the pyramid, the country's socio-economic development will not remain a dream or hard-to-achieve goal. As Burt (2013) argued, poverty elimination at various levels is possible if the government works closely with civil society, firms, and entrepreneurs.

In addition, policymakers must pay more attention to entrepreneurship-related policies that could affect rent-seeking, opportunity exploration, risk-taking, innovative and creative behaviours of potential and existing entrepreneurs (Sánchez-Báez & Avancini-Schenatto, 2017). Motivating entrepreneurs and helping them in exploring, evaluating, and exploiting entrepreneurial opportunities will absolutely affect the total entrepreneurial activity index. Besides, increasing indigenous entrepreneurial activities could improve the entrepreneurial ecosystem (Dana, 2015).

5 Toward the Future

Like several South American countries in which entrepreneurial ecosystems are not mature sufficiently, the Paraguayan government must pay particular attention to developing such an ecosystem. Sanitation conditions are not always optimal (Fig. 19). Many areas still have no running water (Fig. 20). Infrastructure such as good roads is also important; some roads are better (Fig. 21) than others (Fig. 22).

By unleashing the power of [potential] entrepreneurs, many socio-economic problems could be solved, and several entrepreneurial opportunities might be explored, evaluated, and exploited by these change agents of the society. In this chapter, the Mennonite communities and their role in promoting collective entrepreneurial activities have briefly discussed as an example of how the entrepreneurial wave could change the current status.

Besides, policymakers and government officials might expand and promote more initiatives to facilitate this wave of change. By doing so, Paraguayan society could be revitalised, and this might become a U-turn in the history of this country. Also,

Fig. 19 Meat exposed to flies in a small shop; photo © 2021 by Léo-Paul Dana

identifying the formal and informal institutions[11] and considering them in policymaking will improve the entrepreneurial ecosystem of Paraguay. In addition to the policy-related issues, as the research on entrepreneurial activities is relatively

[11] Rules of the game.

Fig. 20 Pumping water; photo © 2021 by Léo-Paul Dana

Fig. 21 A main street in Tobati; photo © 2021 by Léo-Paul Dana

Fig. 22 Dusty; photo © 2021 by Léo-Paul Dana

new in the country, and since, hopefully, Paraguay has recently joined the GEM consortium, researchers could investigate entrepreneurship-related issues more precisely.

6 Case Study

Collective entrepreneurship is "linked to the existence of groups of individual entrepreneurs involved in the development of the business, whilst maintaining the organization and freedom of the individual" (Comeche & Loras, 2010). In other words, it is defined as an association of [potential] entrepreneurs. In fact, the ownership or control rights are shared among entrepreneurs rather than being individually allocated to some of them. Such an approach could exist in all types of collectives, especially in societies with closer connections and relationships (Manouchehrabadi et al., 2021).

For example, collective entrepreneurship exists in a Mennonite[12] community in Paraguay. According to a study conducted by Dana and Dana (2008b), the Mennonite community which migrated to Paraguay has initiated such collective entrepreneurial activities during the past centuries. The Mennonites are very industrious in

[12]Mennonites are "members of a nonconformist church that broke away from Calvin and Zwingli in the sixteenth century" (Renshaw, 2002). "Mennonites adhere to the teachings of the Dutch reformer Menno Simons" (Dana & Dana, 2008b).

Fig. 23 Mennonite factory; photo © 2021 by Léo-Paul Dana

Paraguay (Fig. 23) and they provide jobs to local indigenous people (Fig. 24), many of whom start the day drinking *mate* (Fig. 25). Figure 26 shows a third-grade class of Chaco Indians near a Mennonite community.

Grant and Rosenstock (2006) argued, Mennonite stick to a series of ethno-religious values, which might have been the reason for shaping collective entrepreneurial activities in their community. These values include, but are not limited to, (i) their strong work ethics, (ii) self-efficacy and self-reliance, which are among the main drivers of entrepreneurship, (iii) family cohesiveness and familiness, which are generally an integral part of immigrant minorities in various societies, and (iv) mutual aid and support. In addition to these values, as discussed by Dana and Dana (2008b), "Old Colony Mennonites have traditionally been opposed to two tenets of capitalism; namely, self-interest and the centrality of private property. According to their worldview, Gelassenheit, people should help their neighbours and share resources. Given this communal ethic, cooperatives can receive a high level of support from Mennonites".

Three major Mennonite communities are living in the Paraguayan Chaco, including (i) the Menno Colony, which are the oldest residents of this region, (ii) the Fernheim Colony, which shaped in the 1930s, and (iii) the Neuland Colony, which was established in 1947. These minorities have significantly contributed to the socio-economic development of Paraguay through mechanisms such as the MEDA.[13] In their seminal work, Dana and Dana (2008b) have focused on the entrepreneurial

[13]Mennonite Economic Development Associates.

Fig. 24 Employee; photo © 2021 by Léo-Paul Dana

Fig. 25 Tradional *mate*; photo © 2021 by Léo-Paul Dana

Fig. 26 Class; photo © 2021 by Léo-Paul Dana

activities of these collective entrepreneurs by interviewing 128 Paraguayan entrepreneurs. They have revealed that Mennonite cooperatives in the Chaco were successfully operating in this region, and those entrepreneurs could be role models for those acting in similar societies. Besides, interestingly, their success rate and the number of their success stories were higher than Chaco Indian cooperatives.

References

Abente-Brun, D. (1999). Latin America's imperiled Progress: "people power" in Paraguay. *Journal of Democracy, 10*(3), 93–100.

Ajjan, H., Beninger, S., Mostafa, R., & Crittenden, V. L. (2014). Empowering women entrepreneurs in emerging economies: A conceptual model. *Organizations and Markets in Emerging Economies, 5*(1), 16–30.

Aponte, M., & Álvarez, M. (2017). Cooperative entrepreneurship in Puerto Rico. *International Journal of Entrepreneurship and Small Business, 32*(3), 386–401.

Barclay, W. S. (1909). The river Paraná: An economic survey. *The Geographical Journal, 33*(1), 1–36.

Beck, K., Gawrońska-Nowak, B., & Valdivieso, P. (2019). Public and expert opinions on free trade agreements in South America. *Entrepreneurial Business and Economics Review, 7*(2), 7–25.

Birch, M. H. (1996). Economic policy and the transition to democracy in Paraguay. In *Economic policy and the transition to democracy* (pp. 166–190). Palgrave Macmillan.

Blanc, J. (2015). Enclaves of inequality: Brasiguaios and the transformation of the Brazil-Paraguay borderlands. *Journal of Peasant Studies, 42*(1), 145–158.

Blanco, G., Amarilla, R., Martinez, A., Llamosas, C., & Oxilia, V. (2017). Energy transitions and emerging economies: A multi-criteria analysis of policy options for hydropower surplus utilization in Paraguay. *Energy Policy, 108*, 312–321.

Blinn Reber, V. (1999). A case of total war: Paraguay, 1864–1870. *Journal of Iberian and Latin American Research, 5*(1), 15–40.

Burt, M. (2013). The "poverty stoplight" approach to eliminating multidimensional poverty: Business, civil society, and government working together in Paraguay (innovations case narrative: Fundación Paraguaya). *Innovations: Technology, Governance, Globalization, 8*(1-2), 47–67.

Cano, V. E., Quero, M. C., & Giménez, T. D. H. (2017). EU-MERCOSUR trade agreement: Finding winners products for Paraguay. *Revista de la Facultad de Ciencias Agrarias, 49*(2), 289–302.

Chesterton, B. M. (2013). *The grandchildren of Solano López: Frontier and nation in Paraguay, 1904–1936*. UNM Press.

Comeche, J. M., & Loras, J. (2010). The influence of variables of attitude on collective entrepreneurship. *International Entrepreneurship and Management Journal, 6*(1), 23–38.

Cooney, J. W. (1983). Repression to reform: Education in the Republic of Paraguay, 1811-1850. *History of Education Quarterly, 23*(4), 413–428.

Dana, L. P. (2015). Indigenous entrepreneurship: An emerging field of research. *International Journal of Business and Globalisation, 14*(2), 158–169.

Dana, L. P., & Dana, T. E. (2008a). Tobatí, Paraguay: Indigenous market town revisited. *International Journal of Entrepreneurship and Small Business, 6*(4), 520–535.

Dana, L. P., & Dana, T. E. (2008b). Collective entrepreneurship in a Mennonite community in Paraguay. *Latin American Business Review, 8*(4), 82–96.

Dana, L. P., Salamzadeh, A., Ramadani, A., & Palalic, R. (2022). *Understanding contexts of business in Western Asia: Land of bazaars and high-tech booms.* World Scientific.

Duarte Recalde, L. R. (2017). Democracy and representation in Paraguay. *Partecipazione e Conflitto, PACO, 10*, 1–10.

Esteche, E., Gerhard Wasmuth, Y., & Venialgo Figueredo, M. (2020). Las tradiciones organizacionales, culturales y el financiamiento como factores influyentes. *Revista Argentina de Investigación en Negocios, 6*(1), 85–96.

Fogelquist, D. F. (1949). Paraguayan literature of the Chaco war. *The Modern Language Journal, 33*(8), 603–613.

Gallardo, J., & Raufflet, E. (2014). Extreme poverty alleviation through community-based entrepreneurship: PRODECO in Paraguay. *Development in Practice, 24*(1), 140–146.

García J, E. (2008). Ramón Indalecio Cardozo as a pioneer of psychology in Paraguay. *Interamerican Journal of Psychology, 42*(1), 171–180.
Garvin, P. L., & Mathiot, M. (2017). *The urbanization of the Guaraní language—A problem in language and culture* (pp. 783–790). University of Pennsylvania Press.
Gonzalez, F. L. R. (2019). Entrepreneurship education and the promotion of startup development: The case of Pilar, Paraguay. In *Public policy research in the global south* (pp. 247–269). Springer.
Grant, H., & Rosenstock, M. (2006). Do Mennonites earn less than other Canadians? The role of religion in the determination of income. *Journal of Mennonite Studies, 24*, 73–92.
Grassi, D. (2014). Democracy and social welfare in Uruguay and Paraguay. *Latin American Politics and Society, 56*(1), 120–143.
Grazzi, M., & Vergara, S. (2012). ICT in developing countries: Are language barriers relevant? Evidence from Paraguay. *Information Economics and Policy, 24*(2), 161–171.
Hall, J., Matos, S., Sheehan, L., & Silvestre, B. (2012). Entrepreneurship and innovation at the base of the pyramid: A recipe for inclusive growth or social exclusion? *Journal of Management Studies, 49*(4), 785–812.
Ibrahim, I., Neubert, M., & Van der Krogt, A. (2020). Internationalization behavior of Paraguayan small and medium-sized enterprises. *Innovation Management, Entrepreneurship and Sustainability (IMES 2020).*
Jurik, N. C. (2018). Book reviews: Social collateral: Women and microfinance in Paraguay's smuggling economy. *Journal of Latin American Studies, 50*(3), 735–736.
Krauer, J. C. H. (1982). Proceso económico en el Paraguay de Carlos Antonio López: la visión del cónsul británico Henderson (1851–1860). *Revista Paraguaya de Sociología, 19*, 108.
Kraybill, D. B., Nolt, S. M., & Wesner, E. J. (2010). Amish enterprise: The collective power of ethnic entrepreneurship. *Global Business and Economics Review, 12*(1–2), 3–20.
Lambert, P. (2008). A new era for Paraguay. *NACLA Report on the Americas, 41*(4), 5–8.
Larrouqué, D. (2019). Introduction. Le Paraguay peut-il encore être qualifié de «semi-autoritaire»? *Cahiers des Amériques latines, 90*, 21–38.
Lewis, P. H. (1980). *Paraguay under Stroessner* (pp. 22–24). University of North Carolina Press.
Llamosas, C., Pereira, G., González, A., & Blanco, G. (2021). Energía y desarrollo: explorando el potencial del sector energético para cumplir metas de desarrollo en Paraguay. *Población y Desarrollo, 27*(52), 58–68.
Maak, T., & Stoetter, N. (2012). Social entrepreneurs as responsible leaders: 'Fundación Paraguaya' and the case of Martin Burt. *Journal of Business Ethics, 111*(3), 413–430.
Manouchehrabadi, B., Letizia, P., & Hendrikse, G. (2021). Governance of collective entrepreneurship. *Journal of Economic Behavior & Organization, 185*, 370–389.
Masi, S. D. (2013). Factores determinantes de la actitud emprendedora investigativa en científicos del Paraguay. *Revista Iberoamericana de Ciencia, Tecnología y Sociedad-CTS, 8*(23), 67–87.
McRostie, V. B., Gayo, E. M., Santoro, C. M., De Pol-Holz, R., & Latorre, C. (2017). The pre-Columbian introduction and dispersal of Algarrobo (Prosopis, section Algarobia) in the Atacama Desert of northern Chile. *PLoS One, 12*(7), e0181759.
Nickson, A. (1989). Paraguay. In *The state, industrial relations and the labour movement in Latin America* (pp. 67–98). Palgrave Macmillan.
Nickson, R. A. (2009). Governance and the revitalization of the Guaraní language in Paraguay. *Latin American Research Review*, 3–26.
Pathak, A. K., Carraher, S. M., Lane, S., & Import, L. (2009). International entrepreneurship and strategic risk. *Academy of Entrepreneurship, 15*(2), 1–29.
Renshaw, J. (2002). *The Indians of the Paraguayan Chaco: Identity and economy*. University of Nebraska Press.
Saeger, J. S. (2007). *Francisco Solano López and the ruination of Paraguay: Honor and egocentrism*. Rowman & Littlefield Publishers.

Salas-Pilco, S. Z., & Yang, Y. (2020). Learning analytics initiatives in Latin America: Implications for educational researchers, practitioners and decision makers. *British Journal of Educational Technology, 51*(4), 875–891.
Sánchez-Báez, E. A., & Avancini-Schenatto, F. J. (2017). Innovación y competitividad de los clusters de Paraguay: evidencia de las limitaciones. *Dirección y Organización, 63*, 65–73.
Santiago-Vendrell, A. D. (2018). The Jesuit missions to Paraguay and a cultural history of utopia (1568–1789), written by Girolamo Imbruglia. *Mission Studies, 35*(2), 299–300.
Sarreal, J. J. (2014). *The Guaraní and their missions: A socio-economic history*. Stanford University Press.
Schaub-Jones, D. (2008). Harnessing entrepreneurship in the water sector: Expanding water services through independent network operators. *Waterlines, 27*(4), 270–288.
Schaub-Jones, D. (2011). Market-based approaches in water and sanitation: The role of entrepreneurship. *Waterlines, 30*(1), 5–20.
Simão, F., Ferreira, A. P., Vullo, C., Xavier, C., Huber, G., Quiroz, A., et al. (2017). Paraguay: Unveiling migration patterns with ancestry genetic markers. *Forensic Science International: Genetics Supplement Series, 6*, e226–e228.
Sohn, K., & Kwon, I. (2018). Does trust promote entrepreneurship in a developing country? *The Singapore Economic Review, 63*(05), 1385–1403.
Villalba Benítez, E. F., & Ortega Carrasco, R. J. (2021). The entrepreneurial profile in Paraguay, analysis of the youth population. *Suma de Negocios, 12*(26), 31–40.
Whigham, T. (2018). Court of blood: Treason and terror under Paraguay's Francisco Solano López. *The Americas, 75*(2), 325–348.
Wilhelm, P. G. (2002). International validation of the corruption perceptions index: Implications for business ethics and entrepreneurship education. *Journal of Business Ethics, 35*(3), 177–189.
Williams, J. H. (1977). Foreign Tecnicos and the modernization of Paraguay, 1840-1870. *Journal of Interamerican Studies and World Affairs, 19*(2), 233–257.

Aidin Salamzadeh is an assistant professor at the University of Tehran. His interests are startups, new venture creation, and entrepreneurship. Aidin serves as an associate editor in "*Revista de Gestão*", "*Innovation & Management Review*" (Emerald), "*Entrepreneurial Business and Economics Review*", "*Journal of Women's Entrepreneurship and Education*", as well as an editorial advisory in "*The Bottom Line*" (Emerald). Besides, he is a reviewer in numerous distinguished international journals. Aidin is a member of the European SPES Forum, the Asian Academy of Management, and Ondokuz Mayis University.

Léo-Paul Dana is Professor at Dalhousie University and holds titles of Professor at Montpellier Business School and Visiting Professor at Kingston University. He is associated with the Chaire ETI at Sorbonne Business School. A graduate of McGill University and HEC-Montreal, he has served as Marie Curie Fellow at Princeton University and Visiting Professor at INSEAD. He has published extensively in a variety of journals including *Entrepreneurship: Theory & Practice, International Business Review, International Small Business Journal, Journal of Business Research, Journal of Small Business Management, Journal of World Business, Small Business Economics,* and *Technological Forecasting & Social Change.*

Entrepreneurship in Peru

Armando Borda, Miguel Cordova, and Luis Narro

Abstract

This chapter presents the characteristics of the Peruvian Entrepreneurial environment. First, it describes enduring country conditions affecting the development and evolution of new ventures. Next, the chapter presents recent efforts done by different actors to develop a supportive ecosystem that encourages innovative startups capable of escalating rapidly at the national and regional levels. The chapter presents the case of Quantum Talent, an example of this new type of startup that internationalized early to different countries within the region.

1 Introduction

Located in the west central part of South America, Peru has strong connectivity with the rest of the region. The country borders Ecuador and Colombia in the north, Brazil in the east, Bolivia and Chile in the south and the Pacific Ocean in the west. It is the third-largest country in South America with 1285,216.20 km^2 and it is considered one of the most megadiverse countries in the world (OECD, 2016). Peru has 31 million people (INEI, 2017), mostly concentrated in the pacific coast and in

A. Borda (✉)
ESAN University, Santiago de Surco, Peru
e-mail: aborda@esan.edu.pe

M. Cordova
Pontificia Universidad Católica del Perú, San Miguel, Peru
e-mail: cordova.miguel@pucp.edu.pe

L. Narro
Alaya Capital, Cordoba, Argentina
e-mail: luis.narro@alaya-capital.com

L.-P. Dana et al. (eds.), *Entrepreneurship in South America*, Springer Texts in Business and Economics, https://doi.org/10.1007/978-3-030-97060-4_11

Fig. 1 Panoramic view of Lima, Capital of Peru; © Christian Vinces—Shutterstock, Inc., used with permission

particular in Lima (Fig. 1), the capital, where more than 30% of the total population resides (INEI, 2017).

Since the 2000s, the country has consistently outperformed the average growth rate in Latin America during the 2000–2019 period. Despite being dramatically affected by the COVID-19 in 2020, where the GDP contracted almost 12%, it is expected a strong rebound. Indeed, Thorne and Associates ("Thorne and Associates", 2020) forecast a GDP growth of 10% in 2021 and Euromonitor (2020) mentioned that the economy has the potential to grow at 4% yearly for the next few years. According to the Reserve Central Bank of Peru, the country's GDP by 2019 was US$ 225 million. The country national currency is the Sol (S/PEN), and Spanish is the official language.

In an insightful article, Dana (1988) suggested that understanding the historical context in general and the Inca's business practices in particular could be the root to understand current socioeconomic conditions of the country. In this line, we provide a historical overview next.

2 Historical Overview

Peru is characterized by its exceptionally rich History. Its territory was the cradle for important historical cultures which established their civilizations since 800 B.C. Nevertheless, despite its just nearly 100 years of dominance, the Inca Empire that ruled between 1438 and 1533, it is the most recognized and influential one.

Fig. 2 Aboriginal farmers selling their products; © Léo-Paul Dana, used with permission

The Inca Empire had a centralized economy that was organized in Ayllus, which were the primary unit within the Andean society (Klarén, 2019). The Ayllus imprinted among its constituencies a strong sense of collectivism to organize economic activities. Each Ayllu specialized in particular products with comparative advantages. The surplus was given to the state that would trade the excess (Fig. 2).

It was not until the conquest by the Spaniards that Peruvians were introduced to the concept of small businesses and the promotion of individual initiatives (Dana, 1988). The Viceroyalty of Peru lasted almost 300 years and it was the most important of the Region. Despite agriculture, farming and commerce took place at this time, mining was the most important activity. During the Viceroyalty that ended in 1824, Inca's descendants were progressively attracted by the creation of business and self-employment (Figs. 3 and 4).

According to Llosa and Panizza (2015), between 1890 and 1970, the Peruvian economy has had a slow but constant GDP growth rate (around 1% annually). However, most of this growth was linked to commodities like fish flour, agricultural products and mining-related activities. However, it generates huge inequalities. The dictatorship of Velazco (1968–1975) implemented a model called "state capitalism" by which the government organized the means of production with the goal of reducing the widespread inequality. During that time, the government controlled up to 75% of total exports and the number of public companies represented up to 31% of the total number of existing companies (Llosa & Panizza, 2015). The model has been associated with economic growth, but with large fiscal deficits. External

Fig. 3 Street market and Informal economy photo; © Léo-Paul Dana, used with permission

shocks such as the oil crisis increased the gap in our balance of trade, generating a huge financial crisis.

Following governments during the 1970s and 80s were incapable of dealing with these economic problems with profound GDP deterioration, large fiscal deficits, high inflation rates and increasing inequality. For many Latin American countries, the 1980s are considered "the lost decade" and Peru was not the exception. However, the depth of the recession and the length needed to recover was particularly salient. The GDP decreased as low as 30% in 1987, the accumulated inflation rate was 2,200,200% between 1985–1990 and it took up to 15 years to recover from the 1987 crisis (Llosa & Panizza, 2015).

The situation during the early 1990s was chaotic and required the urgent help of international financial institutions such as the World Bank and the IMF. However, the help was conditioned to the adoption of the "Washington Consensus" a set of rules that countries must adopt to receive the required financial support (Cuervo-Cazurra & Dau, 2009). Fiscal discipline, respect for property rights, market liberalization and privatization were some of the main conditions that Peru needed to adhere to.

The president at that time, Alberto Fujimori, closed the congress and the new parliament enacted a new constitution embracing the recommendations of the Washington Consensus in the economic chapter. While most of the region followed this path almost at the same time (Cuervo-Cazurra & Dau, 2009), most of the countries in the region have had a non-consistent adherence to the recommendations

Fig. 4 Rural economy; © Léo-Paul Dana, used with permission

provided. Peru, in contrast, has adhered to these main tenets for more than 25 years. There are several benefits and drawbacks regarding the economic model implanted.

Regarding the benefits, there is a significant and constant growth rate. Since 1998, the GDP has grown consistently even during the 2008–2009 global crisis. For instance, the average economic growth rate per year in the 2002–2013 period is 6.1% (World Bank, 2018). Furthermore, according to BBC (2017) Peru has reduced poverty dramatically in 50% between 2007 and 2017.

Regarding the drawbacks, it seems that Peruvian governments were unable to mobilize the country's economic welfare into the population's social needs (Ganoza & Stiglich, 2015). The lack of governments' effectiveness derived in a country with socio-political unrest as well as a profound institutional weakness (Vergara, 2018). As in the late 60s and early 70s, the population is complaining about the gap between economic growth and social well-being (Grompone & Tanaka, 2009), representing one of its main challenges on the verge of its 200-year anniversary.

3 Environment for Entrepreneurship

The emergence of dynamic startups is contingent on the existence of favorable systemic conditions that shape both the resources available in a particular market and the new venture creation process (Kantis et al., 2018). Accordingly, to understand the environment for entrepreneurship, we rely on the lenses of comparative institutional systems, where the focus is on enduring institutional features to organize transactions.

Schneider (2013) argued that Latin America is a Hierarchical Market Economy with four important traits: the dominant presence of highly diversified family business groups, Multinational Corporations (MNCs) that heavily invest in manufacturing, financing, and utilities, the existence of atomistic labor relations with weak unions, and finally, low-skill levels of the work force couple with a poor investment on education.

There are strong complementarities among these institutional conditions that reinforce each other preventing change (Schneider, 2013). First, MNCs invest in particular sectors where they can leverage their preferential access to foreign R & D and capital discouraging participation of domestic business groups. Second, Business groups self-select on commodity-related sectors characterized by low R & D activities and low-skilled labor to avoid competition. Consequently, there are weak incentives to conduct R & D activities at the national and firm levels. Peru invests only 0.12% of its GDP in R & D activities (WEF, 2020), lagging all other South American countries. Further, the participation of the private sector in R & D activities remains well below the Latin American average (WEF, 2020), reflecting the relative low interest of established businesses to support innovation.

In turn, companies and individuals do not invest in developing industry-specific skills. Given the inexistence of strong unions, it is expected both a short time tenure and high turnover rates. Individuals move from one sector to the other reducing their interest in fine-tuning their skill sets applicable to a single industry. While Peru imposed one of the most rigid regulations for worker protection in the region (Roldos et al., 2019), its lack of capacity to enforce them trigger high informality rates. Informality in the labor market is one of the highest in the region (WEF, 2020). According to INEI (2018) more than 70% of the total employment corresponds to the grey labor market and only about a third of the formal employment can be considered as permanent. While most of the existing companies in Peru can be considered as micro and small enterprises, more than half of them operate informally (WEF, 2020).

Additionally, individuals do not necessarily invest in high-skill education due to the weak demand for these types of activities and low compensation levels. As dominant business groups self-select on low-skill sectors, highly trained workers face strong difficulties to find appropriate positions. On the opposite side, as firms

Fig. 5 Domestic firm mostly invest in low-skilled sectors; © David Huamani Bedoya/ Shutterstock, Inc., used with permission. Photo © 2021 Shutterstock

struggle to find highly skilled employees, companies favor investments in low-skilled sectors (Fig. 5). According to WEF (2020), Peru has a low-quality human capital where the presence of researchers in the labor force is a third of the average in the region.

As mentioned, all these conditions shaped the nature of the entrepreneurial activity in the country. According to the Global Entrepreneurship Monitor (GEM), Peru is among the countries with the highest total entrepreneurial activity (TEA) in its sample of 49 countries scoring 22.4% (Serida et al., 2020). More than 22 individuals per hundred are actively involved in running early-stage businesses in the country. Peru ranks fifth in the whole ranking and third in LATAM, right after Chile and Guatemala.

Resembling the figure that most companies in the country are micro or small companies, more than 60% of the early-stage ventures are created by only one founder reducing their capacity to get enough resources or access to credit. Indeed, the exit index, or the percentage of the population that has closed a business, is 7.6, significantly above the average of both other Latin American countries and middle-income economies (its natural comparison groups).

Over the last decade, the TEA has remained stable despite the consistent increase of the GDP per capita during this time span. While the GDP per capita (in parity terms) has increased from US$ 8858 in 2008 to US$ 13,084 in 2018, the TEA remains at the same level. Increases in GDP per capita do not have any significant effect on entrepreneurial initiatives.

Fig. 6 Most entrepreneurs target commercial based activities like restaurants; © Christian Vinces/ Shutterstock, Inc., used with permission. Photo © 2021 Shutterstock

Nevertheless, the type of motivation that Peruvians have for starting a new venture has changed. The GEM distinguishes between necessity and opportunity-driven entrepreneurs. During the last decade, two opposite trends can be distinguished. On the one hand, opportunity-based entrepreneurship has grown consistently, while necessity based has decreased significantly.

Despite more Peruvians declare that they started a new venture to exploit an opportunity, 76.7% of the early-stage ventures targeted commercial activities or restaurants (Fig. 6) with relatively low innovation and technology adoption. In the innovation index, a composed measure reflecting the level of competition that early-stage entrepreneurs faced and the novelty of products offered, Peruvian new ventures remained below the average of both comparison groups. This type of early-stage activity may reflect the quality of both the human capital available in the country and the low investment in education at the national level mentioned.

Regarding the access to the financial system, WEF (2020) highlighted that only 43% of adults have a bank account in Peru, recording the lowest access in South America. While insufficient, microfinance institutions have helped in overcoming some of the limitations that SMEs have to obtain financial access. Additionally, there is no space in the formal financial system to fund early-stage businesses. Most entrepreneurs must rely on their own resources or turn to informal sources of financing.

Women are relatively less involved than men in early-stage ventures (53% in contrast to 47% for women). Interestingly enough, there are no differences between men and women when we compare the opportunity/necessity ratio. However, there are at least two instances in which we can identify relevant gender gaps: the type of sectors targeted and the financial inclusion of each group. Regarding the former, women start more business in commercial activities than men. Moreover, the proportion of women starting new businesses in technological, professional, or financial sectors is less than half of the proportion of man. Regarding the latter, the gender gap in Peru is the second largest in South America (after Ecuador). Stereotypes regarding the role of women in the society and consequently, their relative less participation in STEAM type of careers may determine this behavior.

4 Towards the Future

In a relatively recent attempt to modify the current state of affairs, the Peruvian government is aiming to promote an entrepreneurial ecosystem that can be the driver for employability and competitiveness (Kantis & Angelelli, 2020). In this effort, the joint support of private initiatives such as the Entrepreneurship Peruvian Association (asep.pe) and of private incubators and accelerators such as Wayra or Endeavor are worth noticing.

Since 2007, three programs financed by the Peruvian government and the Inter-American Development Bank (IDB) have been conducted. The first one from 2007 to 2012, with US$ 36 MM to stimulate innovation and research. The second ran from 2013 to 2016 with US$ 100 MM in funds. For the first time, a pilot for promoting entrepreneurship was created, allocating US$ 6 MM for this purpose. The last program, currently implemented, has US$ 100 MM available but with US$ 30 MM reserved explicitly for enabling, strengthening, and developing the entrepreneurship ecosystem.

One of the main pillars in this effort was to promote the access to financial resources to dynamic startups. The government created Innovate Peru in 2014 and its flagship program StartUp Peru had already provided more than US$ 10 MM to 400 businesses and exposed those beneficiaries to new rounds of investment. StartUp Peru provides seed capital to either entrepreneurs with a minimum viable products already validated in the market or those with a functioning business model that has the potential to scale up operations. Up to date, there are seven generations of companies supported by StartUp Peru in different sectors such as edutech, agtech, and foodtech (Kantis et al., 2018). In parallel, the IDB-LAB created a US$ 20MM fund for attracting venture capital firms.

A second pillar was the orchestration and promotion of a system of incubators. Nowadays, more than 30 incubators have been co-financed by Innovate Peru. Moreover, currently more than 80% of the incubators created in the country are related to a University. Incubators are one of the main mechanisms of support to startups at early stages. Given the type of new ventures incubated, it is expected an alignment of interest among actors to conduct R & D activities and to pursue education in STEAM careers. Further, most of the mentoring needed by firms backed by StartUp Peru is channeled to one of the incubators associated with

Fig. 7 Example of PECAP supporting activities to the entrepreneurial ecosystem; © Luis Narro used with permission

Innovate Peru. Regarding inclusion and considering that there are more women with university degrees but less incline to Science and Technology (Avolio et al., 2018), the presence of incubators and hubs of innovation within each particular university may help to diminish the gender gap noted before.

The link with universities can also be an opportunity to develop more efficient technologies in sectors where Peru has comparative advantages such as biotechnology, agriculture, fishing, mining, among others. Orchestration of new ventures with established participants in these sectors may represent another area needed to spark the interest in this new breed of startups. The role of the private sector also strength the entrepreneurial ecosystem by providing access to relevant training and network that entrepreneurs can leverage. A case in point is the creation of several networks of investor angels in the country.

The government initiatives have strongly resonated in Lima, the capital, where it manages to attract incubators, accelerators, investors, and associations like PECAP to support the entrepreneurial ecosystem (Fig. 7). However, Peru needs to expand the coverage and impact of its efforts nationwide. Since 2017 it is trying to expand the scope of its activities to different cities across the country. However, this is an avenue that needs to be further developed.

It is expected to have a significant growth of the Peruvian ecosystem in the near future. The recent approval of a law that eases the creation of venture capital firms, the implementation of the crowdfunding law enacted in 2021, the current support of IDB-LAB to enable ecosystems in emerging economies and the evolution of

Peruvian startups support this claim. In relative terms, the Peruvian ecosystem is small in comparison with other markets in the region. However, it has strong annual growth rates (15–20%) with expectations to double these figures in the short term.

5 Case Study: Quantum Talent

Quantum Talent (QT) is an innovative company founded in Lima in 2017 with the aim to be a solution for both low-skilled workers that find difficulties to get an adequate job and companies that are struggling to reduce their turnaround and improve labor productivity. Despite being a Peruvian company that addresses a salient problem in the domestic market, its scope was to be a regional company since its inception. Similar challenges can be found in other Latin American countries that may provide the firm the opportunity to scale its operations.

In LATAM there are around 100 million people without a university degree that are either not employed or employed informally. These people are in jobs that do not provide them any opportunity to succeed or to acquire the relevant skills needed in the labor market. On the other side, the great majority of companies are facing strong difficulties to find the required talent to be more competitive and expand operations.

To address this problem, QT developed a web-based SAAS (software as a service) model with Machine Learning. Firms that adopt QT's solution not only digitize their selection process but also they can accurately predict the fit between candidates and job opportunities. Consequently, companies can improve the tenure of their employees and improve their job performance.

5.1 The Entrepreneur: Carlos Ganoza

Carlos is an economist with an MBA from the University of Chicago. Before founding QT, Carlos has had relevant managerial and entrepreneurial experience. Further, he had served as chief of assessors in the Peruvian Ministry of Economy and Finance (MEF).

Carlos has been manager of strategy and business development in Price Waterhouse and Coopers. After completing his MBA, he worked in a private equity company in Brazil where he got interested in pursuing an entrepreneurial path. Consequently, he and other investors decided to acquire the most prestigious business magazine in Peru, Semana Economica, where he was the CEO. During this period, the company could quadruple its revenues and double its operation margins.

Later, he served as the chief of assessors in the MEF. There, he studied in depth the problems in the labor market and the lack of connection between demand and offer.

Recently, he was recognized as Endeavor Entrepreneur in 2020. This recognition provides a strong signal in the international capital market about the potential scalability of Quantum Talent and the capacity of the founding team.

5.2 Quantum Talent Business Model

Carlos understood that at early stages, it would be difficult for any entrepreneur in Peru to obtain large amounts of capital. Being located in a small market with a relatively new entrepreneurial ecosystem plays against its odds. Therefore, he designed a capital-efficient model to operate.

QT used the model of technology adoption developed by Geoffrey Moore to define its target market. The company focuses on innovators and early adopters. In the first group, QT looked for innovative firms that were already using technology and trying to transform themselves digitally. In the second group, QT looked for those companies that have very high turnover rates.

Despite this careful segmentation process, QT needed to clarify several assumptions associated with its customers. By using a trial and error approach (during part of 2017 and 2018), QT realized that their solution had a better fit with service and retail companies with a relatively large head count. Further, several of its current customers are subsidiaries of multinationals operating in Peru.

Since the value proposition relies on data generation, QT needed to obtain data for the predictive models to work. Based on the seniority of Carlos and its recognition, QT was capable of providing HR consultancy services to target companies. The consultancy services had attractive prices and generated both revenues and the data needed by the company to work. This strategy also gave some initial traction for the client acquisition process. It is important to note that the revenue model is based on monthly subscriptions depending on the number of candidates evaluated per month.

Human talent is the most important but the most difficult resource to get in Peru. As mentioned, R & D investment and the number of people involved in STEM sectors lag other countries in the region. Consequently, QT struggle to find highly talented technical employees at inception, which represented a serious problem for the company. Currently, the company has 26 people with almost 70% being data science, machine learning or software engineers.

To address this problem, QT has worked on developing a sound value proposition to attract young talented employees besides a competitive compensation. Core to its proposition are the autonomy provided, the creative freedom encouraged, and the constant learning opportunities available. Traditionally, when an individual enters a big company, he is not exposed to brand new technologies and have little flexibility to operate. On the contrary, in QT employees work with the latest technology available, they have freedom to experiment, and much more space to grow within the company. QT invests significantly in training with courses available not only in Peru but elsewhere. We found that this value proposition is attractive for high-skill workers and allows QT to compete for talent against established firms.

5.3 Internationalization

The company started its international expansion in 2019. Today, the company is operating in Argentina, Chile, Colombia, Ecuador, Mexico, and Peru. The company's business model requires economies of scale to be sustainable and accordingly, Carlos designed its business model to be a regional multinational from the beginning.

Two factors can explain the rapid internationalization process of QT. First, it secured the support of Grupo Modelo in Mexico. QT won an open innovation contest organized by the brewery that allowed them to develop a fully paid pilot program. In 2019 QT not only signed a contract with Grupo Modelo but also could expand its operations with other Mexican companies such as Palacio de Hierro, the biggest retailer in the country. Second, several multinationals operating in Peru refer QT's services to other subsidiaries within LATAM. For instance, in 2019, Atento, a Spanish contact center, recommends QT services to the subsidiaries in Chile Argentina and Colombia. Also, Arca continental, a Mexican Multilatina operating in Peru, brought the firm to Mexico and Argentina.

5.4 Future Challenges

Despite obtaining US$ 2.5 MM in its first round A investment in 2020 (and the second in Peruvian history), Quantum Talent has several challenges ahead. The COVID-19 has seriously affected the hiring process of its customers and consequently its revenues. Nevertheless, there is still a window of opportunity for the firm. Since several potential customers were forced to digitize their operations faster than expected, it is reasonable to anticipate an earlier recovery of the firm given the growth market potential. Also, while the company needs to increase its participation in Mexico, it can't forget the largest market of the region: Brazil. Language barriers and resources needed to operate represent a major constraint to be solved.

6 Conclusions

Peru has a strong entrepreneurial activity. However, most of the new ventures created have a low potential for escalation and innovation. The Peruvian government with the help of international agencies such as IDB is orchestrating the development of an entrepreneurial ecosystem that both breaks some prevalent institutional conditions and encourages new ventures capable of being the engine of national competitiveness. It seems that a new breed of companies is being created but not in the scale needed. A case in point is the appearance of Quantum Talent, a company with an international scope, based on technology and with the capacity to attract and develop highly skilled employees.

References

Avolio, B., Chavez, J., Vilchez-Roman, C., & Pezo, G. (2018). *Factores que influyen en el ingreso, Participación y desarrollo de las mujeres en las carreras vinculadas a la ciencia, tecnología e innovación*. CIES. https://www.cies.org.pe/sites/default/files/investigaciones/factores_que_influyen_en_el_ingreso_participacion_y_desarrollo_de_las_mujeres_en_carreras_vinculadas_a_la_cti_0.pdf

BBC. (2017, January 8). *Como Peru deslumbro al mundo al reducir mas del 50% de la pobreza en 10 años*. https://www.bbc.com/mundo/noticias-38497627

Cuervo-Cazurra, A., & Dau, L. A. (2009). Promarket reforms and firm profitability in developing countries. *Academy of Management Journal, 52*(6), 1348–1368. https://doi.org/10.5465/amj.2009.47085192

Dana, L. P. (1988). International note: More small business is not the answer for Peru. *Journal of Small Business Management, 26*(3), 68–70. https://search.proquest.com/openview/23bf08eadfe1423b1d78ddb732691cc2/1?pq-origsite=gscholar&cbl=49244

OECD. (2016, May). *Environmental Performance Reviews PERU highlights and recommendations*. https://www.oecd.org/environment/country-reviews/16-00312-environmental%20performance%20review-peru-web.pdf

Euromonitor International. (2020). *Peru: Country Profile*. https://www-portal-euromonitor-com.esan.idm.oclc.org/portal/analysis/tab.

Ganoza, C., & Stiglich, A. (2015). *El Perú está calato. El falso milagro de la economía peruana y las trampas que amenazan nuestro progreso* (1st ed.). Editorial Planeta.

Grompone, R., & Tanaka, M. (2009). *Entre el crecimiento económico y la insatisfacción social. Las protestas sociales en el Perú actual*, 1st ed. Lima: Instituto de Estudios Peruanos (IEP). IMF (2019) file:///D:/Users/aborda/Downloads/LaborMarket.pdf.

INEI. (2017, June). *Peru crecimiento y distribución de la población*. https://www.inei.gob.pe/media/MenuRecursivo/publicaciones_digitales/Est/Lib1530/libro.pdf

INEI. (2018, November). *Producción y Empleo informal en el Peru*. https://www.inei.gob.pe/media/MenuRecursivo/publicaciones_digitales/Est/Lib1589/libro.pdf

Kantis, H., & Angelelli, P. (2020). *Emprendimientos de base científico-tecnológica en América Latina: Importancia, desafíos y recomendaciones para el futuro*. Inter-American Development Bank. https://doi.org/10.18235/0002156

Kantis, H., Federico, J., & Ibarra Garcia, S. (2018). *Condiciones sistémicas para el emprendimiento dinámico: Las brechas abiertas de América Latina: Convergencia o Divergencia* (1st ed.). Asociación Civil Red Pymes Mercosur. https://asep.pe/wp-content/uploads/2019/06/Condiciones-sist%C3%A9micas-para-el-emprendimiento-din%C3%A1mico-PRODEM-2018.pdf

Klarén, P. F. (2019). *Nación y Sociedad en la Historia del Perú* (1st ed.). Instituto de Estudios Peruanos (IEP).

Llosa, L., & Panizza, U. (2015). La gran depresión de la economía peruana ¿una tormenta perfecta? *Revista de Estudios Económicos, 30*, 91–117. https://www.bcrp.gob.pe/docs/Publicaciones/Revista-Estudios-Economicos/30/ree-30-llosa-panizza.pdf

Roldos, J., David, A., Perez, C., & Pienknamura, S. (2019). Labor market dynamics and informality over the business cycle in LAC. *IMF*. https://www.imf.org/~/media/Files/Publications/REO/WHD/2019/October/English/LaborMarket.ashx

Schneider, B. R. (2013). *Hierarchical capitalism in Latin America. Business, labor, and the challenges of equitable development* (1st ed.). Cambridge University Press. https://doi.org/10.1017/CBO9781107300446

Serida, J., Alzamora, J., Guerrero, C., Borda, A., & Morales, O. (2020). *Global Entrepreneurship Monitor: Peru 2018–2019*. https://www.esan.edu.pe/publicaciones/2020/05/07/Final_GEM%202019.pdf

Thorne & Associates: PBI del Peru caerá menos de lo esperado este año por medidas del gobierno (2020, October 7). Gestion.

Vergara. (2018). *Ciudadanos sin república: De la precariedad institucional al descalabro político* (2nd ed.). Editorial Planeta.

WEF. (2020). *Strategic Intelligence: Peru.* https://intelligence.weforum.org/topics/a1Gb00000038pm5EAA?tab=publications

World Bank. (2018, October 13). *Perú: panorama general.* http://www.bancomundial.org/es/country/peru/overview#1

Armando Borda (PhD, Florida International University) is an Assistant Professor at the Graduate School of Business of ESAN University in Peru. His areas of interests focus on entrepreneurship and the internationalization of Latin American firms. In particular on exploring how the role of reputation, business group affiliation and institutional context affects both the process itself and outcomes such as survival, reputation, and performance. His work has been published in prestigious journals and editorials such as Journal of International Business Studies, Journal of World Business, Journal of Business Research and in Multinational Business Review.

Miguel Cordova Associate Professor of Management at Pontificia Universidad Católica del Perú. He holds a PhD in Strategic Management from Consorcio de Universidades in Peru, PhD studies in the Copenhagen Business School, and MBA from Centrum Católica. His research interests are Power and Influence, Sustainable Supply Chain Management, and Entrepreneurship. He was a visiting professor at INSEEC Business School in Paris, UDD in Santiago, ESADE in Barcelona, and UDEM in Monterrey. He is an editorial board member of 360 Management Journal (Peru), CEA Journal (Colombia), and Alcance Journal (Brazil). He received five research funds, one teaching award, and an EFMD's teaching scholarship.

Luis Narro Venture Partner at Alaya Capital, a Latin American venture capital firm. Previously he was Executive Director at PECAP, Peru's Venture Capital Association, and worked at entrepreneurial ecosystem development organizations such as the Swiss Entrepreneurship Program (Swiss EP) and COFIDE, Peru's development bank. Collaborated in the design and negotiation of Peru's first venture capital fund of funds. He is a lawyer and Master in Finance with specialization in capital markets by ESAN Graduate School of Business (Peru) and Pompeu Fabra University (Spain).

Entrepreneurship in Suriname

Aidin Salamzadeh and Marina Alekseevna Romanovich

Abstract

Suriname is a multicultural Caribbean country with a very long historical background. As a factor-driven economy, Suriname relies on its agricultural and natural resources. Nevertheless, entrepreneurs have played a significant role in their economy. Surprisingly, immigrant entrepreneurs from other countries or Surinamese entrepreneurs who have acted as the socio-economic change agents for many years have rarely studied in academic research. Therefore, this chapter provides a better understanding of the country, its historical background, and the environment for entrepreneurship. As shown in this chapter, the entrepreneurship ecosystem is not developed well, but there are many possibilities to explore, evaluate, and exploit entrepreneurial opportunities to create value. Although limited information exists about Surinamese entrepreneurs, the authors introduce a female Surinamese entrepreneur, and finally, the chapter concludes with some future directions and some concluding remarks.

1 Introduction

Republic of Suriname, which is also called Suriname or Surinam, is a tropical country located in the North American region, bordering the Atlantic Ocean. Suriname has two similar neighbours on each side, i.e. French Guiana on its east and Guyana on its west. Also, Suriname is located in the north of Brazil. As a

A. Salamzadeh (✉)
Faculty of Management, University of Tehran, Tehran, Iran
e-mail: Salamzadeh@ut.ac.ir

M. A. Romanovich
Department of Hoist Transport and Road Machines, BSTU Named After V. G. Shukhov, Belgorod, Russia

L.-P. Dana et al. (eds.), *Entrepreneurship in South America*, Springer Texts in Business and Economics, https://doi.org/10.1007/978-3-030-97060-4_12

Fig. 1 Tropical tree Source: © Pixabay https://pixabay.com/photos/palm-tree-tropical-summer-nature-3337325

Caribbean country, with 163,820 km^2 and a population of 586,634 (in 2020), it is the smallest country in the South American region (Andrade, 1985; Kooye, 2014). Most of its population reside in the capital and a number of larger cities around it. Therefore, the northern coast is the most populated area of Suriname. As a tropical country, it benefits from rain forests and local economies shaped based on natural resources, such as gold, bauxite, petroleum, and agricultural products (Landburg et al., 2021) (Fig. 1).

Suriname is a Dutch-speaking country that inhibits people with diverse cultural backgrounds (Stell, 2018). Nevertheless, Surinamese communicate in other languages as well. Although Dutch is used prevalently as the official language in formal instances and places and over 60% of them are native speakers, they use 14 local languages in their daily lives. The first or second language of most Surinamese is Sranan (St-Hilaire, 1999). Both Dutch and Sranan are affected by other languages which various ethnic groups frequently use to communicate. However, Sranan is the vernacular language, and people use Dutch in more formal situations. Sarnami (Caribbean Hindustani) stands in third place, which is a heritage of the British Indians who moved to this region many years ago. In addition to these, Aluku, Amerindian (Arawak, Carib, Tiriyó, Wayana), Aukan, Cantonese, Hakka, Javanese, Kwinti, Mandarin, Matawai, Paramaccan, and Saramaccan are used in some communities (Davis, 2009).

Suriname is a country with diverse ethnic groups that created a unique cultural diversity, with various foods, customs, and traditions (Fig. 2). Looking back through

Fig. 2 Surinamese food Source: © Pixabay https://pixabay.com/photos/surinamese-food-eat-in-banana-leaf-329507

history and based on the existing evidence, one could notice that indigenous people were inhibited in this region around four millennia BC (Tobias & Morrison, 2021). Nevertheless, limited evidence exists similar to many neighbouring countries in this regard. Europeans entered this region back in the sixteenth century, and a new era started for this country (Okumura, 2011). This evolution is discussed in more detail in the next section. Suriname derived its name from its early inhabitants, i.e. Surinen, and the river around which the early communities were shaped (Mugnier, 2021) (Fig. 3).

In terms of political governance, Suriname turned to the Republic of Suriname according to its Constitution in 1987 (Pieters, 2021). The president gets elected every 5 years and appoints the cabinet, including 16 ministers. Besides, a vice-president is also elected for the same period. The High Court of Justice of Suriname, which is called the Supreme Court, is in charge of the judiciary (Mohammed-Davidson, 2016). Due to its history, the country had extensive relationships with the Netherlands. Nevertheless, this relationship has been weakened during the past decade. Suriname is an open country to positive relationships. It has created bilateral agreements with the United States and the European Union to improve its socio-economic status (Sieber et al., 2021). For instance, the US Department of Defence provides funds for military purposes in Suriname (Brana-Shute, 2021). Also, it has established partnerships with Caribbean and African states (van Genderen-Naar, 2008).

Fig. 3 River in Suriname Source: © Pixabay https://pixabay.com/photos/river-maroni-guyana-suriname-1312552

Due to several socio-economic and political challenges, the economic situation of Suriname was unstable before the 1990s (Sedoc-Dahlberg, 2018). Hopefully, the country has diversified its economy after turning to a Republic state. Many countries, especially the Netherlands and the United States of America, helped them create more reliable and bilateral international relationships (Sedoc-Dahlberg, 2021a). They recently signed contracts and agreements with Brazil and China to improve the infrastructures and provide major governmental educational, agricultural, and medical services (Ellis, 2012). Then, as a country with a moderate level of human development, Suriname can be socio-economically developed in the near future (Sanches et al., 2022).

This chapter is structured as follows. First, the historical context of Suriname is reviewed to provide a more comprehensive insight for the readers. Then, the environment for entrepreneurship and doing business is elaborated. Afterwards, the authors provide some insights on the future directions. Finally, a case study is provided, and the chapter concludes with some remarks about entrepreneurship in Suriname.

2 Historical Context

Many native tribes, such as Arawak and Carib peoples, have inhabited the region from almost the fourth millennia BC (Brana-Shute, 1993). Surinen were also among the earliest people who have lived there. Some historians believe the name came from these people, and thus, the country has been named Suriname, as it is called today (McLester-Davis et al., 2021). Like many South American countries, limited information about the early history and its inhabitants are available. Surinen moved to other regions of the Guianas[1] due to conflicts with Indians by the end of the sixteenth century (MacDonald–Ottevanger et al., 2021). Christopher Columbus had already provided Europeans with information about the inhabitants of this region, and some consequent expeditions had led to increasing interest in moving to this region (Simms, 2018). Thus, in the first half of the seventeenth century, many European countries, including Great Britain, the Netherlands, France, and Spain, attempted to invade this region (Blakely, 1998). Nevertheless, their attempts remained unsuccessful as the Indians retaliated and saved their country.

In the 1650s, British people were among the first European settlers in Suriname, whose activities mainly focused on agriculture (Klooster, 2010). They used slaves to plant and harvest agricultural products (Davis, 2011). In the late 1660s, Dutch entered Suriname and exchanged it with New Amsterdam.[2] Then, for many years, the country was ruled by the Dutch and only for two periods, i.e. 1799 to 1802 and 1804 to 1815, the British ruled over this country (Hunter, 1991). Finally, in 1975, Suriname gained its independence (Moore, 2000). Before its independence, the British and Dutch planters had already improved its agricultural sector, and they exploited many relevant opportunities to produce sugar, cacao, coffee, and the like.

Slavery was prominent in this region, from the date the British fleet invaded the country until the mid-nineteenth century (Oostindie, 1993). Therefore, most of the population were slaves until Europeans entered the country and new inhabitants were diversified. Although most of them were from the Netherlands, other groups came from Great Britain, France, Germany, as well as a Jewish minority who moved to this region. The community was diversified itself, as it included jews from Italy, Spain, and Portugal who had earlier immigrated to the neighbour country, i.e. Brazil (Elkin, 1998). This migration wave did not stop, and in 1853 and onwards, the Chinese, Indian, and Indonesian workers moved to Suriname to exploit agricultural opportunities. Hopefully, the abolishment of slavery was officially announced in 1863 (Emmer, 1993). They celebrate this event in Suriname (Fig. 4).

Although the primary products of Suriname were agricultural products, this sector was weakened by the discovery of Aluminium in this country. In 1916, Alcoa[3] began exploiting the reserves, and after World War II, in 1939, Dutch also joined mining activities in Suriname (Messing, 1988). In 1948, the country's political autonomy negotiations were initiated, and the Netherlands offered its new financial aid packages (Hout, 2007). World War II could be considered as a turning point in Suriname's history, as political parties shaped and various ethnic groups began their socio-political activities. The country gained its internal autonomy in 1954, and the packages provided by the Netherlands helped them improve their independence and

[1] The Guianas region includes Guyana, French Guiana, and Suriname.

[2] The New York City.

[3] Aluminium Company of America.

Fig. 4 Celebrating slavery abolishment Source: © Pixabay https://pixabay.com/photos/koti-slavery-abolition-history-218909/?download

socio-economic development (Bal & Sinha-Kerkhoff, 2021; Bissessar, 2017). The political evolutions helped Suriname to become independent in 1975.

Despite its independence, the economy faced many problems in its first years. Issues such as stagnation, a high unemployment rate, and low income worsened the situation (Sedoc-Dahlberg, 2021b). Then, in 1980, a number of army officers took control over the country in an army coup. Surinamese appreciated the new power shift, and the Dutch government facilitated it by financing a new programme (Brana-Shute, 2021). Nevertheless, things did not go as perfect as they thought, and the new government spent resources on military affairs until the economy turned into a closed ecosystem. The conflict rose dramatically, and international financial aid was stopped from the Netherlands and the United States' sides (Bissessar, 2017). The disputes continued, and many people were killed in the next few years (Kruijt, 2020). This led to the migration of many civilians to French Guiana.

A new referendum was held in 1987, based on which they approved a new constitution in the same year (Thorndike, 2021). Then, a non-military government was shaped based on a free election. According to a new series of peace negotiations with the French government, Maroons had to be repatriated from French Guiana (Cbim et al., 2020). They signed an agreement in 1989, but the military forces took control over the country again in the next year. They had to devise a more reliable policy. Then, with the help of the Netherlands, the United States, and France, a new election was held in 1991 (Vander Weyden, 2006). Hopefully, non-military parties won the election, and they passed an act to deprive military forces of any political positions.

Nevertheless, some officials were accused of drug trafficking in the next few years, and instability remained as a fact in Suriname. Based on the IMF[4] reports, Suriname was bankrupt in 2000. A new president was elected in 2000, and the new government attempted to solve the problems despite their intensity and variety (Geesteranus, 1992). Besides, the country had some conflicts with its neighbours, which were mainly due to the boundaries. The socio-economic situation is still volatile, and there is a steady decrease rate in many economic indicators.

3 The Environment for Entrepreneurship

As a factor-driven economy, Suriname depends on producing and exporting its resources, raw materials, and products (Khyareh et al., 2019). As mentioned earlier, agricultural products and minerals are among the primary resources on which its economy relies. Most of the export is related to exporting minerals and the mining sector (Darson & Kroesen, 2017). Based on various reports, the government earns more than 25% of its revenues from this sector which entails 85% of the exports. It makes Suriname more vulnerable as it is highly dependent on its international relations (Gavin, 2019). Also, the GDP has decreased in the last few years, making Suriname more prone to external shocks. The other socio-economic indicators have also been decreasing in the past few years (Alemna et al., 2021).

According to the IMF reports, the country must revise its monetary and fiscal policies to decrease its socio-economic instability. In addition to such reforms, the business environment needs much attention (Ooft et al., 2021). For instance, the ease of doing business indexes reveals that starting and running a business in Suriname is not much easy. The private sector players are less motivated and eager to run a business, and thus entrepreneurship is hindered in this country (Pounder & Gopal, 2021). The following table shows the country profile for Suriname (Table 1).

According to the latest GEM survey in 2014,[5] adult Surinamese who had enough knowledge about entrepreneurial opportunities and would like to start a business in the next 6 months had decreased by 12% in 1 year. This rate was lower than half of the Latin American countries. Nevertheless, their perceptions about running a business were extremely high, and their level of fear of failure was very low. Then, Surinamese were more prone to run a business as they dared to take risks and face their fear of failure. Also, this might be because, in general, people in less developed countries perceive more opportunities and have lower fear of failure rates than people in developed countries. Besides, the desirability of entrepreneurship as a career alternative remained higher than many countries, even the United States and China, but still was lower than in the Netherlands. Suriname was the eighth top country in the GEM report regarding the rate of media attention to entrepreneurship. The country was listed in the middle of the surveyed countries regarding how much

[4] International Monetary Fund.

[5] https://www.gemconsortium.org/economy-profiles/suriname.

Table 1 Country profile for Suriname (Source: World Development Indicators (https://data.worldbank.org/country/suriname))

	1990	2000	2010	2020
General information				
Population, total (millions)	0.41	0.47	0.53	0.59
Population growth (annual %)	2	1.2	1.1	0.9
Surface area (sq. km) (thousands)	163.8	163.8	163.8	163.8
Population density (people per sq. km of land area)	2.6	3	3.4	3.8
GNI, atlas method (current US$) (billions)	0.58	0.93	4.03	2.71
GNI per capita, atlas method (current US$)	1420	1970	7620	4620
GNI, PPP (current international $) (billions)	2.67	3.46	7	8.23
GNI per capita, PPP (current international $)	6590	7340	13,230	14,030
People				
Life expectancy at birth, total (years)	67	68	70	72
Primary completion rate, total (% of relevant age group)	90	–	87	86
School enrollment, primary (% gross)	121.4	106.1	114	109.2
School enrollment, secondary (% gross)	57	75	71	82
Environment				
Forest area (sq. km) (thousands)	153.8	153.4	153	152
Urban population growth (annual %)	2.1	1.3	1	1
Energy use (kg of oil equivalent per capita)	–	1339	1356	–
Economy				
GDP (current US$) (billions)	0.39	0.95	4.37	2.88
GDP growth (annual %)	−4.5	2.1	5.2	−15.9
Inflation, GDP deflator (annual %)	49.9	60.7	7.2	44.9
Agriculture, forestry, and fishing, value added (% of GDP)	8	10	9	8
Industry (including construction), value added (% of GDP)	22	25	35	35
States and markets				
Time required to start a business (days)	–	–	690	66
Mobile cellular subscriptions (per 100 people)	0	8.7	98.5	153.3
Individuals using the internet (% of population)	0	2.5	31.6	48.9
High-technology exports (% of manufactured exports)	–	–	14	13
Statistical capacity score (overall average) (scale 0 - 100)	–	–	71	58
Global links				
Merchandise trade (% of GDP)	243	97	78	127
Net barter terms of trade index (2000 = 100)	–	100	135	149
Net migration (thousands)	−5	−9	−5	−5
Personal remittances, received (current US$) (millions)	1	1	4	124
Foreign direct investment, net inflows (BoP, current US$) (millions)	−77	−97	−256	84
Net official development assistance received (current US$) (millions)	61	34.8	100.8	23.4

people respect entrepreneurs and their status. The level of entrepreneurial intention was also very low.

Suriname's total entrepreneurial activity (TEA) rate was the lowest among Latin American countries included in the GEM 2014 report. Besides, both nascent entrepreneurship and new business ownership rates were the lowest among others. Only 5.4% of the TEA were necessity-driven entrepreneurship, and 39.8% of it were improvement driven. Based on the 2013 GEM survey, most of the main indicators for entrepreneurship framework conditions were above the average for the Latin American countries. Nevertheless, Suriname was ranked as the 162nd country in terms of the Doing Business index in 2020. Then, it could be concluded that doing business, establishing a company, or entrepreneurship could not be straightforward in this country (Rubach et al., 2015; Villegas, 2017).

4 Toward the Future

As discussed earlier, entrepreneurship in Suriname is almost an emerging topic that has been hopefully empowered by activities such as joining the GEM consortium, holding entrepreneurship-related events, and financing entrepreneurial activities and events, primarily using resources endowed by various countries such as the United States (Lachman et al., 2018). Although the GEM reports show many potential improvements are required to improve the ecosystem, the young generation is more prone to become entrepreneurs or run their own businesses as entrepreneurship education and promotion policies are devised and implemented. As mentioned in the historical background of Suriname, the country has transformed from a purely agricultural economy to a more industrial one that mainly relies on minerals and other resources (Malgie et al., 2015). Although still it is categorised as a factor-driven economy, a new entrepreneurship wave could help Suriname make the second transition (Villegas, 2017). According to the extant research, sustainable, agricultural and social entrepreneurship might be considered the country's three primary waves of entrepreneurship policies (de Theije, 2021). Besides, based on the recent explorations, Suriname could produce more oil in the near future, which might be a real two-edged sword (Raghoebarsing & Reinders, 2019). An event that could decrease the speed of entrepreneurial changes- like many oil-producing countries (e.g. Dana et al., 2021; Doshmanli et al., 2018; Guerrero et al., 2014, 2015; Salamzadeh et al., 2017)- or help the country move forward more vigorously. Besides, the young population is becoming well-educated in starting businesses and entrepreneurship. Then, they could become the change agents of their society and provide a better future for Suriname.

5 Case Study

Entrepreneurs deal with various challenges and solve many predicted and unpredicted events, especially in more volatile environments. Surinamese entrepreneurs also act in such an uncertain and risky environment. Due to the Doing Business index, doing business and enterprising are much more challenging for [potential] entrepreneurs. In 2018, the first entrepreneurship award went to Vanessa Grootfaam, who founded the Queens Vans Hair & Nails company. She is a perfect role model for female entrepreneurs in Suriname. She was selected in the Entrepreneur & Manager of the Year election- conceptually borrowed from The Other Business Man in the Netherlands. They initiated this event to motivate entrepreneurs and create role models for future Surinamese entrepreneurs.

Vanessa Grootfaam studied Hair Styling/Stylist and Hair Design at the Monalisa Kapperschool in 2007 and started her business a few years later. Despite all the socio-economic barriers to starting her business, she decided to produce her own products. Starting a local business is always a challenge. It was not an exception for her too. Vanessa took advantage of her background, experience and education to become a successful agripreneur. Her products are made up of garlic oil, ginger, and natural oils. She analyses the customers' hair to ensure the current status and issues, such as hair loss, dandruff, or hair fall. Using their natural products, they offer the best choice to their customers.

She believes that she teaches people to live healthy lives. She expands the idea that the hair does not grow from the outside but the inside. Most people only take care of the outside and the skin when they choose a treatment for their hair. Vanessa loves her entrepreneurial journey and takes advantage of social media platforms to introduce her products to her customers. In an interview, she argues that being an entrepreneur is not easy. She believes that one needs to have a goal in his/her mind, and no matter what comes in ones' way, he/she should find their way. She adds that one must be self-confident and find a solution. Her idea of entrepreneurship is so close to the notion of entrepreneurship as a lifestyle. Vanessa believes that to become an entrepreneur, one must act and compete. Competitors help an entrepreneur grow faster.

Her entrepreneurship journey is a trifold story. Firstly, she is an excellent example of a female entrepreneur who acts in a local economy while considering a global approach toward finding innovative solutions for her customer pains. Secondly, she could be considered as an agripreneur, as she uses agricultural products to develop new products. Last but not least is her intrinsic approach to improving Suriname's creative economy. Besides, like many entrepreneurs, Vanessa cares about her country, people, and their lives. For instance, in 2016, together with 14 young agricultural entrepreneurs, she attended the ninth Regional Planners Forum to discuss the challenges faced by local entrepreneurs in the agriculture sector. They clarified many existing challenges and proposed some suggestions to help those entrepreneurs.

6 Concluding Remarks

Suriname is a country with a fascinating history, which witnessed several ups and downs, peaks and valleys, during millennia. After the Europeans entered the country, a new era began- An era full of fears and hopes. Those years were full of fears of slavery and hopes for change. After its independence, Surinamese were glad to become freer, but it did not take very long, and coups happened by the military. Again they experienced other waves of change. Until the past decade, a young generation with creative minds and more access to technologies would like to change the country. All and all, the country were less able to improve entrepreneurial activities. Nevertheless, with the aid coming from more developed countries, this is changing in recent years. Maybe, as the economy is experiencing fluctuations, potential entrepreneurs could explore, evaluate, and exploit more entrepreneurial opportunities to create value. Also, female entrepreneurs, such as Vanessa Grootfaam, could strengthen the creative economy in Suriname and act as role models for future entrepreneurs. There is great potential to exploit opportunities in the creative industries. Besides, startups and new technology-based firms (NTBFs) could change the entrepreneurship ecosystem. Hopefully, a series of events are being held, and various national and international players provide motivations. These could lead to significant improvements in the entrepreneurship ecosystem of the country. Surinamese policymakers also must devise relevant small and medium-sized enterprises (SMEs) and entrepreneurship policies to help the ecosystem grow. Again, entities such as Global Entrepreneurship Monitor (GEM) officials must provide policy implications and suggestions to help them set constructive policies. Last but not least, there is an evident need to conduct research about entrepreneurship in Suriname. The extant body of the literature provides fragmented insights about the entrepreneurial ecosystem and entrepreneurs in this country.

References

Alemna, D., Artaraz, K., Haynes, P., & Mwale, S. (2021). The complexity and instability of policy conditionality and transfer: IMF interventions in the political economy of South America. *Complexity Governance and Networks, 6*(1), 14–31.

Andrade, J. (1985). Suriname. In *World police & paramilitary forces* (pp. 191–191). Palgrave Macmillan.

Bal, E., & Sinha-Kerkhoff, K. (2021). Ethnic and Religious Identification among Muslim East Indians in Suriname (1898–1954). In *Crescent over Another Horizon* (pp. 63–82). University of Texas Press.

Bissessar, A. M. (2017). Suriname. In *Ethnic conflict in developing societies* (pp. 73–88). Palgrave Macmillan.

Blakely, A. (1998). Historical ties among Suriname, the Netherlands Antilles, Aruba, and the Netherlands. *Callaloo, 21*(3), 472–478.

Brana-Shute, G. (1993). An inside-out insurgency: The Tukuyana Amazones of Suriname. *Journal of Commonwealth & Comparative Politics, 31*(2), 54–69.

Brana-Shute, G. (2021). Love among the ruins: The United States and Suriname. In *The Dutch Caribbean* (pp. 191–202). Routledge.

Cbim, F. R., Aladji, M., & Diop, M. (2020). Long term migratory dynamics and context of a territory: French Guiana. *The Journal of Applied Business and Economics, 22*(12), 60–77.

Dana, L. P., Tajpour, M., Salamzadeh, A., Hosseini, E., & Zolfaghari, M. (2021). The impact of entrepreneurial education on technology-based enterprises development: The mediating role of motivation. *Administrative Sciences, 11*(4), 105.

Darson, R., & Kroesen, J. O. (2017). Suriname. In *The world guide to sustainable Enterprise* (pp. 129–134). Routledge.

Davis, N. Z. (2009). Creole languages and their uses: The example of colonial Suriname. *Historical Research, 82*(216), 268–284.

Davis, N. Z. (2011). Judges, masters, diviners: Slaves' experience of criminal justice in colonial Suriname. *Law and History Review, 29*(4), 925–984.

de Theije, M. (2021). Corporate and migrant investment in a gold-mining development corridor: The case of Suriname. In *Handbook of translocal development and global mobilities*. Edward Elgar Publishing.

Doshmanli, M., Salamzadeh, Y., & Salamzadeh, A. (2018). Development of SMEs in an emerging economy: Does corporate social responsibility matter? *International Journal of Management and Enterprise Development, 17*(2), 168–191.

Elkin, J. L. (1998). *The Jews of Latin America* (p. 191). Holmes & Meier.

Ellis, R. E. (2012). Suriname and the Chinese. *The SAIS Review of International Affairs, 32*(2), 85–97.

Emmer, P. (1993). Between slavery and freedom: The period of apprenticeship in Suriname (Dutch Guiana), 1863–1873. *Slavery and Abolition, 14*(1), 87–113.

Gavin, D. M. (2019). Inflation and economic activity in Suriname. *Journal of Economics Library, 6*(3), 168–185.

Geesteranus, G. M. (1992). Can foreign states be declared bankrupt? The case of Zaire. *Netherlands International Law Review, 39*(S1), 215–226.

Guerrero, M., Urbano, D., & Salamzadeh, A. (2014). Evolving entrepreneurial universities: Experiences and challenges in the middle eastern context. In *Handbook on the entrepreneurial university*. Edward Elgar Publishing.

Guerrero, M., Urbano, D., & Salamzadeh, A. (2015). Entrepreneurial transformation in the Middle East: Experiences from Tehran universities. *Technics Technologies Education Management, 10*(4), 533–537.

Hout, W. (2007). Development under patrimonial conditions: Suriname's state oil company as a development agent. *The Journal of Development Studies, 43*(8), 1331–1350.

Hunter, B. (1991). Suriname. In *The Statesman's year-book* (pp. 1143–1146). Palgrave Macmillan.

Khyareh, M. M., Khairandish, M., & Torabi, H. (2019). Macroeconomic effects of entrepreneurship: Evidences from factor, efficiency and innovation driven countries. *International Journal of Entrepreneurship, 23*(1), 1–21.

Klooster, W. (2010). The Essequibo liberties: The link between Jewish Brazil and Jewish Suriname. *Studia Rosenthaliana, 42*, 77–82.

Kooye, R. V. D. (2014). Case 6: Suriname—The land rights issue and media performance. In *Global journalism practice and new media performance* (pp. 201–213). Palgrave Macmillan.

Kruijt, D. (2020). Suriname: The National Army in Politics. In *Oxford Research Encyclopedia of Politics*.

Landburg, G., Amatamsir, C., Muys, B., & Hermy, M. (2021). Medium and long term effects of logging systems on forest structure and composition in the tropical rainforest of Suriname. *Journal of Forest Research, 26*(5), 328–335.

MacDonald-Ottevanger, M. S., Boyd, A., Prins, M., van der Helm, J. J., Zijlmans, C. W. R., Hindori-Mohangoo, A. D., et al. (2021). Differences in prevalence of hepatitis B virus infection and genotypes between ethnic populations in Suriname, South America. *Virology, 564*, 53–61.

Malgie, W., Ori, L., & Ori, H. (2015). A study of pesticide usage and pesticide safety awareness among farmers in Commewijne in Suriname. *Journal of Agriculture Technology, 11*, 621–636.

McLester-Davis, L. W. Y., Shankar, A., Kataria, L. A., Hidalgo, A. G., van Eer, E. D., Koendjbiharie, A. P., et al. (2021). Validity, reliability, and transcultural adaptations of the Bayley scales of infant and toddler development (BSID-III-NL) for children in Suriname. *Early Human Development, 160*, 105416.

Messing, F. A. M. (1988). C. Lamur, the American takeover. Industrial emergence and Alcoa's expansion in Guyana and Suriname 1914-1921. *BMGN-Low Countries Historical Review, 103*(3), 466–467.

Mohammed-Davidson, R. (2016). Show me the money: Enforcing original jurisdiction judgments of the Caribbean court of justice. *Leiden Journal of International Law, 29*(1), 113–135.

Moore, B. (2000). Decolonisation by default: Suriname and the Dutch retreat from empire. *The Journal of Imperial and Commonwealth History, 28*(3), 228–250.

Mugnier, C. J. (2021). Grids and datums update: Co-Operative Republic of Guyana. *Photogrammetric Engineering & Remote Sensing, 87*(4), 231–232.

Okumura, M. (2011). The end of slavery: Disease patterns and cultural behaviours of African Americans in Suriname. *International Journal of Osteoarchaeology, 21*(6), 631–642.

Ooft, G., Bhaghoe, S., & Franses, P. H. (2021). Forecasting annual inflation in Suriname. *Journal of International Financial Markets, Institutions and Money, 73*, 101357.

Oostindie, G. (1993). Voltaire, Stedman and Suriname slavery. *Slavery and Abolition, 14*(2), 1–34.

Pieters, D. (2021). Suriname. In *Social security law in small jurisdictions* (pp. 237–247). Springer.

Pounder, P., & Gopal, N. (2021). Entrepreneurship and small island economies. *Organisations and Markets in Emerging Economies, 12*(2), 415–439.

Raghoebarsing, A., & Reinders, A. (2019). The role of photovoltaics (PV) in the present and future situation of Suriname. *Energies, 12*(1), 185.

Rubach, M. J., Bradley, D., III, & Kluck, N. (2015). Necessity entrepreneurship: A Latin American study. *International Journal of Entrepreneurship, 19*, 126.

Salamzadeh, A., Arasti, Z., & Elyasi, G. M. (2017). Creation of ICT-based social start-ups in Iran: A multiple case study. *Journal of enterprising culture, 25*(01), 97–122.

Sanches, M., Graafsma, T., & Leckie, G. (2022). Psychology in Suriname. In *Psychology in Oceania and the Caribbean* (pp. 271–281). Springer.

Sedoc-Dahlberg, B. (2021a). Suriname: 19175—89. Domestic and foreign policies under military and civilian rule. In *The Dutch Caribbean* (pp. 17–33). Routledge.

Sedoc-Dahlberg, B. (2021b). Struggle for democracy in Suriname. In *The Dutch Caribbean* (pp. 173–189). Routledge.

Sedoc-Dahlberg, B. N. (2018). Democracy and human rights in Suriname. In *Democracy and human rights in the Caribbean* (pp. 212–229). Routledge.

Sieber, I. M., Campagne, C. S., Villien, C., & Burkhard, B. (2021). Mapping and assessing ecosystems and their services: A comparative approach to ecosystem service supply in Suriname and French Guiana. *Ecosystems and People, 17*(1), 148–164.

Simms, G. G. (2018). Maroon indigenous women circle, Jamaica: Historical recurrences from indigenous Women's perspectives. *Journal of International Women's Studies, 19*(2), 244–247.

Stell, G. (2018). Sociolinguistic indexicalities in ethnic diversity: Perceptions of ethnicity and language in Suriname. *New West Indian Guide/Nieuwe West-Indische Gids, 92*(1–2), 35–61.

St-Hilaire, A. (1999). Language planning and development in the Caribbean: Multi-ethnic Suriname. *Language Problems and Language Planning, 23*(3), 211–231.

Thorndike, T. (2021). Suriname and the military. In *The Dutch Caribbean* (pp. 35–62). Routledge.

Tobias, M. C., & Morrison, J. G. (2021). Cave paintings of the mind. In *On the nature of ecological paradox* (pp. 293–300). Springer.

van Genderen-Naar, J. (2008). The implementation of the Cariforum-EC economic partnership agreement. *Global Watch, 3*(4), 43.

Vander Weyden, P. (2006). The comeback of Désiré Bouterse? General elections in Suriname 2005. *Representations, 42*(3), 235–242.

Villegas, R. V. (2017). Youth entrepreneurship dynamics in the Caribbean region: 2011–2013. *International Journal of Entrepreneurship and Small Business, 30*(3), 287–307.

Aidin Salamzadeh is an assistant professor at the University of Tehran. His interests are startups, new venture creation, and entrepreneurship. Aidin serves as an associate editor in "Revista de Gestão", "Innovation & Management Review" (Emerald), "Entrepreneurial Business and Economics Review", "Journal of Women's Entrepreneurship and Education" as well as an editorial advisory in "The Bottom Line" (Emerald). Besides, he is a reviewer in numerous distinguished international journals. Aidin is a member of the European SPES Forum, the Asian Academy of Management, and Ondokuz Mayis University.

Marina Alekseevna Romanovich is an associate professor of the Department of Host transport and road machines, BSTU named after V. G. Shukhov, Belgorod, Russia. Her interests are energy-saving technologies in the grinding of materials, energy-saving equipment, innovation, new technologies, technological parks, business incubators, startups created based on universities. She has won awards in various innovation-oriented programmes, foreign competitions, and grants.

Entrepreneurship in Uruguay

María Ximena Fernández Delucchi and Nicolás Gambetta Lopassio

Abstract

This chapter provides insight into the entrepreneurial ecosystem and the small and medium-size enterprises situation in Uruguay. The study begins with a historical overview, analyzes the current state of entrepreneurship, the business environment and ends highlighting the challenges and opportunities for entrepreneurs and investors in the country.

1 Introduction

This chapter is about entrepreneurship and small and medium-sized companies in Uruguay, a parliamentary democracy in South America with a small population of 3.5 million people. Administratively, Uruguay is divided into 19 departments covering a total area of 318,000 square kilometers; about 40% of the total population lives in the capital city, Montevideo (Instituto Nacional de Estadística, 2017). The country stands out in the region for being an egalitarian society, showing in 2019 a GINI Index of 0.39 (being USD 9.798 and 0.46 the LATAM average respectively) (Uruguay XXI, 2020a).

Uruguay is positioned among the first places in the Latin America and the Caribbean region in relation to various political and social stability indices: #1 democracy (The Economist, 2019), #1 in inclusive development (World Economic Forum, 2018), #1 in low corruption perception (Transparency International, 2019) and #1 in Rule of law (World Justice Project, 2019). Montevideo is the city with the best quality of life in Latin America (Uruguay XXI, 2019a). Likewise, it leads among emerging markets in the J-ESG-EMBI index (Emerging Markets Bonds

M. X. F. Delucchi (✉) · N. G. Lopassio
School of Management and Social Sciences, Universidad ORT Uruguay, Montevideo, Uruguay
e-mail: fernandez_mx@ort.edu.uy; gambetta@ort.edu.uy

L.-P. Dana et al. (eds.), *Entrepreneurship in South America*, Springer Texts in Business and Economics, https://doi.org/10.1007/978-3-030-97060-4_13

Index) of the financial firm J.P. Morgan, which incorporates a medium-term sustainability perspective in its country risk assessment (Uruguay XXI, 2020b).

All these indicators make of Uruguay a reliable country for foreign investments, and this is backed by the figures: the stock of Foreign Direct Investment (FDI) for the period 1990–2019 represents 49% of the country's GDP (Uruguay XXI, 2020a).

2 Historical Context

Uruguay, prior to its discovery by the Spanish in 1516, was populated by a few thousand indigenous people, mainly "charrúas". The arrival of the Europeans and the cattle and horses that they abandoned at the beginning of the seventeenth century in Uruguayan territory, modified the habitat, demography and customs of these indigenous people. The Banda Oriental, a designation that the Spanish gave to the Uruguayan territory, was a region of late colonization, contemporary especially with the Spain of the Bourbons in the eighteenth century. It was populated for three fundamental reasons: the quality of its natural pasture combined with the multiplication of cattle abandoned by the Spaniards on its plains; the advantages of Montevideo as the only natural port of the Río de la Plata; and the condition of border territory in permanent dispute between the crowns of Spain and Portugal (Barrán, 1995a).

From 1811 to 1814 the Orientals fought against Spain, trying with Buenos Aires help to occupy Montevideo. From 1816 to 1820 he had to face the invasion of the Portuguese monarchy based in Rio de Janeiro. On August 25, 1825, the Chamber of Representatives first declared the absolute independence of the country. In 1830 an elected Assembly approved the Constitution of the new country, officially called, "República Oriental del Uruguay". The legal regime apparently ensured internal order, inspired by European and North American models. The new state would be republican and would guarantee individual rights through the classic separation of the three powers (Barrán, 1995b).

The Uruguay of 1830 barely had 70,000 inhabitants. That of 1875 already had 450,000 and that of 1900 a million. The spectacular growth—the population multiplied by 14 in 70 years—was unmatched in any American country, being the European immigration the crucial factor in the demographic revolution. French, Italians, and Spanish until 1850, Italians and Spanish later, arrived in 4 or 5 waves during the nineteenth century. Uruguay at the end of the nineteenth century thus had economic characteristics that distinguished it in the Latin American context. It produced food—meat—and satisfied two other basic needs of man, his footwear, with leather, and his clothing with wool (Barrán, 1995c).

The third stage of the history of Uruguay in the twentieth century (1959–1985), was characterized by crisis and economic stagnation and, in its final years (1973–1985), by the fall of democratic institutions and the installation of a military dictatorship which concluded in 1984. In 1991, Uruguay went on to found and integrate Mercosur, a customs economic alliance that includes it together with Brazil, Argentina and Paraguay (Barrán, 1995d).

3 The Environment for Entrepreneurship

3.1 Economic and Business Environment

Uruguay shows an annual average growth rate of 3.3% in the period 2009–2019 and a per capita income of USD 17.029 (2019 current USD) (International Monetary Fund, 2020). Investment in Uruguay is declared of national interest by law. Foreign investors are granted the same incentives as local investors, so there is no tax discrimination or restrictions for transferring profits abroad. Uruguay counts with several incentives which adjust to different types of activities, from industrial to commercial and service activities. Some of the main incentive schemes available in the country are free zones, free port and free airport schemes, public-private partnership agreements, industrial parks, and temporary admission. The Investment Law specifies that promotional declaration can fall on a specific sector activity. Furthermore, several sectors enjoy specific incentive schemes including, but not limited to, afforestation, graphic industry, maritime and air navigation, software, vehicles or auto parts, biofuels, communication and housing industry (Uruguay XXI, 2015).

Uruguay is a founding member of MERCOSUR, the Southern Cone trading bloc in which Argentina, Brazil and Paraguay are also members. Uruguay is a country with an investment grade, ratified by the main credit rating agencies, such as Moody's, Standard & Poor's and Fitch Ratings, and is usually identified as a beef and wool exporter. But the 2019 USD 16 billion goods and services exports are diversified in the following main categories: 21% non-traditional services (trading, business services, ICTs), 16% tourism, 15% beef, 12% pulp (wood, paper) and 11% agriculture (soy, rice, malta, wheat, citrus fruits, wine and honey). The destinations of the exports are Asia and the Middle East (36%), South America (24%), Europe (21%), North America (10%) and Africa (5%) (Uruguay XXI, 2020a). Uruguay has one of the highest investments in clean energy in Latin American countries and it is also at the forefront of global production of electricity from wind power. Nearly 97% of electricity is produced from renewable sources of which 38% comes from wind farms (Uruguay XXI, 2020c) (Fig. 1).

Uruguay is taking a bottom-up, country-appropriate approach to the 2030 Agenda, focusing on building a future that is more inclusive, environmentally sustainable, and economically viable for all. Even though there is still limited cross-sector engagement with the Sustainable Development Goals (SDGs), there is growing interest in both public and private sectors, in how multi-stakeholder could be operationalized in practice (Eversole & Gambetta, 2019). Uruguay is making a significant progress towards achieving the SDGs, but in addition to the financing mechanisms and the funds needed to advance significantly in the 2030 Agenda, the country needs a system of coordination and cooperation between public and private agents, and international cooperation for training in techniques and measurement standards associated with sustainability (Gambetta et al., 2019) (Fig. 2).

Fig. 1 Puerto del Buceo, Montevideo. Source: © Nicolás Gambetta

Fig. 2 Aerial view Rambla Armenia, Montevideo. Source © Nicolás Gambetta

3.2 SMEs in Uruguay

The last survey done in Uruguay to understand the status of the SMEs in the country was performed in 2017 by the Ministry of Industry, Energy and Mining (MIEM, 2017). The total number of Micro, small and medium enterprises (MSMEs) in Uruguay was 151.910, up 11% from 136.691 in the 2012 survey. The 51% of these firms are in the services sector, the 39% are in the trade sector and the remaining 11% in the industrial sector, while the 50% of all these firms are located in the capital city. Regarding the ownership, only the 35% is owned by women, but the MSMEs owners' educational level is high compared to the Uruguayan population, as the 33% shows studies higher than secondary level (secondary, undergraduate and postgraduate level). Figures show that the employment share of the

Uruguayan MSMEs is around 40% of the country's total, but the contribution to the national GDP is lower because of low productivity levels (MIEM, 2017).

The survey identifies some challenges these companies face to scale their business, being the access to financing sources the most relevant: only 8% of the MSMEs have access to financing sources without problems, another 19% access to financing sources but with some difficulties, 20% is not able to get financing and 53% of the SMEs prefers not to get financing from third parties. The difficulties to get funds are explained by limited income, lack of financial information and low credit ratings. Additionally, the MSMEs have limited access to business networks; less than 40% of these companies are involved in a commercial network. Other significant difficulties the MSMEs show are lack of technology, lack of trained human resources and low scale of production (MIEM, 2017).

In 2018, the core of goods exporting companies in Uruguay was made up of 764 companies, of which 77% are MSMEs. Despite its numerical importance, MSMEs represent only 7% of the exported value. It is important to note that exporting MSMEs generate 22% of the jobs in the exporting companies, which is representing approximately 13,521 people (Uruguay XXI, 2019b). Exporting MSMEs have a lower export survival rate than large companies. Only 28% of the exporting MSMEs exported 15 years uninterrupted. This percentage rises to 66% in the case of large companies. This shows the importance of public policy in the design of support tools aimed at promoting the internationalization of this type of company (Uruguay XXI, 2019b).

In this line, the Uruguayan government recently launched a programme to promote the SMEs' inclusion into Global Value Chains (GVCs), (ANDE, 2019).

3.3 The Entrepreneurial Ecosystem

Uruguay has attracted some attention this year with the emergence of DLocal as its first unicorn and the development of a COVID-19 app within a week to track active cases (Financial Times, 2020).

Based on a software industry that began to develop in the 1980s (CEPAL, 2016), Uruguay is the leading software exporter per capita in South America, and the third in absolute terms behind Argentina and Chile, selling to 52 markets, with USA as first destination (ICEX España Exportación e Inversiones, 2019)".

The country has gained a reputation for Information Technology Outsourcing (ITO) service, consolidating as a strategic platform for implementation and testing of potential global solutions. With the arrive in 2002 of the leading Indian offshore services company Tata Consultancy Services (TCS), "Uruguay has expanded its presence as a regional shared services provider, logistics hub and financial services centre" (CEPAL, 2016, p. 15).

The World Bank position Uruguay 101 out of 190 in the "Easy to doing business ranking 2020".

The favourable regulatory framework, and its technological infrastructure, with high internet penetration and one the of fastest download speed of broadband in

Latin America (Statista Research Department, 2020), "make Uruguay the Latin American leader in ICTs and a first-class business centre" (Serron, 2018).

With a strong statist culture, people in Uruguay value the state as a main actor to solve problems for the population (Kantis & Federico, 2005). According to Hofstede's model Uruguay is a collective society with a 99 out of 100 score in uncertainty avoidance which shows the fact that "innovation is not really encouraged, and security is an important element to individual motivation" (Burleson et al., 2018).

Entrepreneurship is not a highly valued activity, since the "High Status to Successful Entrepreneurs" rate—percentage of 18–64 population who agree with the statement that in their country, successful entrepreneurs receive high status—is 49.5% compared with a global rate of 69.5% (GEM, 2018).

According to the last Global Entrepreneurship Monitor report, the Total early-stage Entrepreneurial Activity (TEA) in Uruguay is 15.7% (GEM, 2018) compared with a regional average of 18.2%. The results show an increase of nascent and new entrepreneurs' rate, but a decrease in the established business owners rate, setting a ratio of opportunity to necessity entrepreneurs in 2.4 (Veiga et al., 2016). In terms of female entrepreneurship, there is a marked difference in the level of entrepreneurial activity between men and women in Uruguay, with a TEA of 12.3% for women vs. 19.4% for man (GEM, 2018). Women see themselves less capable than men, identify fewer opportunities and have more fear to failure, which translates in fewer intentions and less entrepreneurial activity (Veiga, 2020). Labour segregation and gender wage gaps are structural characteristics of the labour market in Uruguay, both very related, the first is determined by the strongest feminization of certain occupations and the second caused by the "glass ceiling" (Espino, 2017, p. 131).

Recently, a study presented by Global Ecosystem Dynamics (GED), affiliate to D-LAB Local Innovation Group of the Massachusetts Institute of Technology (MIT), has recognized Uruguay's entrepreneurship ecosystem like the most collaborative in Latin America. The study, an ecosystem mapping shows that the city of Montevideo counts with the largest amount of collaborations in the region, with more than 751 mapped collaborations between 198 identified stakeholders, giving Montevideo a collaboration index of 6.9, concluding that Montevideo "presents itself with solid foundations to be recognized as a leading innovation-based entrepreneurship ecosystem in Latin America", (Tedesco et al., 2020, p. 6).

The Index of Systemic Conditions for Dynamic Entrepreneurship (ICSEd-Prodem) is a tool that helps to identify the main strengths and weaknesses of countries for the emergence and development of dynamic enterprises, those that have the greatest capacity to create quality jobs and diversify the productive structure of the region (Kantis et al., 2018). Uruguay ranks 49 out of 64 globally and ranks fifth in Latin America, right behind Chile, Mexico, Argentina and Costa Rica (Kantis et al., 2019). This latest report highlights particularly Uruguay's conditions for digital development due to the internet access and the digital competences of the population.

With 90+ actors, Uruguay entrepreneurial ecosystem seeks to articulate policies and action from the public sector, academia and the civil society. The National

Development Agency (ANDE) created in 2017, coordinates the Support Network for Future Entrepreneurs (RAFE) and the "Uruguay Emprendedor", which is a contact platform that links the entire system, where entrepreneurs can get the support they need, contact the institutions of the ecosystem and exchange with other entrepreneurs (Kantis et al., 2019, p. 52).

The National Research and Innovation Agency (ANII) is a governmental entity that promotes research and the application of new knowledge to the productive and social reality of the country. ANII makes available to the public funds for research projects, national and international postgraduate scholarships and incentive programmes for innovative culture and entrepreneurship, both in the private and public sectors. ANII is the main source of financing for new ventures projects through the support to Entrepreneurship Sponsoring Institutions (IPEs) which carry out the dissemination, capture, implementation and evaluation of contest and monitoring of projects that wish to carry out a Business Idea Validation. In 2019 ANII launched a call to escalate ventures of the region from Uruguay called Meet the Entrepreneurs. Through this mechanism, ANII approved 160 projects, 8 co-investment founds and 11 incubators; and also launched the platform Trama.uy, a social network to connect entrepreneurs, researchers, businesspeople, investors and talents to share experiences and allows finding contributors, enables promotion and attracts investors (ANII, Annual Report, 2019).

4 Toward the Future

At the end of 2019, Uruguay approved a new legal framework: The Law N° 19.820 for the Promotion of Entrepreneurship. The regulation provides authorization for collective financing platforms and simplified share companies, the promotion of the "Uruguay Entrepreneur" brand and the creation of an Entrepreneurship Advisory Council. The new law declares of interest the consolidation of the entrepreneurial ecosystem, the dissemination of the entrepreneurial culture and the promotion of associative ventures and aims to increase the scope of public policies for entrepreneurial promotion. The text also emphasizes the relevance of constant articulation with the educational system. The legal entity type, the Simplified Joint-Stock Companies ("SAS"), allows companies that have an annual turnover of less than USD 100,000 (approximate conversion to USD) to register as simplified joint-stock companies. Also, for the SAS, the registration time and costs will be reduced, with an entirely digitalized process.

Signalling a course change after 15 years of a centre-left coalition government, Luis Lacalle Pou, son of the former president Luis Alberto Lacalle de Herrera and leader of the centre-right National Party, assumed the presidency of Uruguay in March 2020 backed by a multi-party coalition. In the middle of the COVID-19 pandemic, the government of Luis Lacalle Pou seeks to attract a significant flow of foreign investments, relaxing tax residency requirements and extending the tax holiday regime. According to decree 163/020, foreigners who live at least 60 days a year in Uruguay and buy real estate valued currently the equivalent to USD

380.000 or invest certain amount of money in a business and create at least 15 full-time jobs will qualify for tax residency. Considering the regional social and economic instability, the prospect for Uruguay looks promising.

5 Case Study

Bracco Bosca is a totally hands-on Uruguayan family boutique winery, focused on the production and export of fine wines, located in the wine-growing region of Canelones.

The Canelones area is a small area near the capital city of Montevideo that concentrates the 60% of Uruguay's grapes production, which benefits from coastal breezes and cooler temperatures of the Atlantic Ocean, favouring the production of both, red and white wines.

While Bracco Bosca was founded in 2005, its vineyards have been in the family for five generations since the family arrived from Piedmont, Italy to Uruguay and established in the region aimed to continue the winery tradition.

It was Darwin Bracco and Mirtha Bosca who decided to buy the land where today the vineyards are located and became the base for the construction of the winery. The 11 hectares are located in Laguna del Cisne, a protected area that supplies drinking water to more than 22,000 households and where they plant varieties such as Merlot, Cabernet Franc, Cabernet Sauvignon, Tannat, Moscatel, Ugni Blanc, Syrah and Petit Verdot.

Since Fabiana Bracco, −one of the most charismatic and energetic leaders of the Uruguayan wine industry-, took over the management of the family business in 2016, they have conquered important foreign markets devoting 80% of their 80,000 l production to export. Today Bracco Bosca winery is present in 18 countries including Canada, the USA, Mexico, Brazil, Peru, Costa Rica, Panama, Paraguay and have a hub in Germany, that redistributes the brand to Austria, Switzerland, UK, Ireland, and France (Figs. 3 and 4).

The Tannat classic of the brand received two awards: the "Decantater of Englan", one of the best among 72 wines, with 92 points, and one of the 100 best wines in the world under US$ 15, with 91 points in the list of "Wines and Spirits". Also, the Cabernet Franc, received many awards, including the "Best Cabernet Franc in Latin America", by the "Tasting Guide" and the "Cabernet Franc Revelation", by the "Descorchados Guide". This year, besides Covid effects, Bracco Bosca winery has exported to Brasil and thanks to "Sembrando"—a governmental programme that seeks to strengthen entrepreneurial initiatives—is getting their wine placed on exclusive supermarket shelves available exclusively for products of Uruguayan entrepreneurs. Being a very difficult year due to the Covid-19 crisis, Bracco Bosca Winery took a big step into the wine tourism sector and inaugurated a Nordic-style cabin, stylish with their own imprint based on sustainability, named "Viña Viva by Bracco Bosca" that allows guests to live the experience of nature and wine production in the middle of the vineyard.

Fig. 3 BRACCOBOSCA family vineyard @ 2021 BRACCOBOSCA

Uruguay stands out in the world for its commitment to build a sustainable economy that promotes efficient use of natural resources, in terms of wine production according to INAVI (the local wine industry regulator), the country counts today with 100% of the Uruguayan vineyards georeferenced, which allows having a geographical viewer of the vineyards, as well as moving towards the traceability of the country's wine production. "Being in a protected area helps a lot when it comes to selling abroad, buyers are attracted by the traceability of the product and this constitutes a competitive advantage for our winery", expresses Fabiana.

6 Conclusion

The evolution of the Uruguayan entrepreneurial ecosystem in the last decades is leading the country to a new era. The country was seen in the past as a welfare state, bureaucratic and full of regulations, characteristics that together hamper formal entrepreneurship (Dana, 1997). In the 2020 edition of the United Nations' E-government Survey, Uruguay ranks 26 in the world and second in the Americas behind the United States (United Nations, 2020). In this line, the President of the Chamber of Representatives launched in 2020 the "Legislative Modernization Programme" which proposes to expressly repeal obsolete laws that generate interpretive difficulties and to identify those that are inapplicable in practice due to lack of

Fig. 4 Monitoring harvest time @ 2021 BRACCOBOSCA

regulation. The main objective of the programme is to simplify the national regulatory system and adapt the national legal system to the reality of the twenty-first century, incorporating the use of new technologies (Poder Legislativo, 2020). And as an example of how a small country can make the difference in the global stage, an Uruguayan virologist is the only Latin American on this year's list of " Nature's 10: ten people who helped shape science in 2020, a selection of 10 individuals who, according to the prestigious British scientific publication,", were part of some of the biggest events in the world of science in 2020 ". In this case, Gonzalo Moratorio and his team from the Pasteur Institute and the Universidad de la República, designed a coronavirus test and a national programme for administering it.

Add to this modern and innovative profile of the country its social and economic stability and its approach to sustainable development. All these ingredients make of Uruguay the perfect country to innovate and use the country as a platform to launch and scale projects globally.

More investment is needed in research and development, multi-stakeholders partnership must be reinforced and the education system needs to be modernized urgently. But, viewed as a serious country worldwide, Uruguay is respected and well positioned to attract foreign direct investments and support form multilateral credit agencies to overcome its budgetary constraints.

Do not look for quantity in such a small country, you will get quality. The SMEs are calling the attention of the government as their relevance in the economy is appreciated by the public sector and the community, mainly in regional Uruguay. A great example of this is our case study, the Bracco Bosca family boutique winery, a respected family-owned business taking the name of Uruguay to the world.

References

Agencia Nacional de Investigación e Innovación (2019). *ANII Annual Report 2019. Building the Uruguay of the future*. Retrieved January 12, 2021, from https://www.anii.org.uy/upcms/files/listado-documentos/documentos/memoria-2019-ingl-s.pdf

Barrán, J. P. (1995a). *El Uruguay indígena y español*. Red Académica Uruguaya. Universidad de la República. Retrieved January 14, 2021, from https://www.rau.edu.uy/uruguay/historia/Uy.hist1.htm

Barrán, J. P. (1995b). *El Uruguay pastoril y caudillesco en la primera mitad del siglo XIX*. Universidad de la República. Retrieved January 14, 2021, from https://www.rau.edu.uy/uruguay/historia/Uy.hist2.htm

Barrán, J. P. (1995c). *El nacimiento del Uruguay moderno en la segunda mitad del siglo XIX*. Universidad de la República. Retrieved January 14, 2021, from https://www.rau.edu.uy/uruguay/historia/Uy.hist3.htm

Barrán, J. P. (1995d). *Uruguay siglo XX*. Universidad de la República. Retrieved January 14, 2021, from https://www.rau.edu.uy/uruguay/historia/Uy.hist4.htm

Burleson, R., Zhou, P., Mawji, A., Herrera, G., & Masrour, S. (2018). *Comparing Cape Verde, USA, & Uruguay* (p. 60). Global Business Research.

Comisión Económica para América Latina y el Caribe, CEPAL. (2016). *Employment Situation in Latin America and the Caribbean: Global supply chains and decent work*. UN/ILO.

Dana, L. P. (1997). A contrast of Argentina and Uruguay: The effects of government policy on entrepreneurship. *Journal of Small Business Management, 35*(2), 99.

Espino, A. (2017). Gender equality in Uruguay. In *Gender equality in a global perspective* (pp. 140–165). Routledge.

Eversole, R., & Gambetta, N. (2019). Reimagining development institutions for the SDG era: Pathways to impact. In F. W. Leal, A. Azul, L. Brandli, P. Özuyar, & T. Wall (Eds.), *Partnerships for the goals. Encyclopedia of the UN sustainable development goals*. Springer. https://doi.org/10.1007/978-3-319-71067-9_48-1

Financial Times. (2020). *Thriving tech scene allows Uruguay to shine during pandemic*. Accessed January 1, 2021, from https://www.ft.com/content/c0d64a95-8cda-40d7-9cdc-08cf1ea06542

Gambetta, N., Azadian, P., & Hourcade, V. (2019). Reyes, M.E. The financing framework for sustainable development in emerging economies: The case of Uruguay. *Sustainability, 11*, 1059.

GEM Global Entrepreneurship Monitor. (2018). *Reporte Nacional de Uruguay del GEM 2018*. IEEM Centro de Emprendimiento. Retrieved from https://www.ieem.edu.uy/pdf/noticias/392/reporte-nacional-gem-2018.pdf

ICEX España Exportación e Inversiones. (2019). *El mercado del software en Uruguay*. Retrieved January 12, 2021, from https://www.icex.es/icex/es/navegacion-principal/todos-nuestrosservicios/informacion-de-mercados/estudios-de-mercados-y-otros-documentos-de-comercioexterior/DOC2019833701.html

Instituto Nacional de Estadística. (2017). *Anuario Estadístico. (2017)*. Montevideo, Uruguay.

International Monetary Fund. (2020). *World Economic Outlook: The Great Lockdown*. Washington, DC, April.

Kantis, H., & Federico, J. (2005). *Empresarialidad y contexto emprendedor en Uruguay*. Inter-American Development Bank, Regional Operations Department I.

Kantis, H., Federico, J., & Ibarra, S. (2018). *Condiciones sistémicas para el emprendimiento dinámico en América Latina*. Asociación Civil Red Pymes Mercosur. Digital book file:///C:/Users/dell/Downloads/InformePRODEM2018.pdf

Kantis, H., Federico, J., & Ibarra, S. (2019). *Condiciones sistémicas para el emprendimiento en América Latina: emprendimientos y digitalización: una agenda común de posibilidades y desafíos*. Asociación Civil Red Pymes Mercosur. Digital book https://prodem.ungs.edu.ar/wp-content/uploads/2019/11/Informe-PRODEM-2019-VF-28.11.pdf

Ministerio de Industria, Energía y Minería. (2017). *Encuesta Nacional de Mipymes industriales, comerciales y de servicios*. Tercera edición. Ministerio de Industria, Energía y Minería

Poder Legislativo. (2020). *Programa de modernización legislativa recibirá aportes de la ciudadanía*. Retrieved January 14, 2021, from https://parlamento.gub.uy/noticiasyeventos/noticias/node/92796

Serron, C. (2018). *Uruguay: The Silicon Valley of South America. Medium*. Retrieved from https://medium.com/bros/uruguay-the-silicon-valley-of-south-america-8cdef0bbcadc.

Statista Research Department. (2020). *Average download speed of broadband internet in Latin American countries from July 2019 to June 2020*. Accessed January 1, 2021, from https://www.statista.com/statistics/1010977/internet-download-speed-latin-america-by-country

Tedesco, M. S., Serrano, T., Sánchez, V., Ramos, F., & Hoffecker, E. (2020). *Ecosistemas de Emprendimiento Basados en Innovación en Iberoamérica: Resumen ejecutivo Ciudad de Montevideo*. MIT D-Lab.

The Economist. (2019). *The Economist Intelligence Unit's Democracy Index*. Retrieved January 14, 2021, from https://www.economist.com/graphic-detail/2020/01/22/global-democracy-has-another-bad-year

Transparency International. (2019). *Corruption Perceptions Index*. International Transparency. Retrieved January 14, 2021, from https://www.transparency.org/en/cpi/2019/results

United Nations. (2020). *United Nations E-Government Surveys: 2020 Digital Government in the Decade of Action for Sustainable Development*. United Nations Department of Economic and Social Affairs. United Nations.

Uruguay XXI. (2015). *Investment promotion schemes. Investors' guide*. Uruguay XXI.

Uruguay XXI. (2019a). *Montevideo is the South American city with the highest quality of life*. Uruguay XXI. Retrieved January 14, 2021, from https://www.uruguayxxi.gub.uy/en/news/article/montevideo-es-la-ciudad-sudamericana-con-mayor-calidad-de-vida/

Uruguay XXI. (2019b). *Caracterización de las Mipymes exportadoras de bienes en Uruguay. Documento de Trabajo No12. Departamento de Inteligencia Competitiva*. Instituto Uruguay XXI.

Uruguay XXI. (2020a). *Invest, export, work, live*. Uruguay XXI.

Uruguay XXI. (2020b). *Uruguay, el país emergente más atractivo para invertir*. Uruguay XXI. Retrieved January 14, 2021, from https://www.investinuruguay.uy/es/noticias/articulo/uruguay-el-pais-emergente-mas-atractivo-para-invertir/

Uruguay XXI. (2020c). *Why Uruguay?* Uruguay XXI. Retrieved January 14, 2021, from https://www.investinuruguay.uy/es/noticias/articulo/uruguay-el-pais-emergente-mas-atractivo-para-invertir/

Veiga, L. (2020). El emprendimiento femenino en Uruguay. *IEEM Revista de Negocios*. Retrieved January 14, 2021, from https://www.hacerempresa.uy/el-emprendimiento-femenino-en-uruguay/

Veiga, L., Chaquiriand, I., & Bartesaghi, A. (2016). Las barreras a la actividad emprendedora en Uruguay. *IEEM Revista de Negocios, 19*(4), 38–42.

World Economic Forum. (2018). *The inclusive development index*. World Economic Forum.

World Justice Project. (2019). *Rule of Law Index 2019*. The World Justice Project.

Professor María Ximena Fernández Delucchi is Director of postgraduate degrees in human resources management at Universidad ORT Uruguay. Her research interests include organizational culture and climate, entrepreneurship in higher education and gender. Member of AFIDE, the Association for Training, Research and Development of Entrepreneurship. She teaches female leadership at undergraduate level and research workshops at postgraduate level. Professor Fernández Delucchi qualifications: BS in sociology (Universidad de la República, Uruguay) and PhD in Research Methods in Education (Universidad Complutense de Madrid, Spain).

Professor Nicolás Gambetta is Director of postgraduate degrees in accounting and taxation at Universidad ORT Uruguay. His research interests are assurance services and auditing, social and environmental accounting, sustainable development, and banking. His research has been published in leading journals such as The British Accounting Review, Journal of Business Research, International Review of Economics and Finance, Service Business, among others. He is also the executive advisory board member of the Australian Studies Centre at Universidad ORT Uruguay. Professor Gambetta qualifications: BBus (Universidad de la República, Uruguay), MBus (University of Technology Sydney) and PhD in Accounting (Universidad de Valencia, Spain).

Entrepreneurship in Venezuela

Nunzia Auletta, Urbi Garay, Patricia Monteferrante, and Aramis Rodríguez-Orosz

Abstract

Venezuelan entrepreneur's face an enormous challenge in surviving both an economy that has collapsed (with an estimated cumulative GDP decline of 75% between 2014 and 2020), and a notorious absence of public policies aimed at promoting and consolidating a healthy entrepreneurship ecosystem. In spite of this, several remarkable dynamic initiatives prove that opportunities may arise for those with the motivations, right skills, and capabilities. The reconstruction of the Venezuelan business sector and its economy necessarily requires supporting and nurturing these types of individual initiatives. This effort requires that all actors of the ecosystem create opportunities for collaboration, as well as increasing the participation of new actors, such as the large and increasing Venezuelan diaspora.

1 Introduction

In 2011, Venezuela was one of the leading countries in the rankings of early entrepreneurial activities. This apparent good news was shadowed by the poor survival rates of new initiatives and their lack of impact on employment and economic development. In what has become one of the worst-performing economies in the world, the entrepreneurship potential in the country is yet to unfold.

N. Auletta · P. Monteferrante · A. Rodríguez-Orosz
Entrepreneurship Center, IESA Business School, Caracas, Venezuela
e-mail: nunzia.auletta@iesa.edu.ve; patricia.monteferrante@iesa.edu.ve; aramis.rodriguez@iesa.edu.ve

U. Garay (✉)
Finance Center, IESA Business School, Caracas, Venezuela
e-mail: urbi.garay@iesa.edu.ve

L.-P. Dana et al. (eds.), *Entrepreneurship in South America*, Springer Texts in Business and Economics, https://doi.org/10.1007/978-3-030-97060-4_14

However, a reservoir of entrepreneurial talent and a sample of successful ventures indicate that a proper development of an entrepreneurship ecosystem could foster sustainable private initiatives, based on specific capabilities, and focused both on economic performance and on social impact.

This chapter presents an overview of entrepreneurship in Venezuela and is organized as follows. Section 1 provides a historical and economic context for Venezuela. Section 2 is on the environment for entrepreneurship, looking at its entrepreneurial ecosystem. Section 3 hypothesizes about the future for entrepreneurship in Venezuela, considering that the country has been recently taking steps away from a centrally controlled economy, and toward a more market-friendly environment. Finally, we present a case study based on Venemergencia, a Venezuelan health care initiative that has gone from the emergency room to become a global health service provider, and brief conclusions.

2 Historical and Economic Context

Basic information and statistics about Venezuela:

Capital: Caracas
Largest cities (population, INE, 2011): Caracas (2,904,376), Maracaibo (1,906,205), and Valencia (1,396,322)
Population (2019): 28 million (IMF)
Area: 916,445 km^2 (353,841 square miles)
GDP (INE, 2010): USD 471.1 billion (current prices)
GDP: USD 204.3 billion (current prices).
Exports (BCV, 2018): USD 33.7 billion (Figs. 1 and 2)

Venezuela is a country located on the northern coast of South America. It is bordered on the north by the Caribbean Sea, on the west by Colombia, on the south by Brazil, on the east by Guyana, and on the northeast by Trinidad and Tobago.

The territory occupied by Venezuela today was colonized by Spain in the early XVI century. The economy started to become diversified in the XVII century, and cocoa and tobacco were cultivated on large plantations and sent to Spain. In 1728, the *Compañía Guipuzcoana de Caracas* began operations in Venezuela as a privileged trading company, until it was dissolved in 1785. Coffee, indigo, and cotton were introduced during those years (Dana, 1996). In 1811, Venezuela became one of the first territories in the Americas to declare independence from Spain (initially as a department of the Gran Colombia, and gaining full independence in 1830). The rest of the XIX century was a period of political instability, including the Federal (Civil) War (1859–1863). The first steps toward democracy were taken in 1935, when General Juan Vicente Gómez passed away, after a 27-year dictatorship. Democracy was finally gained in 1958, although the country has recently receded dramatically on that front.

Fig. 1 Map of Venezuela. Source: Taken from 123rf.com

Fig. 2 Caracas. Source: Authors' own

The Venezuelan economy has been based primarily on the production and export of petroleum for almost 100 years. This helped the country to become the fastest growing economy in the world between 1927 and 1977. Ample oil income during that period aided modernize a country that had been very poor until oil was discovered, helped to reduce poverty and lead to the surge of a large middle class.

Vast amounts of resources were spent on public programs such as education, health care, transport, and food subsidies. Venezuela became one of the most urbanized countries in Latin America.

Between the 1950s and the 1980s, the economic development model was based on the distribution of income generated by oil exports to the different sectors of the economy and on the adoption of an import-substitution model, like other Latin American and other developing countries, whereby the imports of final products were forbidden, to stimulate the creation of a national industry, which could import intermediate parts (Baptista, 1984). The import-substitution model collapsed in the late 1980s when oil prices declined and the national industry became highly uncompetitive. The economy was briefly opened in the 1990s, including the oil industry, only to be closed again at the beginning of the new millennium, when Hugo Chávez was elected President, and an inward-oriented model, as well as general price controls, exchanged rate controls, and massive expropriations of private companies were adopted, among other measures and policies, which were implemented at a time when oil prices were booming (2004–2014).

Venezuela has the world's largest known oil reserves and has been (until recent times) one of the world's leading oil exporters. Venezuela is one of the founding members of the OPEC (Organization of the Petroleum Exporting Countries). Oil has represented about a third of GDP, around 80–90% of total exports, and about half of government revenues during the past decades. Until the first decade of this century, Venezuela also manufactured and exported heavy industry products such as steel, cement, and aluminum. The Guri Dam, located in the south of the country, and one of the largest dams in the world, provides around 75% of electricity to Venezuela.

Venezuela received around 800,000 immigrants from Europe (Dana, 1996), mostly from Spain, Italy, and Portugal in the late 1940s and in the 1950s, at a time when the total population of Venezuela was only around four million people (early 1940s). Many Europeans were looking for a more promising future outside a continent that had been ravished by the Second World War. Venezuela also received very large immigration from other Latin American countries between the 1960s and the 1980s.

Faced with the collapse of oil production in recent years (in April of 2020 production was just 600 thousand barrels per day, in 1998 it was 3.2 million bpd), after years of mismanagement at Petróleos de Venezuela (PDVSA), the state-owned oil company, the economy has suffered an unprecedented collapse in the history of the continent, with a staggering estimated cumulative drop in GDP per capita of 75% between 2014 and 2020. The fall was of such magnitude that the GDP of Venezuelans has fallen back to the levels it had in the 1940s (Fig. 3). As a result of this collapse, the agricultural and industrial sectors have been working with an idle capacity greater than 70% (ANCE, 2020). By 2020, 64.8% of Venezuelan households experienced "multidimensional poverty" (Encovi, 2020), and the UNHCR registered that more than five million Venezuelans had left the country to "escape violence, insecurity and threats as well as lack of food, medicine and essential services."[1]

[1] https://www.unhcr.org/venezuela-emergency.html.

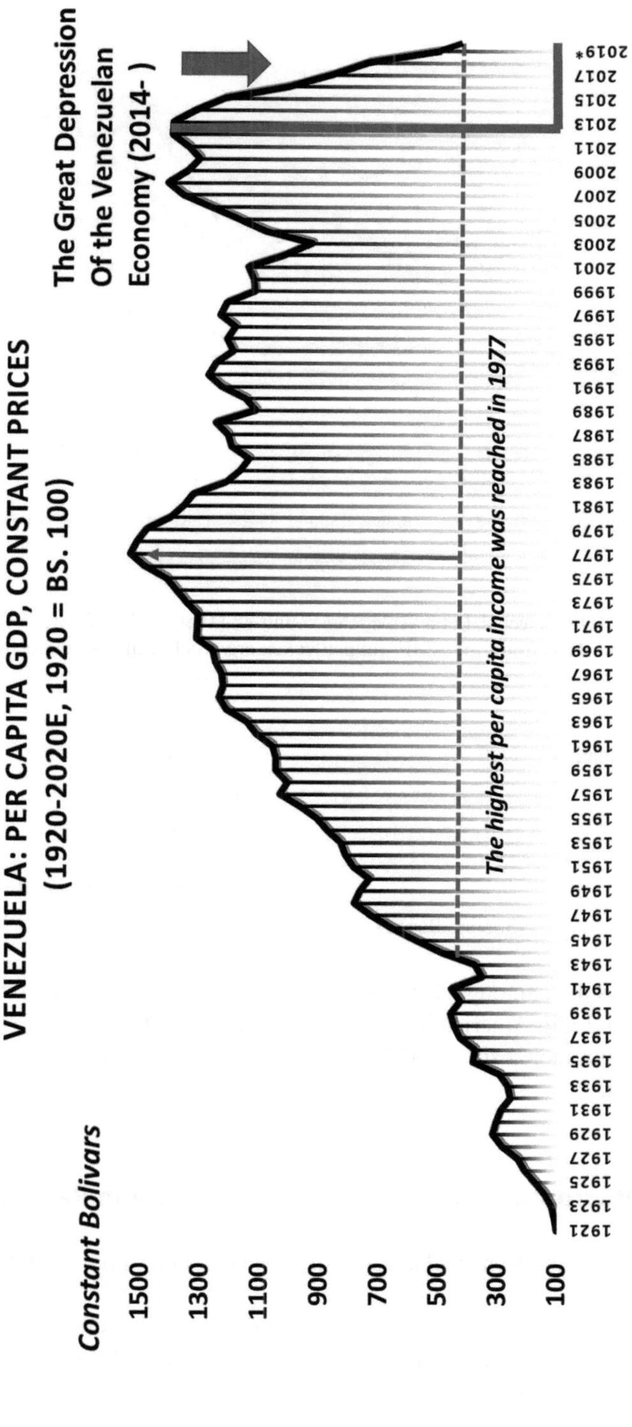

Fig. 3 Per capita GDP (Venezuela, 1920–2020). Sources: (1) GDP: From 1920 to 2008: Baptista (2011), from 2009 to 2018E: BCV, 2019E and 2020E: IMF. (2) Populatiion: From 1920 a 1979: Baptista (2011), from 1980 to 2020: IMF. Own calculations. @urbigaray

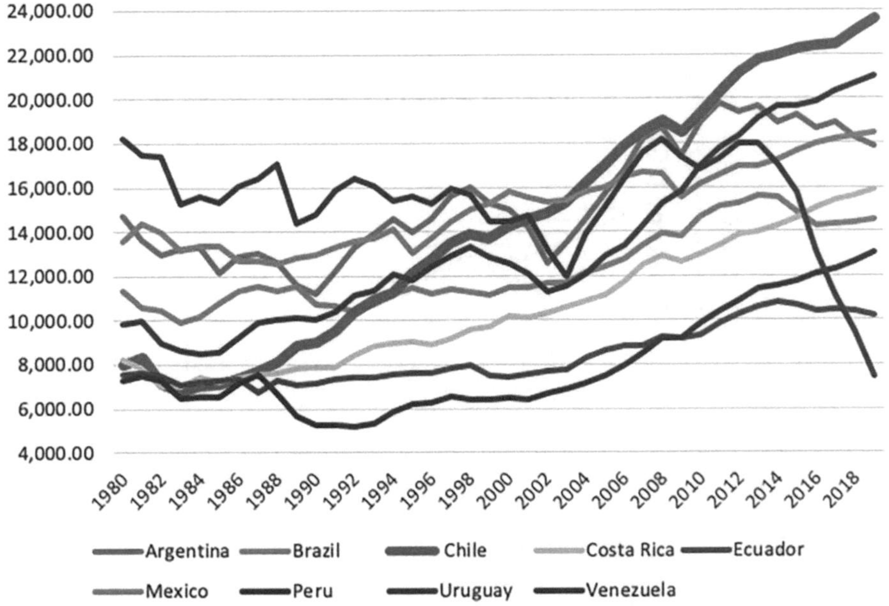

Fig. 4 Per capita GDP, selected Latin American countries (1980–2019). Source: Taken from Edwards, based on data from the IMF (https://voxeu.org/article/chile-s-insurgency-and-end-neoliberalism)

Table 1 Annual inflation rates

2016: 274%
2017: 863%
2018: 130,060%
2019: 9586%
2020: 6500% (estimation by the IMF)

Source: Banco Central de Venezuela

Figure 4 shows that, among a list of selected countries, Venezuela had the largest GDP per capita in Latin America in 1980. However, by 2019 it had the lowest GDP per capita, has plummeted since 2014, and at a time when the rest of the countries were catching up.

2.1 The Macroeconomic Situation in Venezuela in Recent Years

Since October 2017, the Venezuelan economy has been in a situation of hyperinflation (Table 1).

This hyperinflationary process has been accompanied by an unprecedented loss of value of the bolivar, which has led to an increasing (informal) dollarization of the economy, especially since 2018. It is estimated that at the end of 2020, two-thirds of the transactions inside Venezuela were being conducted in US dollars (Ecoanalitica, 2020). At the financial level, since the beginning of 2020 there has been a situation of illiquidity in the economy (marginal banks reserves have been placed at 100%), which has reduced financing to companies, in an environment of controlled interest rates.

Venezuela remains closed to international financial markets due to the selective default situation in which both PDVSA and the Republic have found themselves since the end of 2017. Total external debt rose (mid-2019), according to some private estimates, to about $160 billion (financial and nonfinancial debt). The external debt was equivalent to a staggering 200% of GDP. The budget deficit, which has already dragged on for 15 consecutive years, reached 20% of GDP in 2018, aggravated by the decrease in oil production (ANCE, 2020).

In 2019, the government started to free foreign exchange controls (which have been in place since 2003) to spur the economy. However, economic sanctions applied by the US Government and the European Union during the past few years, including a prohibition of oil imports from Venezuela in the USA, have negatively affected an economy that had already been in a downward spiral.

3 The Environment for Entrepreneurship

The environment for entrepreneurship in Venezuela can be understood through a look at its entrepreneurial ecosystem, which has been deemed as one of the least sophisticated in Latin America (Acs et al., 2018; Sela, 2016). The institutions in charge of formally building the reward structures for entrepreneurs have mainly been able to promote and determine unproductive entrepreneurial activity (Toro, 2020), understood as the generation of organizations that use their skills to compete for resources that already exist without increasing them, and without improving the country (Soltan Acz, according to Toro, 2020).

For almost a decade, the GEM[2] study has registered a high rate of early entrepreneurial activity (18.5% in 2011), but most Venezuelan startups end up becoming small or micro companies with a limited possibility of growth and survival (Auletta & Rivera, 2011; Auletta, Rodríguez and Vidal, 2010). The most relevant programs to support entrepreneurship in the Venezuelan entrepreneurial ecosystem focus their offer on traditional need-driven initiatives instead of fostering dynamic ones (Kantis et al., 2017; Sela, 2016), while in Latin America there is a more articulated and institutional effort in favor of ecosystems suitable for dynamic initiatives (Sela, 2016).

Unlike Venezuela, the entrepreneurial ecosystems of other Latin American countries have reached some development. Mexico and Colombia are working on their institutional framework, Uruguay and Peru's ecosystems are specializing, while Chile and Brazil have very mature ecosystems. Their State policies emphasize the

[2] Global Entrepreneurship Monitor Venezuelan Report (2011-2012).

development of dynamic entrepreneurship promoting a mix of support programs for different sectors, expanding the offer of financing for early entrepreneurship, strengthening the accompaniment through incubation and effective acceleration, and generating the necessary culture and spaces for networking and entrepreneurial social capital. Eight large groups of actors represent the bases of all ecosystems in Latin America and the Caribbean: venture capitalists, angel investors, generators of competitions and contact networks, mentors and consultants, business incubators, business accelerators, trainers, and service providers and coworking spaces.

In Venezuela, these actors lack completely from government support and public policies, and tend to operate in isolated initiatives that too often struggle to survive. This is the case of EneVenezuela (Venezuelan Entrepreneurial Ecosystem), a private initiative that in 2011 united more than 60 higher education institutions, foundations, NGOs, incubators, and financial institutions to promote entrepreneurship. Unfortunately, the worsening of economic conditions has weakened this initiative and has diminished its potential impact. As compared to its Latin American peers, the Venezuelan entrepreneurial ecosystem is made up of immature actors that are not supported by institutional programs (Sela, 2016).

The health of the entrepreneurial ecosystem in Venezuela has been estimated using the Global Entrepreneurship Index (GEI), which suggests that Venezuela has the lowest quality entrepreneurial ecosystem in Latin America (Acs et al., 2018). The index includes three aspects of entrepreneurial ecosystems: attitudes of the country toward entrepreneurship, entrepreneurial capabilities, and entrepreneurial aspirations. Out of these three dimensions, Venezuela presents better perspectives in attitudes toward entrepreneurship. Entrepreneurship is well regarded in the country, and entrepreneurs enjoy legitimacy and social status. This seems to be in line with the finding that, for more than 15 years, an increasing number of actors in the ecosystem have been specializing in disseminating entrepreneurial activity and training people who wanted to create businesses (Ojeda & Rodríguez, 2011). This, apparently, is reflected in the latest GEI measurements which highlight that one of the positive factors of the Venezuelan entrepreneurial ecosystem is in the pillar of startup skills. In fact, many of the people who start new ventures in Venezuela have a formal education and possess systematic and specialized training in technology, management, and business. However, such well-trained human capital often decides to migrate seeking opportunities to scale and to take their business ideas to a higher level. For instance, the founding team of Kavak, the first Mexican unicorn startup (valued at US $1.15 billion) (Medina, 2020), graduated from the Venezuelan educational system, but migrated to grow and develop as entrepreneurs. Loreanne García, Kavak's founder, commented that there is good talent in Venezuela, but that other essential factors such as capital, resources, and community are required to create a good entrepreneurial ecosystem in the country (LEI, 2020).

Most experts agree that Venezuelan entrepreneurs tend to be proactive, curious, take risks, and can manage few resources very efficiently. They also tend to be very resilient since they had to learn how to adapt quickly to a hostile environment. This potential could eventually lead to the emergence of dynamic ventures that in current times represent more the exception than the rule.

4 Toward the Future

The future of entrepreneurship in Venezuela looks quite uncertain and complex, considering the difficult political, social, and economic situation of the country. A large proportion of both formal and informal Venezuelan emerging initiatives are a response to the hostility of the environment, specifically to the low capacity of the economy to generate high-quality jobs. Thus, entrepreneurship in Venezuela is more need-based than opportunity-based, preventing its positive impact on economic development through employment, innovation, and welfare (Acs et al., 2019).

The presence of good entrepreneurial skills, highlighted by the GEI results, fuel success stories that evidence an opportunity-driven entrepreneurial movement with good potential for growth. For example, in 2019, more than 30 startups backed by the technology accelerator Wayra[3] managed to obtain financing. Similarly, in that same year, Venezuela was the Latin American winner of the Technovation Girls Challenge, a nonprofit organization that promotes young women to become technology entrepreneurs (Montacuti, 2020).

Digital technology has become instrumental to address both the economic collapse of Venezuela and the COVID-19 crisis. For example, Ubii Pagos, founded in 2013, offers an innovative mobile payment platform, so that small and large businesses can receive card payments, through smart devices, also feeding a business intelligence system. Likewise, Ubii Go delivery service application (available on App Store and Google Play) connects quarantined consumers to a wide network of allied businesses, contributing to operational continuity in the supply chain.

Social entrepreneurship is also playing a leading role in Venezuela, operating in the vacuum of public services and welfare systems. Thus, it is possible to find a venture like Leather Heart, the first certified B-Corp in Venezuela, which recycles textiles to make stuffed animals, t-shirts, and masks, employing women from excluded communities to promote their personal and family development and donating part of its production and sales to feed vulnerable children. An example of a hybrid venture is Venemergencia, an innovative health system (about which we will comment later), that operates in an intertwined manner with Venemergencia Foundation, its educational and social impact arm.

Many of these new ventures are closer to the so-called dynamic initiatives, that is, those that identify a business opportunity with high growth potential, on a regional or global scale, and that contribute significantly to the economic development of the country, in addition to generating new and better jobs (Hidalgo et al., 2014). However, what is it that makes it possible for dynamic ventures to emerge in such an unfavorable environment for the growth of private initiatives? Once again, we believe that this has to do with skills, but also with motivations and experiences of the founding entrepreneurial teams. Some Venezuelan entrepreneurs possess dynamic capabilities, defined as "the abilities to reconfigure a firm's resources and routines in the manner envisioned and deemed appropriate by its principal decision-

---

[3] The investment, open innovation, and entrepreneurship arm of Telefónica in Latin America.

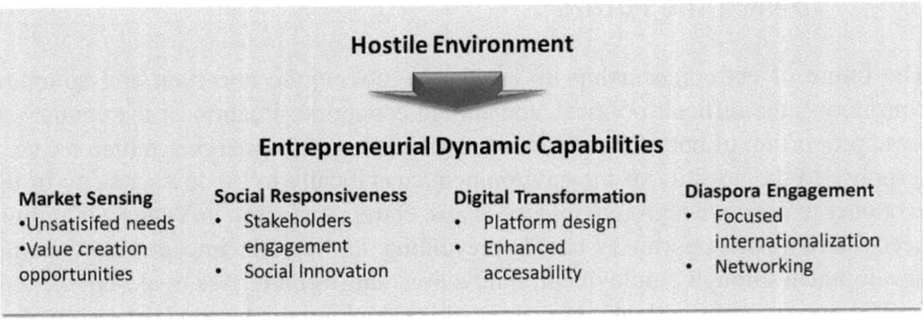

Fig. 5 Dynamic entrepreneurial capabilities. Source: Authors' elaboration based on Venezuelan cases

maker" (Zahra et al., 2006, p. 918), that allows them to seek opportunities and reconfigure resources to produce changes both at a business and at a social level. Specifically, four types of dynamic capabilities were found: market sensing, social responsiveness, digital transformation, and diaspora engagement (Fig. 5).

Market sensing, understood as the ability to perceive and react to the market environment and changes in terms of technological advance, consumer tastes and demands, innovation and value offer (Likoum et al., 2020), is a characteristic that is present in most of these Venezuelan entrepreneurial initiatives. The appearance of different technological platforms to respond to the payment needs of consumers and businesses are a specific example of this type of capacity. The responses to COVID-19, both in terms of product delivery and the provision of different services (e.g., hospitalization services and home medical consultation), are examples of these types of capacities.

Social responsiveness, the ability and willingness to take corrective actions to a social need and to contribute to the well-being of others, as well as to the improvement of society and the environment, is also a driver that is present in this group of Venezuelan entrepreneurial initiatives, particularly in the absence of a State capable and willing to guarantee the minimum rights and services for the population (e.g., Leather Heart and Venemergencia).

Digital transformation also seems to occupy an important place in such initiatives, allowing startups to take full advantage of digital technologies to improve current organizational systems, prepare for future changes, and achieve long-term profitability. The digital health and virtual medicine services offered by Venemergencia, as well as other digital platforms that are emerging in Venezuela to facilitate financial transactions, are examples of this type of capability.

Diaspora engagement, a distinctive type of market engagement, allows these ventures to build on a valuable network of Venezuelan talent in the world as well as to serve specific unsatisfied needs of Venezuelan migrants. For these entrepreneurial initiatives, the diaspora also constitutes a lever for the internationalization of products and services, considering that Venezuelans abroad are key players that can help promote market penetration.

5 Case Study: Venemergencia: From the Emergency Room to a Global Health Service

Venemergencia, a Venezuelan health care conglomerate, was founded in 2004 by Andrés Simón González-Silén[4] and Luis Velásquez Díaz, two young medical students inspired by their experiences in the emergency room. They worked long hours in the overcrowded services in public hospitals, where the resource limitations and low attention capacity resulted in patients subjected to long waits or hopelessly being taxied by ambulances from one hospital to another. They soon realized that many patients arrived in desperate conditions that could have been relieved by first aids, while others could have been treated at home or by a primary care network, avoiding ER overcrowding.

Their first business idea, teaching first aid courses, soon evolved into selling first aid kits and providing emergency medical services to businesses and events, expanding in a couple of years into occupational medicine. Always reinvesting their revenues in the business, they bought and refurbished a used ambulance, and by the time they became doctors, in 2007, they were managing a small venture with around 30 employees. What started as a combination of a hobby, moonlighting, and social concern, had become a profitable business with a long-term vision that demanded full attention. Recalling those times Dr. González-Silén commented:

> I come from a family of doctors, my father and grandfather, and all I always wanted to be a doctor. But Luis and I realized that either we were doctors, or we continued with the company. We faced that dilemma, thought about it for a week and decided to give up practicing as doctors since both things were incompatible if we wanted to succeed as entrepreneurs.

5.1 Business Growth and Digital Transformation

By 2020, Venemergencia registered a 60% annual growth in an economic context of steep recession and hyperinflation. They claimed to be "the most modern and efficient health system in Venezuela"[5] operating at preventive and primary level, and offering services focused on preventing unnecessary visits to clinics, providing the best quality of care for final users, and reducing operating costs for their two main segments of insurance companies (80% of revenue) and business clients (20% of revenue).

[4] Dr. González-Silén completed medical school at the Universidad Central de Venezuela and also holds an MBA from the Instituto de Estudios Superiores de Administración (IESA). His achievements have been recognized by the World Economic Forum's Young Global Leaders in 2015, Young Presidents Organization, Venezuelan Chapter in 2015, Millenium Leader 50—Group of Fifty in 2015, Venezuela Sin Límites and Schwab Foundation's Venezuela's social entrepreneur of the year in 2014, and Global Shapers in 2012.

[5] https://venemergencia.com/venemergencia.

Their main services included 24/7 primary care, ambulances, paraclinical exams, telemedicine and digital health, as well as home hospitalization, expanding on a national basis through a network of more than 50 allies. They employed more than 300 people including 150 response units (motorcycle and ambulances) with doctors and paramedics, 50 medical call center positions, bioanalysts, and a team of in-house developers who constantly improved the features of their digital health services. They were market leaders with 3.5 million affiliates nationwide, and the first to have a quality management system ISO 9001:2015 certification. Dr. González-Silén considered that their main differentiator was "the ability to set high standards and a sense of competition towards our own ideas."

As the company grew, professionalized, and went through different stages of digital transformation and operational optimization, they focused on data analytics, measuring the rate of use and data generated in their services. They provided their clients with detailed financial analysis about the return on investment, savings that were achieved by reducing patients' visits to clinics by more than 80%, and with a Global Index of satisfaction of 96%.

Telemedicine has proved to be a very cost-efficient way of granting access to health services. Of all the callers, just under 10% are emergencies requiring an ambulance, 30% can be solved by telemedicine, and the remaining 70% can be managed by a house call (out of which only 5% need to go to a clinic or to a hospital). The system produced savings of about USD five million per month for insurance companies and clinics.

5.2 Hybrid Organization and Public Health Services

Since its beginning, Venemergencia Group had the characteristics of being a hybrid organization, mixing the values and logics of a profit-generating venture, with the concerns of a social foundation, in which Venemergencia employees also acted as volunteers.

By 2020, Venemergencia Global Foundation had trained more than 18,000 people in first aid courses in low-income neighborhoods, creating Community Emergency Medical Brigades, which could attend a birth, or a heart attack and acting in first aids and classification of the injured. In 2014, they created a Certificate for Paramedics in alliance with Universidad Simón Bolívar (a public university in Caracas), with 200 theoretical-practical hours, to contribute to field operator professionalization which has successfully graduated five cohorts.

In 2019, the group developed the Public Access Telemedicine (TAP) service to provide free health care consults to Venezuelans nationwide on a 24-hour basis, signing alliances with local administrations interested in granting better access to social medicine to their residents. Commenting on TAP, Dr. González-Silén explained: "We are committed to everyone's health and this is one more step that we are taking to consolidate our social commitment to Venezuela, the engine that moves us as a company."

5.3 Diaspora Engagement and Internationalization

As a result of the Venezuelan diaspora many families have been divided, with younger members seeking opportunities abroad and parents and grandparents staying in the country and frequently surviving thanks to the remittances from emigrated relatives.

Mixing again their capability to identify market opportunities with their social commitment, the Group launched Asistensi Global Insurance, to support people in the diaspora to take care of their loved ones with immediate medical attention, and hospitalization and emergency insurance for people aged up to 99 years, in alliance with Mercantil Seguros, one of the leading insurance companies in Venezuela.

During COVID-19 pandemic, the Public Access Telemedicine services, now COVID SOS, has expanded to serve all Venezuelans in the world that need to quickly talk to a doctor about their symptoms, the probability of having been infected and receive home treatment recommendations. In only a few months this service has reached more than 120 thousand Venezuelans in the world, connecting doctors and patients in the diaspora. As Dr. Gonzalez-Silén commented:

> We launched an internal hackathon to develop the SOS program in only 5 days. With two clicks you can talk unlimited to a doctor. We may have a patient in Berlin talking to a doctor in Texas, since many Venezuelan doctors abroad, even those retired, have volunteered to participate. . . .We are working on the health service of the future and it is no coincidence that we are from our generation and we have been doing it from Venezuela.

This experience, along with the market success of Asistensi, was moving Grupo Venemergencia toward a steadier internationalization, expanding the concept of "taking care of your loved ones from abroad" to other migrant Latin American communities.

6 Conclusions

There is no doubt that Venezuelan entrepreneurs face a colossal challenge in surviving both an economy that has collapsed and an environment that is characterized by the lack of public policies toward the consolidation of a healthy entrepreneurship ecosystem. However, several outstanding dynamic initiatives show that, even in the midst of a deep crisis, opportunities may arise for those with the right skills, motivations, and capabilities. These initiatives are still scarce in Venezuela. However, and as suggested by Acs et al. (2019), in entrepreneurship, quality matters more than quantity.

Promoting the reconstruction of the Venezuelan business sector and its economy necessarily requires supporting and fostering these types of individual efforts. However, it is also essential to strengthen and expand the entrepreneurial ecosystem, taking a cue from the steps that have already been taken by other Latin American countries that have succeeded on that front. This endeavor necessarily requires that

Fig. 6 Venemergencia services

all actors of the ecosystem generate opportunities for collaboration, as well as enhancing the presence of new actors, such as the Venezuelan diaspora (Fig. 6).

References

Academia Nacional de Ciencias Económicas ANCE. (2020). *La pandemia del COVID-19 encuentra a la economía venezolana ya postrada*. Informe CESLA-Red Econolatin, Enero. Junio, p. 8.

Acs, Z. J., Szerb, L., Lafuente, E., & Márkus, G. (2019). *The global entrepreneurship index*. The Global Entrepreneurship and Development Institute.

Acs, S., Szerb, L., & Lloyd, A. (2018). *The global entrepreneurship index*. The Global Entrepreneurship and Development Institute. Retrieved from https://thegedi.org/wp-content/uploads/dlm_uploads/2017/11/GEI-2018-1.pdf

Auletta, N., Rodríguez, A., & Vidal, R. (2010). *Global entrepreneurship monitor. Informe Venezuela 2005*. Centro de Emprendedores del IESA.

Auletta, N. & C. Rivera (2011). Un ecosistema para emprender. In *Debates IESA*, Volumen XVI, Número, p. 4.

Banco Central de Venezuela (BCV). (2018). Informe Económico (Ediciones BCV, Caracas). Available in: http://www.bcv.org.ve/publicaciones/informe-economico

Baptista, A. (2011). *Bases cuantitativas de la economía venezolana 1830–2008*. Fundación Artesanogroup.

Baptista, A. (1984). Más allá del optimismo y del pesimismo: las transformaciones fundamentales del país. In *En El caso Venezuela: una ilusión de armonía*. Ediciones del IESA.

Dana, L. P. (1996). Devaluation, entrepreneurship. Innovation, and change in Venezuela. *Entrepreneurship Innovation, and Change, 5*(3), 245–251.

Ecoanalitica. (2020) Informe de Coyuntura Cambiaria, Diciembre, Año 16, 17 p.

Encovi. (2020). Retrieved from https://www.proyectoencovi.com/informe-interactivo-2019

GEM Report Venezuela. (2011-2012). *Center for Entrepreneurs*. IESA.

Hidalgo, G., Kamiya, M., & Reyes, M. (2014). *Emprendimientos dinámicos en América Latina. Avances en prácticas y políticas*. Serie Políticas Públicas y Transformación Productiva N°16. Editor CAF.

Instituto Nacional de Estadística. (2010). *Situación y Dinámica Demográfica*. INE. http://www.ine.gov.ve/documentos/Demografia/SituacionDinamica/Proyecciones/html/PoblacionEntFed.html

Instituto Nacional de Estadística. (2011). *XIV Censo Nacional de Población y Vivienda*. INE.

Kantis, H. Federico, J., & S. Ibarra-García (2017). Condiciones Sistémicas para el Emprendimiento Dinámico 2017. *Prodem*. Retrieved from https://prodem.ungs.edu.ar/wp-content/uploads/2018/05/Resumen-2017.pdf

LEI. (2020). *Soñando Nuestra Venezuela: Líderes Empresariales Innovadores (LEI)*. Evento llevado a cabo en GotoWebinar por EY Venezuela en el marco de la 5ta Edición de LEI. Retrieved from https://register.gotowebinar.com/recording/3385324145812401167

Likoum, S. W. B., Shamout, M. D., Harazneh, I., & Abubakar, A. M. (2020). Market-sensing capability, innovativeness, brand management systems, market dynamism, competitive intensity, and performance: An integrative review. *Journal of the Knowledge Economy, 11*(2), 593–613.

Medina, A. (2020). Plataforma de autos usados Kavak es el nuevo 'unicornio' latinoamericano. *Forbes Colombia*. https://forbes.co/2020/10/01/emprendedores/plataforma-de-autos-usados-kavak-es-el-nuevo-unicornio-latinoamericano/

Montacuti, V. (2020). *Entrepreneurship in Venezuela: Starting a Company in the Third Most Difficult Country in the World to Run a Business*. Retrieved from https://www.techstars.com/the-line/pov/entrepreneurship-in-venezuela-difficult

Ojeda, E. & A. Rodríguez (2011) El Ecosistema Nacional de Emprendimiento. *Debates IESA*, Volumen XVI, Número 4.

SELA. (2016). *Experiencias recientes sobre programas de emprendimiento e incubadoras de empresas en América Latina y el Caribe: Hacia la creación de una economía impulsada por el emprendimiento*. SELA. Retrieved from http://s017.sela.org/media/2303968/experiencias-recientes-programas-de-emprendimiento.pdf

Toro, H. (2020). ¿Puede el emprendimiento conducir al desarrollo? Entrevista a Soltan Acs. *Revista Foro., 5*(5), 1–7.

Zahra, S. A., Sapienza, H. J., & Davidsson, P. (2006). Entrepreneurship and dynamic capabilities: A review, model and research agenda. *Journal of Management Studies, 43*(4), 0022–2380.

Nunzia Auletta holds a PhD in Political Science from Universidad Simón Bolívar (Venezuela), an MBA from IESA, and is a Politologist from Universitá di Roma "La Sapienza". She is a Full Professor of Innovation and Entrepreneurship and Development Director at IESA Business School (Venezuela) since 2008 and a visiting professor at Latin American and European schools. She is an editor of books and business journals and author of more than 50 articles, book chapters, and cases published in peer-reviewed publications and research networks.

Urbi Garay holds a PhD in Finance from the University of Massachusetts (Amherst), has a Master's degree in International Economics and Development from Yale University, and is an Economist from Universidad Católica Andrés Bello. He is a Full Professor of Finance at IESA Business School (Venezuela) since 2000, a visiting professor at EGADE-Tec. Monterrey (Mexico) and at Universidad de La Sabana (Colombia). He is a Chaired Member of the National Academy of Economic Sciences of Venezuela and is the author of seven books and more than 40 peer-reviewed journal articles.

Patricia Monteferrante holds a PhD in Management from Tulane University (New Orleans, Louisiana), has a Master's degree in Management from the same University, a Master's degree in Public Policies from IESA Business School (Venezuela), and is an Economist from Universidad Católica Andrés Bello (Venezuela). She is a Full Professor of Family Businesses and Human Resources Management at IESA Business School (Venezuela) since 2005, and is also Coordinator of the Center for Innovation and Entrepreneurship at IESA.

Aramis Rodríguez-Orosz has a Doctorate in Business Science from the Nebrija University of Madrid (Spain), and a Master's degree in Marketing from IESA Management School (Venezuela). He is a full-time Professor of Entrepreneurship and Innovation at the IESA since 2009. His line of research is related to entrepreneurship within companies, paradoxical thinking, and ambidextrous organizations.

Shadow Banking Services for Entrepreneurs

Les Dlabay

Abstract

Informal financial services ranging from loans with family members to community-based savings groups serve entrepreneurs and households in South America. With several hundred million people lacking access to formal banking services in the region, varied alternative financial services are offered by informal and semiformal providers. Individuals and small business owners seek loans, savings services, and payment activities through shadow financial sources influenced by tradition, cultural norms, and economic necessity.

1 Introduction

A *tanda* in Mexico can provide a group member with needed funds to buy a used oven for a home-based bakery business. In rural Bolivia, a person hides *bolivianos* in the wall of her thatch hut, or buries banknotes in the ground, to conceal money from family members or friends who might demand financial assistance. In a produce market in Buenos Aires, a street entrepreneur borrows 2300 pesos for 2 days from a moneylender to cover the cost of inventory.

These situations reflect shadow financial activities among households and entrepreneurs in Latin America and the Caribbean (LAC). Serving the *unbanked* (no formal financial services), *debanked* (previous users of formal financial services), and *underbanked* (limited use of formal financial services), informal financial service providers operate outside the formal banking system. Driven by cultural tradition and a limited financial infrastructure, these "off the books"

L. Dlabay (✉)
Lake Forest College, Lake Forest, IL, USA
e-mail: dlabay@lakeforest.edu

L.-P. Dana et al. (eds.), *Entrepreneurship in South America*, Springer Texts in Business and Economics, https://doi.org/10.1007/978-3-030-97060-4_15

transactions serve millions of households and entrepreneurs with an assortment of alternative banking services (Adams & Fitchett, 1992).

2 Informal Economic Activities

In every economic setting, business activities occur beyond formal, registered enterprises. These informal economic activities can range from 10 to 20% of the economy in industrialized nations to over 60% in developing economies. In Latin America, based on estimates using International Labor Organization data, the portion of jobs in informal sector enterprises ranges from about one-fourth in Brazil to nearly 60% in Honduras (Williams & Youssef, 2014). These business activities are known by a variety of terms that vary based on the nature of the transaction, culture, and the political environment.

The most common terms used to refer to this business segment are:

- informal economy
- shadow economy
- black market
- unregistered business
- cash, street economy
- underground economy
- unreported economy
- off the books
- unregulated economy
- bazaar markets
- extra-legal economy
- unofficial economy

In contrast, lesser-known descriptors of informal economic activities include:

- dual, parallel economy
- survival employment
- hidden economy
- undocumented business
- subsistence economy
- unstructured economy
- economy of affection
- under the table
- alternative economy
- undercover economy
- evasive economy
- invisible economy

Financial services and monetary transactions are a commonly overlooked element of informal economic activities. Unbanked, debanked, and underbanked individuals and small business owners commonly use financial services outside the scope of the formal banking system.

3 Informal Financial Services in Latin America

A limited financial infrastructure along with cultural traditions in many developing economic environments result in alternative banking services (Adams & Fitchett, 1992). These financial products serve business needs among the poor in rural and urban settings. "Off the books" financial activities, also referred to as *shadow banking,* serve millions of entrepreneurs and households.

In Latin America, a very limiting environment exists to open a bank account that may include proof of a job and citizenship, other financial documents, and, in some situations, the applicant must be in the top 20% income bracket. These restrictions along with many hidden fees targeting the poor result in an estimated 70% of the population being unbanked or underbanked (Martins, 2020).

While informal financial services often charge higher rates and may not be as reliable as more established sources, Collins et al. (2009) point out that the appeal for nonconventional channels for banking products includes:

- no access to formal banking institutions
- loans from friends, family members are more flexible, possibly interest free
- no travel expense to formal financial institutions
- comfortable doing business with a local moneylender, personally known in the community
- greater availability of funds for personal reasons, not just business
- a need for large unexpected events, such as illness, funerals, productive asset loss (livestock)
- the poor usually save small and irregular amounts
- ability to quickly obtain short-term loans when cash flow problems occur (*capital smoothing*)

With the presence of diverse informal financial activities, Adams and Fitchett (1992) advocate use of a continuum to delineate among the market participants. As shown in Table 1, shadow banking service providers may be viewed in three major categories:

(1) *Semiformal* providers, with a legal business status but may not be subject to the financial regulations in a country.
(2) *Individual informal* providers participate in unregulated activities to offer financial services.
(3) *Group-based informal* providers serve community financial needs through a cooperative effort based on social connections and shared networks.

Table 1 Nonformal (Shadow) Financial Service Providers in Latin America

	Semiformal	Informal: Individual	Informal: Group-based
Types of organizations	• Credit cooperatives • Pawnshops • Postal service • Non-government organizations (NGOs) • Microfinance institutions (MFIs) • Mobile banking networks	• Family members, friends • Market moneylenders • Shop owners • Loan sharks • Deposit collectors, moneyguards • Informal currency traders	• Self-help groups (SHGs) • Rotating savings, credit associations (RoSCAs) • Accumulating savings, credit associations (ASCAs) • Village savings, loan associations (VSLAs) • Remittance networks
Description, social collateral (degree of trust)	Usually has legal business status, but not extensive financial regulations; may use unrefined credit screening, reporting system	*Social collateral* essential; screening by individual lenders based on personal knowledge of the borrower or recommendations from previous clients	Trust-based group or network, with group consensus regarding personal character as the basis for membership and extending credit
Target audience served; geographic reach	Underbanked households and business owners in a geographic region and perhaps across a country	A limited number of unbanked individuals and small business owners, usually living in close geographic proximity	Individuals and entrepreneurs living in relatively close proximity are in need of expanded financial services
Services provided	Mainly extends loans with some transfer of funds services	Emphasis on borrowing with some savings deposit activities	Strong emphasis on savings in addition to loan availability
Capital source	External/group	Individual	Group
Financial regulatory restrictions	Minimal	None	None

As noted by Wilson (2010), in relation to Haiti, when cash is needed, people will borrow from neighbors, buy food on credit, go to a pawnshop, or use a moneylender, often called a *poignard*, literally a "dagger." A *mutuelle* is a group organized to save money and make loans to group members. A *borlette* is a nationwide, lottery-based gambling scheme in which players hope to "win" as their savings strategy.

In the LAC region, *social collateral* is crucial for the success of informal financial services due to the required trust-based relationship. Personal knowledge of a potential borrower along with guidance from trusted clients are used to determine credit merit (Dlabay, 2015).

4 Semiformal Financial Service Providers

While not normally subject to formal government financial regulations, semiformal financial service providers still function under the jurisdiction of general and commercial laws. These include credit cooperatives, pawnshops, the postal service, financial nongovernmental organizations (NGOs) and microfinance institutions (MFIs), and mobile banking networks.

4.1 Credit Cooperatives

Serving regional financial needs, credit cooperatives offer loans, and sometimes savings accounts, to member owners. The financial nonprofit cooperative is common in Asia, including savings and credit cooperatives (SACCOs) and the Small Farmers Cooperatives Limited (SFCLs) in Nepal (Mercy Corps, 2008); State Cooperative Banks (SCB), District Central Cooperative Banks (DCCB), Primary Agricultural Credit Societies (PACS), and Primary Cooperative Agriculture and Rural Development Banks (PCARDB) in India; and rural cooperatives in China with a "quasi legality" status (Tsai, 2004).

In Latin America, diverse financial cooperatives serve urban, rural, and agricultural entrepreneurs. A study covering Argentina, Chile, Cuba, and Mexico identified several types of coops organized by workers, business owners, and individuals to provide loans, savings accounts, and other banking services (Giovannini & Vieta, 2017).

In Haiti, financial cooperatives, *caisses populaires* (credit unions), have attempted to assist the marginalized poor. The availability of microfinance loans and other services provides evidence for enhanced economic democracy and improved quality of life. The culture of collective banking through cooperatives and credit unions best serves needs of the country's tradition (Hossein, 2014).

A comprehensive study of credit unions in the region (Westley & Branch, 2000) resulted in these observations:

- Credit unions were a major source of credit funding for microenterprises.
- Originally organized by religious and nonprofit organizations, many credit unions lacked professional management to ensure ongoing viability.
- Often larger than village banks, credit unions are better positioned to serve low-income clients.
- Village banks often depended on external donor funding, while credit unions may not encounter the same volatility of capital acquisition with deposits from local sources.

4.2 Pawnshops

For centuries, pawnshops have offered short-term, small loans secured by a physical asset (collateral), such as gold, jewelry, or high-demand, high-value consumer goods. The item may be later sold to recover any past due loan amount. Pawnbrokers often operate a retail store to sell goods that are not redeemed (Ledgerwood, 2013). Interest rates are often exorbitant, often as high as 20 percent a month. In Haiti, most small towns have one or more pawnshops, called *bric-a-brac* shops to get quick credit (Wilson, 2010).

4.3 Postal Service

Operating as a counterpart with the formal banking system, post offices in many countries offer financial services for unbanked people. The postal service as a financial service provider has traditionally been common in African and Asia countries. In Latin America, however, offering postal payment and savings services is limited. In Brazil and the Antilles, postal savings accounts are used by a small portion of the population. More common, although still a very small number of total remittances, money transfers in Argentina, Brazil, Chile, and Uruguay are processed through the postal service. While the number of post offices is comparable to the number of bank branches, post offices are found in locations with no bank facilities. Advocates for improved financial inclusion suggest expanded use of postal financial services to complement the existing formal financial sector infrastructure (World Bank Group, n.d.).

4.4 Non-governmental Organizations (NGOs) and Microfinance Institutions (MFIs)

An array of relief and development organizations facilitate financial services in informal economic settings. Non-governmental organizations (NGOs) and microfinance institutions (MFIs) operate in many areas of Latin America through a physical or an online presence. Some MFIs are licensed to offer financial services such as savings plans and loans, while others guide groups of individuals and households (Mercy Corps, 2008). In over 20 countries in the LAC region, Accion, CRS, CARE, FINCA, Grameen Foundation, Hope International, Opportunity International, Oxfam, and World Vision guide the creation of savings groups and other financial services. In Haiti, various organizations have addressed the special needs of low-literacy people with the development of a memory-based system of financial recordkeeping (Wilson, 2010).

4.5 Mobile Banking Networks

The majority of unbanked people around the world have access to a mobile device. In LAC, nearly all Internet connections occur through mobile devices creating expanded opportunities to serve the financial service needs of the unbanked in the region.

Recent developments to offer financial services through a third party, rather than a formal institution, may be referred to *open banking*. This technology allows low-income, unbanked, and rural consumers to receive, send, and borrow funds. Cellphone transactions, often connected to a bank account, are becoming more common through nonbanking entities such as telecommunications companies. Mobile money systems provide informal entrepreneurs with access to banks, cash machines, and credit cards (Mas & Radcliffe, 2010).

FinTech activities, involving technology-enabled banking and financial services, continue to evolve with apps for budgeting, saving, credit reporting, financial advice, and flexible loan repayment. In Argentina, Brazil, Chile, and Mexico hundreds of fintech startups are developing innovative banking solutions. Many of these apps and software are aimed to serve small business owners and individual entrepreneurs (Crunchbase News, 2019).

An extension of FinTech is *neobanks*, which operate through digital channels and mobile apps, and typically do not have a physical location. Benefits include lower costs to serve underbanked and unbanked consumers along an easy loan approval, technology-based process. The neobank trend could help provide financial inclusion on a larger scale, bringing a greater portion of the LAC region population into the formal economy. In Brazil, with much of its population spread across varied rural areas, mobile banking will provide entrepreneurs with many advantages (Fintech Futures, 2018).

Concerns associated with FinTech activities for the unbanked in LAC and elsewhere include:

- Lower levels of personal contact than with traditional microfinance transactions. Most clients have a high degree of trust with loan officers to assess creditworthiness. The low-income customer has greater faith in the individual than in the institution.
- Traditional lending has greater transparency while the proprietary nature of algorithms is rarely disclosed.
- Breaches of personal data, failure to obtain prior consent, technology and network risks, and weak regulatory enforcement (Escobar de Nogales, 2018).

5 Informal: Individual Provided Financial Services

Providing loans and storing money with family and friends is the foundation of individual-based informal finance services. Beyond personal acquaintances, informal financial entrepreneurs offer borrowing, saving, and other services.

5.1 Family and Friends

In collectivist societies, typical of Central and South America, family members and friends frequently provide loans and money storage. In these communal-oriented cultures, people are often willing to sacrifice individual resources (time, money, other items) for the benefit of others. This *social capital* associated with a society is the basis of many financial relationships and transactions.

5.2 Market Moneylenders

In informal economic settings, loans may be obtained for both personal and business needs. Most moneylenders use their personal funds to provide loans for small amounts. Loans are usually unsecured, based on an individual acquaintance or recommendation; however, assets such as gold, jewelry, or land may serve as collateral.

In Mexico, for example, moneylenders are a vital financial intermediary for *ejidatarios* (farm peasants), who also often sought loans from other lenders. The agricultural and economic uncertainties faced by these itinerant farmers require them to interact with both informal and other nonbank financial service providers. The negative reputation of moneylenders results from unscrupulous actions that include: (1) encouraging higher levels of debt without monitoring how borrowed funds are used; (2) charging high-interest rates; (3) not providing information and access to a fair price for crops; (4) confiscating animals, seeds, clothes, and the use rights to the *ejidal* land plot; and (5) engaging in violence to force debtors to make payments (Mottier, 2018).

Additional evidence of moneylender activities in Latin America over the years comes from Nisbet (1971). A preference for this informal credit source was the result of a simple application process for obtaining a loan. Borrowers talked directly with the moneylender about their financial needs as the informal lender had an ongoing connection with the rural community.

Worth noting are two variations of moneylenders that operate in the Asian-Pacific region:

- In the Philippines, *5–6 moneylenders* operate in market areas. Borrowers obtain five pesos for a week, or just a day, payback six; resulting in a 20 percent interest rate for the time period. This can result in an annual interest rate exceeding 1000 percent. Most 5–6 borrowing involves short-term loans to bridge the time between current expenses and future business revenue (Kondo, 2003).
- In Indonesian fishing communities, traders provide loans to fishermen. No interest is charged; traders buy some fish from the borrower at 5–10 percent below the market price. The trader profits when fish are processed and sold. Loans are repaid when fishermen sell the remaining catch to other traders (Mohammad & Yunaningsih, 2014).

5.3 Shop Owners and Loan Sharks

In many villages and small-town settings, retailers extend credit to shoppers. Amounts owed are usually due within a few days or at the end of the month.

Common throughout the world is *loan sharks*, illegally charging exorbitant interest rates. An extensive Colombian loan shark network hired agents to operate in Mexico and nine other Latin American countries. These illicit lenders offered credit to workers and small businesses with a 20 percent interest rate for 20 days. A failure to pay often resulted in threats, attacks, and robbery. Murders have also been attributed to the loan shark network (Lakic, 2017).

5.4 Deposit Collectors

As a result of collectivist values in some cultures, funds may be requested by family and friends. To evade these situations, storing money elsewhere is common. With no access to a formal banking institution, for a fee, people may make use of *deposit collectors*, or *moneyguards*. The amount charged for this service can be as high as 10 percent of the amount saved resulting in a negative rate of return.

Risks associated with deposit collectors are not being able to obtain the money when needed, and the collector may depart a community with the funds (Ledgerwood, 2013). Common in Ghana, *susu collectors* serve marketplace traders since few banks offer low-balance savings accounts. Collins et al. (2009) report moneyguarding common among households in Bangladesh, India, and South Africa. In Latin America, this money storage service may be provided by friends and distant family members rather than an entrepreneurial deposit collector.

5.5 Informal Currency Traders

To facilitate transactions, the US dollar has traditionally been accepted in many informal market settings. Beyond that, the US dollar is the official currency in Ecuador and El Salvador, while in Panama the dollar is a *parallel currency* with the *balboa*.

Often, unregistered banknote exchange services operate in locally owned shops serving as a "front" for currency transactions that are not government sanctioned. These informal currency traders compete with the foreign exchange services at banks, hotels, airports, and rail stations. A survey of US embassy representatives by Dlabay and Reger (2007) concluded that nations with lower levels of economic development experienced greater levels of informal foreign exchange activities. Other findings in this study included:

- The use and acceptance of the US dollar in Central and South America, both formally and informally, was present on a regular basis.

- *casas de cambio* (exchange houses) in rural Mexico are small, usually family owned, foreign exchange businesses that serve local workers and people working in the United States.
- In Paraguay, individuals representing *casas de cambios* were observed along the borders with Argentina and Brazil offering to exchange currencies.
- The US dollar was reported as commonly accepted in Peru, along with the presence of *casas de cambios* changing currency in the street in a fashion that might resemble street vending; they are "less formal to completely informal." (b) Plenty of opportunities exist to exchange; you see individuals on many corners in cities changing money (mostly local to US dollars and vice versa).
- In Uruguay, markets were viewed as extremely *dollarized* with the US dollar being highly acceptable.
- The recent extreme economic difficulties in Venezuela resulted in expanded acceptance of the US dollar in black market settings.

6 Informal: Group-Based Financial Service Providers

Community-based groups extend the financial services provided by family, friends, and other individuals. These locally formed and self-managed assemblies fit cultural norms and regional business practices, and may be referred to as "informal credit markets" (Ghate, 1992).

6.1 Self-Help Groups (SHGs)

To facilitate entrepreneurial activities among women, self-help groups (SHGs) provide social and economic empowerment. Popular in Asia, especially India, SHGs involve 15 to 20 women in rural villages organized for savings and lending with a commitment to financial and business development (US AID, 2008). Benefits of SHGs include enhanced financial security, greater self-confidence and respect, increased literacy, and improved social status (Sinha 2010).

To expand saving among SHG members using technology, urban micro-entrepreneurs in Chile received a text message to encourage regular deposits. Since most in the study did not have a savings account, the text commitment motivated informal-sector entrepreneurs to save for needed supplies and tools. Those who received text messages made more deposits, indicating that regular feedback and follow-ups create accountability for expanded savings (Kast et al., 2018).

6.2 Rotating Savings and Credit Associations (RoSCAs)

Serving the need for financial services in more than 70 countries, rotating savings and credit associations (RoSCAs) are described by Ardener and Burman (1996) as "an association formed upon a core of participants who make regular contributions to a fund which is given in whole or in part to each contributor in turn." At the RoSCA meeting, a set amount is submitted by each member with the total distributed to one person. People otherwise unable to save or obtain credit receive needed money for medical bills or business expenses. RoSCAs may dissolve after each member receives the money once, but the group may continue or form a new group. The RoSCA provides a strong community support system for economic and social empowerment.

Around the world, RoSCAs have varied names that include *arisans* (Indonesia), *chit funds* (India), *ekub* (Ethiopia), *osusu* (Nigeria), and *tontines* (in several Asian and African countries) (Bouman, 1995). In the LAC region, these include:

- Bahamas: *Esu*
- Barbados: *Meetings*
- Belize: *Syndicate, Tanda*
- Bolivia: *Pasanacu*
- Brazil: *Consorcio, Pandero, Syndicates*
- Curacao: *Sam, Hunga sam*
- Dominican Republic: *San*
- Guatemala: *Cuchubal, Cuchuval*
- Guyana: *Throw a box, Boxi money*
- Haiti: *Sol*
- Jamaica: *Partners, (Throw a) Box, Susu*
- Mexico: *Tanda, Cundina, Mutualista*
- Panama: *Pandero*
- Peru: *Pandero*
- Surinam: *Kasmonie*
- Tobago: *Susu*
- Trinidad: *(E)susu, Sou sou, Hui, Chitty*
- West Indies: *Susu*

RoSCAs are known as *tandas* in central and southern Mexico, and *cundinas* in northern Mexico and the Southwest United States (Vélez-Ibáñez, 2019). These social lending groups that meet each week or month build lifelong friendships and help members who may encounter short-term financial needs. An estimated 30 percent of the people in Mexico participate in a *tanda*.

In recent years, an online version of the *tanda* was available, connecting people in varied worldwide locations. With this digital platform, the payout was guaranteed, reducing risk; however, a fee is charged, with the amount depending on where a person was in the payout time schedule. This fee was often less than the rate charged by most credit cards. On-time payments for the online system are often reported to credit services to help people build their credit scores (Edmondson, 2020).

A *sol* is a RoSCA in Haiti that usually operates in a marketplace, and is organized by someone referred to as the *sol mother*, *manman sol,* or simply "banker." In this setting, group members may contribute to the pool more than once in a day based on a higher velocity of cash flow from their business. Most *sol* participants use funds immediately for business or personal expenses. Others use their savings for land or livestock, or to secure a market stall location (Wilson, 2010).

RoSCAs also operate in immigrant communities of industrialized societies. *Kye* is the Korean version used in the Los Angeles area. Many of South Asian descent participate in RoSCAs in Oxford. RoSCA was also observed among Somali women living in the United Kingdom (Ardener & Burman, 1996). *Tandas* and *cudinas* are common among Latino and Chicano populations in the United States (Thompson, 2014).

6.3 Accumulating Savings and Credit Associations (ASCAs)

A variation of RoSCAs, accumulating savings and credit associations (ASCAs) place an emphasis on savings rather than just loans. At each meeting, group members make deposits of an amount of their choosing with funds used for loans to group members. A major difference with RoSCAs, ASCA money is not paid out unless a loan is requested (Rutherford & Arora, 2009). Earnings from interest on loans are ultimately distributed to the group members.

ASCAs are often time-bound, with members saving, borrowing, and repaying for a predetermined amount of time, usually 6 to 12 months. At which time, the *share-out* occurs. These cycles often reflect the seasonality of agricultural cash flows. In many Latin American settings, the share-out is every 12 months and coincides with Christmas and the New Year. Elsewhere, groups may receive share-outs just before planting time, when school fees are due, or when religious or cultural events occur. CARE, Oxfam, and other non-governmental organizations (NGOs) have promoted thousands of these savings groups, especially in Africa and Latin America (Allen & Panetta, 2010).

In Haiti, the *mutuelle* is a group of 10–50 members that accumulate funds over time. Members set rules for the amount and frequency of deposits as well as late fees. Common purchases made by *mutuelle* participants include coffins, bicycles or medical expenses, and school tuition. As the savings funds increase members may access loans for larger sums. Some *mutuelles* are formed by churches and NGOs, but most are self-selected. Communities also benefit from the groups working to reduce crime and assist orphans. *Mutuelles* facilitate vital financial services among micro-entrepreneurs in poor and rural areas (Wilson, 2010).

6.4 Village Savings and Loan Associations (VSLAs)

More formalized community-based financial groups are the self-managed village savings and loan associations (VSLAs). Using a time-bound model, members save and request loans from the collected funds. After 9 or 12 months, the *share-out* occurs with amounts saved and interest earned paid to group members. Then, the VSLA may reform with a new cycle. VSLAs have strong transparency and accountability. In the presence of members, deposits and loans occur at group meetings, creating witnesses for every financial transaction.

Economic development and microfinance organizations serve to create VSLAs in several regions of the world. In recent years, CARE organized VSLAs in Ecuador, El Salvador, and Haiti, while World Relief was active in Haiti and Nicaragua. World Vision has also used the VSLA-model in various Latin American countries.

Income-generating activities may be integrated into the VSLA program. Business ventures have included the sales of solar lanterns and other items to address community needs. Microenterprises were also created to distribute seeds, fertilizer, and other agricultural inputs (Rippey & Fowler, 2011).

6.5 Remittance Networks

In many areas of the world, informal money transfer activities operate under names such as *hundi* (South Asia), *fei chien* (China), *hui kuan* (Hong Kong), *padala* (The Philippines), *phei kwan* (Thailand), and *hawalas* (Middle East and Asia) (Isern et al., 2005). These informal remittance networks are commonly used by migrant workers to send funds back to their home countries.

In Latin America, more formal services are used for remittances, such as Western Union and MoneyGram. The use of PayPal, Remitly, and other money transfer apps is expanding. These remittance service providers (RSPs) compete with informal sources, such as *casas de cambios* (exchange house) that are getting more involved in the remittance business.

Despite the economic downturn from the coronavirus pandemic, remittances held steady or increased in this $100 billion industry. The many migrant workers employed in essential categories (health care, agriculture, food production, food processing) were able to continue to send money to families. Remittances not only came from industrialized countries, but also from within Latin America. With a mass exodus to surrounding countries, remittances become a major source of income for the people of Venezuela. Departures from Haiti, Cuba, Nicaragua, and Colombia also increased the trend, with funds coming primarily from Chile and Costa Rica (Schechter, 2020). After the 2010 earthquake in Haiti, cash came back to the homeland from Chile, sent by former Haitians who settled in the Andean area (Rauls, 2020).

Growth in online remittances through apps and digital wallets will continue to expand. Several hundred new and local LAC startups have entered the market to offer payment and money transfer services for use by those with a limited credit history but with access to a cellphone (Rauls, 2020).

7 Concluding Observations

Semiformal and informal financial service providers fill the gap for unbanked participants in the informal economy. Addressing unmet needs, unregistered banking activities create a financial infrastructure for entrepreneurs.

7.1 Policy Actions

In LAC, shadow financial services provide capital and cash flow for millions of people. To expand and improve these product offerings for informal entrepreneurs, several actions might be considered by business, government, development agencies, and nonprofit and community-based organizations to enhance the vitality of the region:

1. Enact and enforce regulatory actions to prevent fraud and exploitation by illicit lenders.
2. Develop formal–informal financial service linkages for expanded business opportunities, job creation, and improved quality of life.
3. Enhance *financial inclusion* initiatives. Working with underserved populations is My Oral Village (www.myoralvillage.org), which promotes tools to understand financial records.
4. Implement programs for financial literacy, business skills, and technical training for entrepreneurs.
5. Continue expansion of mobile banking and digital services for business activities and household needs.

7.2 Suggested Further Research

With a significant number of business transactions in Latin America involving informal financial services, expanded scholarship might be considered related to these topics:

- How do volatile economic conditions and changeable political environments affect alternative financial services?
- What cultural factors influence operations of group-based financial service providers such as SHGs, RoSCAs, ASCAs, and VSLAs?
- What metrics might measure the economic and social impact of alternative financial services?
- How can social collateral be assessed among informal financial service providers in Latin America?
- What regulations should be considered for digital informal financial services?
- What factors create effective informal–formal connections among financial service providers in Latin America?

- How might microfranchising be used to deliver financial services in various Latin American settings?
- How might unethical and illegal financial service practices be assessed to avoid personal and social costs associated with fraudulent activities?

Reliable financial services are vital for the extensive number of people living, working, and doing business in the informal economy of Latin America and the Caribbean. With limited access to formal financial institutions, enterprising individuals and entrepreneurs have implemented a variety of informal, unregistered banking activities.

Financial, economic, and political stability will create a foundation for a nation's reputation to facilitate global trade and attract foreign investment. The lack of a consistent financial infrastructure that serves all people will result in many banking activities continuing to be "off the books."

Acknowledgment The author is grateful to Udit Mehta for his strong contribution in researching and identifying key ideas related to informal financial services in LAC.

References

Adams, D. W., & Fitchett, D. A. (Eds.). (1992). *Informal finance in low-income countries*. Westview Press.

Allen, H., & Panetta, D. (2010). *Savings groups: What are they?* The SEEP Network Savings-Led Financial Services Working Group.

Ardener, S., & Burman, S. (Eds.). (1996). *Money-go-rounds: The importance of ROSCAs for women*. Berg Publishers.

Bouman, F. (1995). ROSCA: On the origin of the species. *Savings and Development, XIX*(2), 129.

Collins, D., Morduch, J., Rutherford, S., & Ruthven, O. (2009). *Portfolios of the poor: How the world's poor live on $2 a day*. Princeton University Press.

Crunchbase News. (2019). *What's driving the digital banking boom in Latin America*. Retrieved April 11, 2022, from https://news.crunchbase.com/news/whats-driving-the-digital-banking-boom-in-latin-america/

Dlabay, L. (2015). Informal financial services: A proposed research agenda. In P. Godfrey (Ed.), *Management, society, and the informal economy*. Routledge.

Dlabay, L. R. & Reger, G. (2007). *A regional comparison of informal foreign exchange activities: A qualitative analysis*. Paper presented at the annual meeting of the Midwest Chapter. Academy of International Business, Chicago.

Edmondson, B. (2020). *What is a tanda?* Retrieved April 11, 2022, from https://www.thebalance.com/how-do-tandas-work-4582180

Escobar de Nogales, X. (2018). Fintech for the financially excluded? *Stanford Social Innovation Review*. Retrieved April 11, 2022, from https://ssir.org/articles/entry/fintech_for_the_financially_excluded

Fintech Futures. (2018). *An overview of neobanks in Latin America*. Retrieved April 11, 2022, from https://www.fintechfutures.com/2018/09/an-overview-of-neobanks-in-latin-america/

Ghate, P. (1992). *Informal finance: Some findings from Asia*. Asian Development Bank Press, Oxford University Press.

Giovannini, M., & Vieta, M. (2017). Co-operatives in Latin America. In J. Michie, J. R. Blasi, & C. Borzaga (Eds.), *The Oxford handbook of mutual, co-operative, and co-owned business*.

Retrieved April 11, 2022, from https://www.oxfordhandbooks.com/view/10.1093/oxfordhb/9780199684977.001.0001/oxfordhb-9780199684977-e-23

Hossein, C. S. (2014). Haiti's caisses populaires: Home-grown solutions to bring economic democracy. *International Journal of Social Economics, 41*(1), 42–59.

Isern, J., Deshpande, R., & Van Doorn, J. (2005). *Crafting a money transfers strategy: Guidance for pro-poor financial service providers.* CGAP.

Kast, F., Meier, S., & Pomeranz, D. (2018). Savings more in groups: Field experimental evidence from Chile. *Journal of Development Economics, 133*(C), 275–294.

Kondo, M. (2003). *The Bombay 5-6: Last resource informal financiers for Philippine micro-enterprises.* Kyoto Review of Southeast Asia. Retrieved April 11, 2022, from https://kyotoreview.org/issue-4/the-bombay-5-6-last-resource-informal-financiersfor-philippine-micro-enterprises/

Lakic, V. (2017). *Colombia loan shark network booming in Mexico.* Retrieved April 11, 2022, from https://www.occrp.org/en/daily/6910-colombia-loan-shark-network-booming-in-mexico

Ledgerwood, J. (Ed.). (2013). *The new microfinance handbook: A financial market system perspective.* The World Bank.

Martins, P. (2020). *The future of payments in Latin America and the Caribbean.* Retrieved April 11, 2022, from https://blog.2checkout.com/the-future-of-payments-latam/#:~:text=In%20some%20Latin%20American%20countries,is%20either%20unbanked%20or%20underbanked

Mas, I. & Radcliffe, D. (2010). *Mobile payments go viral: M-PESA in Kenya.* Retrieved April 11, 2022, from https://papers.ssrn.com/sol3/papers.cfm?abstract_id=1593388

Mercy Corps. (2008). *Mercy Corps Nepal microfinance assessment: scope of meso-level technical service provision to MFIs in Nepal.* Retrieved April 11, 2022, from https://drive.google.com/file/d/1VZtGmpzT126GVOoDmFsiUxkVKE39r9YO/view

Mohammad, G. & Yunaningsih, R.D. (2014). *Lessons from informal financial systems: Indonesian perspective.* Retrieved April 11, 2022, from http://blog.microsave.net/lessons-from-informal-financial-systems-indonesian-perspective/

Mottier, N. (2018). Moneylending in myth and practice in twentieth-century Mexico. *Mexican Studies, 34*(2), 143–164.

Nisbet, C. T. (1971). Moneylending in rural areas of Latin America: Some examples from Colombia. *The American Journal of Economics and Sociology, 30*(1), 71–84.

Rauls, L. (2020). *Latin America's changing remittance landscape.* Retrieved April 11, 2022, from https://www.americasquarterly.org/article/latin-americas-changing-remittance-landscape/

Rippey, P., & Fowler, B. (2011). *Beyond financial services: A synthesis of studies on the integration of savings groups and other developmental activities.* Aga Khan Foundation.

Rutherford, S., & Arora, S. S. (2009). *The poor and their money: Microfinance from a twenty-first century consumer's perspective.* Practical Action Publishing.

Schechter, P. (2020). *How COVID-19 has reshaped Latin American remittances.* Retrieved April 11, 2022, from https://www.brinknews.com/how-covid-19-has-reshaped-latin-american-remittances/

Sinha, F. (2010). *Microfinance self-help groups in India: Living up to their promise?* Practical Action Publishing.

Thompson, N.A. (2014). *Short-term loans and long-term benefits: Tandas are "no-interest, short-term loans" that can help Latina entrepreneurs and job-creators.* Retrieved April 11, 2022, from http://www.latinpost.com/articles/10321/20140410/shortterm-loans-benefits-latinas-tandas-no-interest-loans-latina-entrepreneurs-job-creators.htm

Tsai, K. S. (2004). *Back-alley banking: Private entrepreneurs in China.* Cornell University Press.

US AID. (2008). *Nepal inclusive economic growth assessment: Microenterprise development.* Retrieved April 11, 2022, from http://pdf.usaid.gov/pdf_docs/PNADN015.pdf

Vélez-Ibáñez, C. G. (2019). *Tandas and cundinas (Mexico and south-western USA).* Retrieved April 11, 2022, from https://www.in-formality.com/wiki/index.php?title=Tandas_and_cundinas_(Mexico_and_south-western_USA

Westley, G. D., & Branch, B. (Eds.). (2000). *Safe money: Building effective credit unions in Latin America*. Johns Hopkins University Press.

Williams, C. C., & Youssef, Y. (2014). Tackling informal entrepreneurship in Latin America: A critical evaluation of the neo-liberal policy approach. *Journal of Entrepreneurship & Organization Management, 3*(1), 1–9.

Wilson, K. (2010). *Haitian informal finance*. Retrieved April 11, 2022, from https://silo.tips/download/haitian-informal-financeby-kim-wilson-april

World Bank Group. (n.d.). *The role of postal networks in expanding access to financial services, worldwide landscape of postal financial services: Latin America and the Caribbean region*. Retrieved April 11, 2022, from http://documents1.worldbank.org/curated/en/136451468339640534/pdf/694520ESW0P0850279B00PUBLIC00000LAC.pdf

Les Dlabay Professor of Business Emeritus, taught at Lake Forest College, Lake Forest, Illinois, for 35 years. He taught 30 different courses and has presented over 300 workshops and seminars to academic, business, and community organizations. Dr. Dlabay has authored or has adaptations of more than 40 textbooks in the United States, Canada, India, and Singapore. His research emphasis involves informal and alternative financial services in cross-cultural, global settings. Professor Dlabay has a BS (Accounting) from the University of Illinois, Chicago; an MBA from DePaul University; and an EdD in Business and Economic Education from Northern Illinois University.

MIX
Papier aus verantwortungsvollen Quellen
Paper from responsible sources
FSC® C105338

If you have any concerns about our products,
you can contact us on
ProductSafety@springernature.com

In case Publisher is established outside the EU,
the EU authorized representative is:
Springer Nature Customer Service Center GmbH
Europaplatz 3, 69115 Heidelberg, Germany

Printed by Libri Plureos GmbH
in Hamburg, Germany